Discovering
The Old Testament

John E. Egglet

Trinity Publishing House
Rossmor Building
500 N. Robert St., Suite 534
St. Paul, Minnesota 55101

Discovering The Old Testament
Copyright © 1978 by John E. Eggleton

All rights reserved. No parts of this book may be reproduced without permission of the publisher. Printed in the United States of America.

All Biblical quotations are from the Revised Standard Version, unless otherwise indicated.

First Edition, 1978
Second Edition, 1980

*To my wife, Phyllis, and my sons:
Phillip, Paul, Steven*

Table of Contents

Foreword i
Introduction iii

Chapter I
The Creation 1
(Genesis 1:1-2:24)

Chapter II
The Fall 8
(Genesis 3:1-5:32)

Chapter III
The Flood 15
(Genesis 6:1-11:26)

Chapter IV
Abraham 21
(Genesis 11:27-25:10)

Chapter V
Jacob 28
(Genesis 25:11-49:33)

Chapter VI
Joseph 35
(Genesis 37:1-50:26)

Chapter VII
Moses 43
(Exodus 1:1-18:27)

Chapter VIII
Israel at Sinai 52
(Exodus 19-40; Leviticus 1-27)

Chapter IX
Israel in the Wilderness 60
(Numbers 1-30; Deuteronomy 1-34)

Chapter X
Joshua 68
(Joshua 1-24)

Chapter XI
The Era of the Judges 76
(Judges 1-21; Ruth 1-4)

Chapter XII
Samuel and Saul 85
(I Samuel 1-31)

Chapter XIII
David 94
(II Samuel 1-24; I Chronicles 1-29)

Chapter XIV
Solomon 102
(I Kings 1-11; II Chronicles 1-9)

Chapter XV
The Divided Kingdom 111
(I Kings 12; II Kings; II Chronicles 10-36)

Chapter XVI
The Prophet of the Ninth Century B.C. 123
(I Kings 17; II Kings 13; Jonah; Joel)

Chapter XVII
The Prophets of the Eighth Century B.C. in Israel 135
(Amos 1-9; Hosea 1-14)

Chapter XVIII
The Prophets of the Eighth Century B.C. in Judah 147
(Isaiah 1-66; Micah 1-7)

Chapter XIX
The Prophets of the Seventh Century B.C. 159
(Zephaniah 1-3; Habakkuk 1-3; Nahum 1-3; Jeremiah 1-52)

Chapter XX
The Prophets of the Sixth Century B.C. 173
(Obadiah; Ezekiel 1-48; Daniel 1-12; Lamentations 1-5)

Chapter XXI
The Prophets of the Restoration 184
(Haggai 1-2; Zechariah 1-14; Malachi 1-4)

Chapter XXII
The Books of Ezra, Nehemiah and Esther 191
(Ezra 1-10; Nehemiah 1-13; Esther 1-10)

Chapter XXIII
The Book of Job 199
(Job 1-42)

Chapter XXIV
The Book of Proverbs 209
(Proverbs 1-31)

Chapter XXV
The Book of Ecclesiastes and Song of Songs 215
(Ecclesiastes 1-12; Song of Songs 1-8)

Chapter XXVI
The Book of Psalms 221
(Psalms 1-150)

Bibliography 229
Appendix 235
   The Divided Kingdom 235
   Weights, Measures, & Coins 242
   Map of the Ancient World 245
   Map of the Exodus 246
   Map of the Conquest of Canaan 247
   Map of David's Wanderings 248
Subject Index 249

Foreword

This book has been written to serve as a basic general introduction to the content and meaning of the Old Testament. In writing, I have tried to avoid the extremes of being too superficial or technical. The book is designed for the general reader, especially for the person who is interested in understanding the Old Testament on its own terms. It is my hope that this book will challenge the reader to a deeper study of the Old Testament. The book should prove useful for group or individual study. Bible classes in churches will find the twenty-six chapters a convenient two quarter study, although a shorter or longer period may be used. The book is also intended as a college textbook for Old Testament survey courses.

While many people have contributed to the growth and development of this book, a few should be especially mentioned. In particular, I would like to thank my former teachers who inspired me to acquire a deep appreciation for the Old Testament. Included are: Lloyd Schupbach, Kentucky Christian College; T.W. Nakarai of Butler and Emmanuel Schools of Religion; Rolland Wolfe of Case Western University, and J. Kenneth Kuntz of the University of Iowa. Whatever good qualities the book possesses are due to their influence, the weaknesses are all mine. In addition, I would like specifically to thank Lisa Hiatt, Sharna Gibbons, and Dorothy Kimbro for their patience and ability in typing both the rough and final drafts of the book.

Finally, this work is dedicated to my wife, Phyllis, whose love and understanding made the book possible.

Introduction

Discovering the Old Testament

This book seeks to introduce the reader to the overall content and meaning of the Old Testament. No attempt is made to cover all of the Old Testament. Selected material has been chosen by the author with the intent of emphasizing key ideas, events, and people in the Old Testament. The survey ranges from the Creation to the restoration of Israel as a nation following the Babylonian Exile. Hopefully, this material will prove to be a stimulus for further study of the Old Testament. The diversity and depth of the Old Testament makes a thorough coverage of the Scripture impractical. Although this book has been designed to serve as a text for a three-hour one semester course in Old Testament survey, the material is adaptable to a longer or shorter period of study.

Attitudes toward the Old Testament

Various approaches to the study of the Old Testament have validity, but, by themselves, may prove misleading. For example, some see the Old Testament as simply a literary product of the ancient Hebrews, but it is surely more than this! It is, in addition, a record of the history and heritage of an ancient people who survive to this day. Obviously, the Old Testament is religious literature and, in that regard it is unique. The Old Testament is, moreover, a book that has both human and divine dimensions. Several dozen men wrote and compiled the books of the Old Testament over a period of roughly one-thousand years. These men wrote with divine guidance and produced a book that is God's Word for all people.

The approach of the writer will be to take the words of the Old Testament on their own merit. For the most part, the material will be taken to mean what it says unless there is good reason for seeing it figuratively or symbolically. The emphasis will be more upon understanding the text than interpreting it. Ideally, the meaning will be drawn out of the text rather than read into it. The only presupposition with which the writer begins is that the Old Testament is God's revelation of Himself to mankind who have alienated themselves from the Creator. Ultimately, God through His kindness, love, and mercy restores sinful man, through Christ, to the Paradise that was lost in the Garden. Thus, the primary aim of this study is avowedly religious -- to come to know and understand God's Word and purpose more adequately.

Chronology of the Old Testament[1]

(1) Early History
?? to ca. 4000 B.C.
(Genesis 1-5)

From the Creation to the Flood

(2) Postdiluvian
ca. 4000 to 2000 B.C.
(Genesis 6-11)

From the Flood to the call of Abraham

(3) Patriarchal
ca. 2000 to 1843 B.C.
(Genesis 12-45)

From the call of Abraham to the migration to Egypt

(4) Egyptian (Bondage)
ca. 1843-1446 B.C.
(Genesis 46-Exodus 11)

From the migration to Egypt to the Exodus

(5) Wandering
ca. 1446 to 1406 B.C.
(Exodus 12-Deut. 34)

From the Exodus to entering of Canaan

(6) Conquest
ca. 1406 to 1380 B.C.
(Joshua 1-24)

From the entering of Canaan to the death of Joshua

(7) Era of Judges
ca. 1380 to 1050 B.C.
(Judges 1-I Sam. 7, Ruth)

From the death of Joshua to the anointing of Saul as King of Israel

(8) The United Kingdom
ca. 1050 to 931 B.C.
(I Samuel 8-I Kings 11-
I Chronicles)

From the anointing of Saul to the death of Solomon

(9) The Divided Kingdom
ca. 931-586 B.C.
(I Kings 12-II Kings 25-
II Chronicles)

From the death of Solomon to the Fall of Jerusalem

(10) The Two Kingdoms
Israel (North)
ca. 931 to 722 B.C.
prophets Jonah, Amos Hosea

From the accession of Jeroboam to the Fall of Samaria

[1]Based on an outline by B.S. Dean **(An Outline of Bible History)**, Cincinnati: Standard Pub., 1912

Judah (South) ca. 931 to 586 B.C. **prophets** Joel, Isaiah Micah, Zephaniah, Nahum, Jeremiah, Obadiah	From the accession of Rehoboam to the Fall of Jerusalem
(11) Babylonian Exile ca. 586 to 516 B.C. (II Kings 24-25) **prophets** Daniel, Ezekiel	From the Fall of Jerusalem to the return and rebuilding of the Temple
(12) Post-Exilic ca. 516 to 400 B.C. **prophets** Ezra, Nehemiah, Haggai, Zechariah, Malachi, (Esther)	From the rebuilding of the Temple to the end of the Old Testament canon

The chapters that follow should be studied with the Bible at hand. Specific Scripture reading is suggested at the beginning of the chapter. In addition, particular passages are cited as the lesson develops. There is simply on substitute for the actual reading of the Bible. All comments are based primarily on the content of the Scripture itself. The student will find his study more enlightening if more than one translation is consulted.

The Pentateuch

In the Hebrew Bible the first five books of the Old Testament are known as the Torah. Although the word Torah is usually translated "law," the better translation is "instruction" because the Torah is more than legislation. The Torah contains God's instructions and guidance for the whole life of the people of Israel. In addition to the religious dimension of life, political, social and even medical assistance is given. Significantly, the essential structure of the Torah is based on a covenant of faith and love between Yahweh and Israel. The designation Pentateuch is a later development derived from two Greek words meaning five volumes (or books).

Authorship of the Pentateuch has been a debated question only in modern times. Both the Biblical record and Jewish tradition is unanimous in ascribing the Torah to Moses. While modern scholars generally hold to a multiple authorship based primarily on a literary anaylsis of the first five Old Testament books, the evidence is not conclusive. For the basic arguments in favor of the Documentary Hypothesis see Ernst Sellin and George Fohrer's

Introduction to the Old Testament (trans. David E. Green, Abingdon Press). Roland K. Harrison's *Introduction to the Old Testament* (Eerdmans Publishing Co.) presents significant criticisms of the Documentary explanation of the Pentateuch. Perhaps the most useful summation of the arguments in favor of the Mosaic authorship is to be found in Merrill F. Unger's book *Introductory Guide to the Old Testament* (Zondervan Publishing House).

Since the main purpose of this book is to acquaint the reader with the basic content and religious value of the Old Testament, no attempt will be made to detail the complex arguments of authorship and date of the various books of the Old Testament. Such questions are better discussed in an Old Testament Introduction.

While the approach to the Old Testament text will be topical, the basic development of the material will follow, as far as possible, the probable chronological order of the Scripture. Essentially then, the sequence of events will be more historical than topical in arrangement.

Abbreviations

ANET	Ancient Near Eastern Texts (Princeton)
BW	Biblical World (Baker)
EC	Encyclopedia of Christianity (National Foundation for Christian Education)
IDB	Interpreter's Dictionary of the Bible (Abingdon)
ISBE	International Standard Bible Encyclopedia (Eerdmans)
NBC	New Bible Commentary (Eerdmans)
NBD	New Bible Dictionary (Eerdmans)
TOTC	Tyndale Old Testament Commentary (InterVarsity)
WBC	Wycliffe Bible Commentary (Moody)
WBE	Wycliffe Bible Encyclopedia (Moody)
ZPBD	Zondervan Pictorial Bible Dictionary
ZPED	Zondervan Pictorial Encyclopedia of the Bible

CHAPTER I
The Creation
"And God said..."

Readings: *Genesis 1:1-2:3; 2:4-24*

The Beginning: 1:1-2

In "beginning" God created the heavens and the earth! The Bible simply asserts the fact of God's creation. No attempt is made to present logical arguments nor historical evidence. The declaration is one of affirmation and faith. Some have argued, without sufficient evidence, that creation is a process of evolution. Others attempt to ignore the issue by simply saying that the creation of the world is an unknown factor. However, the Bible positively declares that God "created the heavens and the earth." The word create (bara') is used exclusively of God in the Old Testament and implies that the creation was **ex nihilo** (out of nothing). Genesis 1:1 does not clearly indicate that creation took place out of pre-existing material. If so, then God surely created this "material." It is the "Spirit" of God that moves upon the face of the waters which He has created.

Creation is by fiat! God speaks and the world comes into being. Genesis chapter one stresses that creation is the sole work of God. Creation is recounted in terms of command and fulfillment. No less than eight times does God say, "and let there be" with the response "and there was." Six times in the first chapter of the Bible the affirmation is "and it was so." This phrase emphasizes the fact that God's purpose and intention are carried out fully.

God's Week of Work: 1:3-31

The actual work of creation falls into a hexameron or period of six days. The Hebrew word "day" (yom) does not always mean a twenty-four hour period of time, but is often used to designate various lengths of time. Day in Hebrew, as is often the case in

English, simply refers to a period of time. In Genesis chapter one it is best to see the word "day" as a reference to the creative "day" of God. (See Gen. 2:4, Zech. 14:7, Deut. 7:1 where the word "day" does not mean a literal twenty-four hours.) In addition, it is important to keep in mind that God is not limited by either space or time (see Ps. 90:4, II Pet. 3:9) while God's creation is limited by both. Since God is the Creator of the universe, it is necessary that the Bible student avoid imposing his limitations on the Deity.

Throughout the account of creation the key emphasis is that "it was good!" At the end of the sixth day the declaration is even more emphatic--"and it was very good!" Contrary to popular opinion, the Old Testament does not teach that the world is evil in itself, rather the problem lies with mankind's misuse and abuse of the creation. What God creates is good! Here the clear assertion is that God is not the author of evil, but the Divine Creator of a good world. It is through mankind's disobedience that the earth has become corrupted. Ultimately, it is through God's Son that it will be redeemed.

Days One and Two: 1:3-8

God's creative week begins with the calling forth of light. God speaks and there is light! Then, He separates the light from the darkness and the first day is concluded. On day two the creation of a firmament (or expanse) takes place. This "firmament" refers to the establishment of a layer of air or atmosphere about the earth. The Hebrews referred to this "firmament" as one of the heavens.

Day Three: 1:9-13

During the third day of creation dry land is separated from the waters (seas). Vegetation, including plants and trees, is the next item of creation. At this point the principle of propagation is introduced. Each plant is to reproduce "after its kind." Later, this principle will also include animals and human beings as well. In contrast to most evolutionary theories, the Bible declares that reproduction is within the species. No crossover is implied even on a long term basis. Limited evolution is certainly possible since change and development do take place within a species. For example, all of the varieties of tomato have originated from just one member of the night-shade family. This same principle can be applied to citrus trees, animals, and even people. Here we are dealing with a horizontal evolution (i.e. change within a species) as over against Darwinian evolution which is vertical (i.e. change and development from the simplest to the most complex form of life with one single line of evolution). In the Bible change takes place only within a species, never from one species to another. At the close of the third day the assertion is "and it was good."

Days Four and Five: 1:14-23

On the fourth day, the luminaries are created. Literally the word "luminary" means "light holder." In the case of the sun, moon, and stars the primary function is to produce light. The sun was also created to produce heat. These luminaries were to aid mankind in such matters as planting, growing crops, and working. Both the sun and the moon were to assist in the utilization and understanding of seasons, directions, and time.

Sea animals and birds come into existence on the fifth day. As in the case of plants, each animal was to reproduce "after its kind." Obviously the multiplicity of sea creatures and birds in our day is to be accounted for on the basis of change and development within the various species. In this regard the Genesis account is not at variance with science as such.

Day Six: 1:24-31

Land animals and human beings are created on the sixth and final day of creation. Each animal is created "according to its kind." Human beings are a special and distinct creation. In fact, both male and female humans are created in the "image of God." This likeness is evidently a spiritual and not a physical one. Humans are like God because they have a "soul." Genesis 2:7 says, "then the Lord God formed man of dust from the ground, and He breathed into his nostrils the breath of life, and man became a living being." In contrast to animals, humans are rational and morally responsible beings since they are in the "image" and "likeness" of the Creator.

The phrase "let us make man in our likeness" in Genesis 1:27 has been variously interpreted as a reference to (1) the "trinity," (2) God's heavenly court (angels), and as (3) the Hebrew plural of majesty. Of the three, the third is the most probable since it is characteristic of the Hebrew language to use the plural to indicate greatness and power. For example, the generic word for God in Hebrew is **Elohim,** the plural of **El,** (God). In order to express the power and majesty of One God, the plural is normally used. Apparently, this is also the reason for the plural in Genesis 1:27. Certainly there is no implication of polytheism. The idea of the "trinity" at this early stage in God's dealings with man would not be understandable at all, although it is possible that the plural would include the "heavenly court." In any case, the key point is that mankind is created in the "image" of God.

God's injunction to mankind in 1:28 is to "be fruitful and multiply, and fill the earth and subdue it..." Both responsibility and privilege are placed upon the human race. Finally, after the sixth creative day everything which God had created is declared to be "very good," a positive description of God's excellent creation which is later to be marred by sin.

Day Seven: 2:1-3

On the seventh day God rests from the work of creation. This "rest" is not an absolute one, but a rest from the activity of creation (see Jn. 5:17). The word Sabbath is derived from the word translated "rest" in Genesis 2:2. God blessed and sanctified the seventh day because it celebrated the end of His work of creating the world. Interestingly, there is no mention of "evening" on the seventh day. Some have taken this to be a mystical reference to heaven where there will never be any night (see Heb. 4:4, Rev. 21:22-25).

Creation in Genesis chapter one follows a clear line of development from the least complex to the more complex. This is demonstrated in the arrangement of organic life from plants to sea animals and birds, then upward to land animals, and finally humans. On the surface this might appear to be a telling argument for organic evolution; but the Biblical account indicates that the creation is limited in its capacity for change and development. Each plant and animal is commanded to reproduce "after its kind." No crossover of species is intimated, or even permitted, in Genesis. Since modern science is still unraveling the riddle of creation, there is no reason to suspect that science and the Bible are in serious conflict. (See James Jauncey's discussion of the subject in his book **Science Returns to God**.) The order of creation is logical for light precedes the existence of plants, animals, and even the sun! This primeval light, while to some degree uncertain in its nature, is directly provided by God. Such a feat is no more mysterious than man's ability to produce artificial light for plants.

Creation of Adam and Eve: 2:4-24

A more detailed account of the creation of human beings is given in Genesis chapter two. Some have seen this as a second account of creation or as a reworking of a "priestly myth." However, the two accounts (Gen. 1,2) are complementary. Genesis chapter two simply gives a more detailed account of God's supreme creation. It has been objected that Genesis chapter two is too anthropomorphic (i.e. it seems to describe God as a man), but the description is given in a figurative sense so that the account would be more understandable. In fact, how else can we relate to God except in human terms? It is also true that the Genesis Two narrative is geocentric as some assert, but this is so in a religious sense and not scientifically. No significant scientific problem arises with the creation story in Genesis, if the account is taken at face value.

From a social viewpoint, the original pair were monogamous. The closeness between husband and wife was ordained from the beginning. From Adam's rib came his wife and they were both to "cleave" to one another becoming a marital unity (i.e. "one flesh").

Extra-Biblical Creation Stories:

Several ancient Near Eastern cultures have accounts of creations. In some respects these are similar to the Genesis account, but in others they differ from the Biblical one. For example, in the Babylonian story known as the **Enuma Elish**, it is asserted that the world was made by god Marduk from the carcass of the slain sea monster Tiamat. He then shapes the earth and sky out of her lifeless body. Humans were then fashioned out of the blood of Kingu, Tiamat's consort. The whole narrative is grossly polytheistic in contrast to the monotheistic Genesis account. The latter reflects an advanced philosophical and scientific viewpoint. (For further study see Alexander Heidel's, **The Babylonian Genesis.**) The Genesis record is an affirmation of God's direct creation. God speaks and the world is. God created the earth for the habitation of human beings who are then given an opportunity to serve Him.

Discussion - Questions to consider:
1. What is the significance of the order of creation? Why seven days?
2. Does the Biblical account of creation conflict with modern science?
3. What is the religious meaning of creation?
4. Why is light created on the first day of creation? How can there be light without the sun, moon and stars?
5. In what way is man created in the "image" of God (Gen. 1:27)?
6. What is the distinction between the physical body and the soul (Gen. 2:7)?
7. Why did God create the universe and human beings?
8. Would extra-biblical accounts of creation be an indirect proof of validity of the Biblical one? Would the extra-biblical creation stories point to a probable common knowledge of the "creation" in the ancient world?
9. What similarities and differences do you see between the Genesis account of creation and modern evolutionary views?

10. Do scientists know the actual nature of creation?

Resources for additional study:

B.W. Anderson, "Creation," *IDB*

Robert P. Benedict, *Journey Away from God* (Revell)

R. K. Harrison, "Creation," *ZPEB*

Alexander Heidel, *The Babylonian Genesis* (University of Chicago Press)

James Jauncey, *Science Returns to God* (Zondervan)

Derek Kidner, *Genesis* (Intervarsity - TOTC

James Lindsay, "Creation," *ISBE*

K. C. McKay, "Creation," *NBD*

Allan A. MacRae, "Creation," *ZPBD*

Henry M. Morris, *The Bible and Modern Science* (Moody)

Francis A. Schaeffer, *Genesis in Time and Space* (Intervarsity)

Jack Wood Sears, *Conflict and Harmony in Science and the Bible* (Baker)

Edward J. Young, "Creation," *EC*

CHAPTER II
The Fall
"What is this that you have done?"

Readings: Genesis 3:1-4:26; 5:1-32

The Tempter: 3:1-5

Sin is disobedience of God's law! The first sin was committed when the progenitors of the human race ate of the forbidden tree. Of course Adam and Eve were led astray by the Serpent, but they were responsible for their action. The Serpent subtly suggested that God had restricted the "tree of knowledge" for selfish reasons. He declares that "eating of the tree" will make them like God. This half-truth failed to indicate that "knowledge of good and evil" brings responsibility as well as privilege. Through an act of disobedience our first parents lost not only their status of "innocence" but the blessings and benefits of the Garden. Likewise, the assertion of the Serpent that death would not occur from eating the forbidden fruit was also a half-truth. Immediate death did not result, but both physical and spiritual death became a reality because of the act of disobedience. The ability of the Serpent to speak may seem strange to us, but it would no more have appeared so to the first man and woman in their primeval innocence than to a small child today. The Serpent is surely Satan in disguise. Knowledge did come as the Serpent promised, but so did death!

The Test: 3:6-7

The tree in the "midst of the garden" was there to test Adam and Eve. Clearly there was no valid reason to eat of the "tree" since the produce of the garden was more than adequate for sustenance. Some have raised the question, why have the "tree" at all? Such a question fails to take into account that God wants people to serve him voluntarily and not by coercion. If no opportunity for choice had been given, then we would be less than human, no more than intelligent animals. Perhaps even androids--creatures without a soul. God tested the loyalty and self-control of Adam and Eve by giving them a choice. Such was the purpose of the "tree of knowledge of good and evil." The first pair are without excuse since they committed an unnecessary act of willful disobedience. It was ambition and pride that led to their downfall. A simple trust and faith in the Deity would have deterred them from their tragic decision. Disobedience brought an awareness of the potential for evil as well as good.

The Tragedy: 3:8-24

Notice the development of sin. The Tempter appears in **disguise** and instills **doubt** about God in the minds of the original pair. This **doubt** then leads to a **desire** for the forbidden fruit that eventuates in the decision to **disobey** their Creator and Companion. Until the moment of disobedience, they had intimate fellowship and communication with the Deity himself. Adam and Eve were on probation in the Garden of Eden, but they violated the trust placed in them.

With the disobedience of God's will came nakedness--both physical and spiritual because they now found themselves without God's presence and protection. The shame of their nakedness was so great that when God arrives in the Garden they unsuccessfully attempt to hide themselves. In response to God's query about eating of the restricted tree Adam blames his wife and she, in turn, attempts to pass off her guilt to the Serpent. However, no such evasion is possible. Each was individually responsible. Some interpreters have speculated that the sin of Adam and Eve was the sex act. Such a view is obviously in contradiction to God's direct command to "be fruitful and multiply, and fill the earth..." (Gen. 1:28). Reproduction, even the sex act itself, is not wrong in the sacred state of matrimony (see Gen. 2:24-25). In addition, it is highly improbable that the tree of "knowledge" was an "apple" tree since the word apple is derived from the Latin word for fruit. There is no need to assume that the tree was magical either. The point of the Genesis 3 account is that sin began through an act of disobedience. Whatever the exact nature of the tree, it is clear that Adam and Eve violated the express command of God.

Sin brought judgment! First, on the Serpent who was condemned to crawl on his "belly." The Serpent was once a reptile with legs. However, the Serpent was used by Satan and suffered the penalty of the association. On the woman, the judgment was not only banishment from the privileges of the Garden, but hardship in childbirth as well. The man, too, lost paradise and was condemned to earn his "bread" by the "sweat of his face." Even the ground would oppose him with thorns and thistles.

Included in the expulsion from the Garden is the pronouncement of death--"you are dust, and to dust you shall return." Physically mankind began to die when banished from the Garden. The "tree of life" was not available outside the Garden. From the moment of birth, death became the assured end of life. Death means "separation" and sin deprived mankind of eternal life. Although spiritual death also accompanied the banishment, a promise is made for the future restoration of human beings. God declares to the woman that her "seed" would bruise the "head" of the serpent (i.e. the Messiah will be born of a woman and will destroy the power of Satan and sin--see Gen. 3:15). Although the Fall brought the human race to a low moral state, the new awareness arising from the disobedience in the Garden did bring mental growth. Now, there is a new dimension to knowledge, i.e. an understanding of the nature and consequence of sin. "Man is still to attain to immortality, but it must now be through struggle, sorrow, penitence, faith, and death" (R. Payne Smith). Because of disobedience mankind is banished from the Garden and access to the "tree of life" there. Later, through Christ, the "tree" will be restored and once again available for all people (see Rev. 22:2).

The Temptation--True or False?

Some Bible scholars see the account of the Fall as a myth or legend. Such a view, however, fails to take into account the full implication and meaning of sin in human life. If the Fall is not real, then what is the significance of sin? While it is granted that the names Adam (mankind) and Eve (living) have symbolic meaning, yet this is equally true of almost every name in the Old Testament since Hebrew names consistently have symbolic significance. Too much can be made of the meaning of a name. In addition, Adam and Eve are mentioned as the first created humans in Genesis 2. The account is not presented as legend, but as history. The truth of the tragedy in the Garden is seen in the tragic results so obviously apparent in human life. Mankind stands before God naked, polluted with sin, and guilty because each person like Adam of old has sinned against God and his neighbor. Some have asserted that not only has mankind inherited the consequences and influences of the "first sin," but has inherited the very sin itself, and is born a sinner. This theological view known as "original sin" holds that each individual actually carries the sin of Adam and Eve. Such a view distorts both mankind's responsibility and God's justice since it declares the "innocent" guilty on the basis of paternal relationship alone. The Scripture does teach that one is born into a world of sin where sin is the predominant influence, but nowhere does the Scripture state that one is born a sinner (see Ps. 51:5). It is to be granted that human beings have a tendency toward sin, but this results from the limitations of the physical body and the influence of others. In addition, the human race is deprived of free will and condemned before any wrong act is committed, if one is born a sinner. While many sincere people do opt for "original sin," nevertheless such a capricious view of God is out of harmony with the Bible as a whole which teaches that God is just, loving, and kind.

Admittedly, the ability of the Serpent to speak is unusual, but certainly not an impossibility, especially when it is remembered that the animal was a mouthpiece of Satan. Mankind had been appointed as steward of all God's creatures, but the Serpent seeks to rise above the man and woman. That the Serpent was a mouthpiece of Satan is no legend since both Paul (II Cor. 11:3) and John (Jn. 8:44) see the event as historical. It has been argued by some that Genesis 3 is a legend that reveals the true sinful nature of mankind. However, the Fall must surely be more than this! If the account of the origin of sin is legend, then would not our redemption be no more than legend? The truth is that both the Fall and salvation through Christ are **real**!

The Tragic Tale of Two Brothers: 4:1-26

Genesis chapter four details the growth and development of sin from the murder of Abel to Lamech's arrogant Song of Hate. The progression of sin from Adam to Cain and finally to Lamech is not only real but tragic. The influence of Adam and Eve's disobedience on Cain is obvious although it is hardly appropriate to imply that this was a direct inheritance. All people, like Cain, have the tendency and propensity for sin, but the disease is acquired environmentally, not biologically.

Cain's sin, as Adam's, was one of disobedience. There is no valid reason to think that Cain's sacrifice was rejected simply because it was not a "blood" offering. The Hebrew writer declares that Abel's offering was more acceptable than Cain's because it was offered "by faith" (Heb. 11:4). This verse could imply that Cain had deliberately offered a vegetable sacrifice in contradiction to God's express command to bring a "blood sacrifice." The contention however is an argument from silence since the Scripture nowhere records such a command. In fact, later, at the time of Moses, provision is made for the very poor to substitute "flour" for a "blood" sacrifice in the sin offering (Lev. 5:11). Not all sacrifices were blood offerings, as some have asserted (see Lev. 1-5).

Cain's sin was really one of pride that degenerated into a jealous rage. Abel's death was apparently a deliberate act by Cain. After the foul deed, Cain attempts to avoid responsibility for his action, but he cannot escape from his act nor from God. Because he feared the consequences of his deed, God placed a "mark" upon Cain to protect him from blood-revenge. There is no ground at all for assuming that the "mark" on Cain was punishment for his act. Even less probable is the view that Cain's skin color was changed. Even if this were the case, and there is no evidence for it, Cain and his descendants were destroyed by the Flood; only Noah and his family survived.

The old question as to where Cain got his wife really merits little discussion since it is obvious that she was a woman and not an ape. Whether Cain's wife was a sister or the result of an additional creation by God is really immaterial. In the early days of man's history intermarriage between relatives would not necessarily have created a serious problem, morally or physically. Of course the possibility that God created other human beings cannot be discounted outright even though the Bible is silent on the matter. Cain's line of descendants degenerated morally to the point where Lamech, who was not only a bigamist, but even killed a young man for merely striking him. He then boldly brags that his sin was ten times worse than that of his forefather Cain. In fact, the family of Cain continued toward self-destruction until finally destroyed in the Flood at the time of Noah.

The True Descendants of Adam (the line of Seth): 5:1-32

With the murder of Abel, God gives Adam and Eve another son, Seth. Then a son, Enosh, was born to Seth. In contrast to the line of Cain, "men began to call upon the name of the Lord." The family of Seth had a number of people of notable godliness. In particular, "Enoch walked with God; and he was not, for God took him" (Gen. 5:24). The implication is that Enoch never experienced physical death, but was taken by God directly to be with Him. This "translation," though unusual, was undoubtedly an honor bestowed because of Enoch's godliness. Elijah's ascension to heaven in a "whirlwind" is the only other recorded instance of translation (see II Kings 2:11).

Many people have been troubled by the longevity of the descendants of Seth. Methusaleh, the longest living person on record, lived a total of 969 years! Even Adam lived to be 930. Attempts have been made to rationalize these extraordinary life spans. It has been suggested that the years were really months. If so, Enoch became the father of Methusaleh at the age of five years and five months, an improbability not even worthy of comment. Another common suggestion is to argue that the ages are obvious exaggerations. This suggestion raises at least two problems. First, specific ages are given of the father at the time of the son's birth as well as at the death of each of the patriarchs. Second, such long lives are not nearly so improbable as they once were. Modern medical science now predicts a possible lifespan of 600 or more years. During the early history of mankind, when the population of the world was small, and less polluted, long lives would have been quite possible. In any case, after the Flood the length of life gradually decreases from the 950 years of Noah to the 175 years of Abraham and, finally, to the three score and ten in Psalms (90:10). The extraordinary length of life in Genesis is not impossible for God.

This section demonstrates the universality of death. With the exception of Enoch, all died regardless of longevity. Death, a fact of life and the result of sin, is finally conquered through the Messiah (Christ).

Discussion - Questions to consider:

1. Why didn't God create man so that he could not sin?
2. Why did God put the Tree of "knowledge of good and evil" in the Garden of Eden?
3. What are the consequences of the first sin for mankind?

4. What evidence do we have for connecting the Serpent with Satan?
5. Are there any problems with the view that the Fall was a legend or myth?
6. What was the nature of the sin of Adam and Eve?
7. Why was Cain's sacrifice rejected?
8. What is the significance of the "mark" placed upon Cain?
9. What does Lamech's arrogance and attitude say about the power of sin?
10. How do you account for the long lives in the early period of mankind's history?

Resources for additional study:

James O. Bushwell, "Sin" *ZPBD*

C.C. Crawford, *Genesis, Volume I* (College Press)

J. Daane, "Sinner," *ZPEB*

F.E. Davidson, ed. *The New Bible Commentary* (Eerdmans)

S.J. DeVries, "Sin," *IDB*

Charles Erdman, *Genesis* (Revell)

Joseph P. Free, *Archaeology and Bible History* (VanKampen)

Derek Kidner, *Genesis* (Intervarsity - TOTC)

John E. Kuzenga, "Sin" *ISBE*

Herbert Lockyer, *All the Doctrines of the Bible* "Sin" (Zondervan)

J. Murray, "Sin" *NBD*

J. Barton Payne, *Theology of the Older Testament* "The Origin of Sin" (Zondervan)

Charles Pfeiffer, Everett Harrison, "Genesis," *WBC*

C.C. Ryrie, "Sin," *WBE*

Geerhardus Vos, *Biblical Theology* (Eerdmans) pp. 37-55

E.J. Young, *Genesis 3* (Banner of Truth Trust, and Presbyterian & Reformed)

CHAPTER III
The Flood
"My Spirit shall not always strive with man..."

Readings: *Genesis 6:1-9:29; 10:1-32*

Reason for the Flood: 6:1-8

Genesis six depicts the universal condition of mankind without God! "Every imagination of the thoughts of his heart was only evil continually." With the exception of Noah and his family, the human race was in a state of total rebellion against its Creator. The tragic results of this defection are seen in the intermarriage of the "sons of God" with the "daughters of men." The usual suggestion that these "sons of God" were angels has little merit since the Scripture nowhere indicates that angels are capable of reproduction. Jesus, himself, clearly describes angels as non-sexual beings. He says that angels "neither marry nor are given in marriage" (see Matt. 22:30, Lu. 20:34-36, Mk. 12:25). The more probable answer is that the "sons of God" represent the "godly" descendants of the line of Seth and that the "daughters of men" were the children of the descendants of Cain. Apparently, the negative influence of the line of Cain was so dominating the world that every person's thoughts were constantly on Evil. The situation became so bad that God had to call a halt to the normal operation of the world with a massive flood. The actual **cause** of the flood was the sinfulness of mankind. God was disappointed with the whole of his creation. Corruption and violence permeated the world. What was once innocence had now become decadence. Not only is paradise lost, even the remaining descendants of Adam are about to be destroyed. However, one man did find "favor in the eyes of the Lord." It is Noah who proves to be the nucleus of a faithful remnant. Noah, like Enoch of old, "walked with God."

A Remnant Saved: 6:9-10, 18-20; 7:1-3, 7-9, 13-16; 8:16-19

Contrary to popular opinion, the purpose of the Flood was not to destroy mankind. If this had been the actual purpose, then not even Noah and his family would have been saved! The ark would have been a useless boat. As it was, Noah, his family, and the animals in the ark were spared. It was the extreme wickedness, which was so rampant in the world of Noah, that God erradicated. The lesson here is that God did not totally reject or even destroy his creation. He dramatically removed the cancerous sin of rebellion in mankind that had become intolerable. The result of the flood was that a thoroughly representative remnant was saved out of the whole of God's creation.

The Raging Deluge: local or universal? 7:1-24

God brought a great flood upon the earth to destroy the wickedness of mankind. The actual date of this catastrophic event is uncertain. Estimates range from 2000 to 4000 B.C. with the latter date more probable in light of geological data. Considerable evidence is available for a massive flood, but some have contended that the Noahic flood was a local one limited to the Mesopotamian Valley. The argument is that a universal flood would not have been possible. But this view presupposes the present geological configuration of the earth. If the earth's land area was radically different at that time (i.e. a surface that is more level than presently exists), then theoretically the whole earth could have been covered by water. According to the Scriptures, the water came not only from rain, but also through the upward movement of underground streams (see Gen. 7:11). Those who argue for a universal flood insist that the Bible clearly declares that the flood covered the whole earth to fifteen cubits (22½ feet) above the mountains (7:17-22). In addition, Genesis 7:23 says that God "blotted out every living thing that was upon the face of the earth." On the other hand, it is averred by some Bible students that the word "mountain" refers to artificial mountains made of stone known as ziggurats (an ancient temple tower of the Babylonians in pyramidal form). Nevertheless, the Genesis account specifically states that the "ark" came to rest on "the mountains of Ararat" (8:4). However, one problem does arise for the "universal flood" view. The word earth (eretz) does not normally refer to the planet earth but to the inhabited land, particularly the immediate area of the Middle East.

Three significant factors concerning the flood should be kept in mind. First, the flood lasted over a year (371 days); second, the flood rose 15 cubits above the mountains; and third, "all flesh died that moved upon the earth" with the exception of those in the Ark. All of these points argue in favor of a massive flood of universal proportions. Nevertheless, the key point of the Genesis account is not the area covered by the deluge, but the intent which was to remove the extreme wickedness of mankind from the earth. Therefore, the flood would have needed to cover only the "inhabited" area of the earth. If, at the time of Noah, mankind had not moved out of the Mesopotamian Valley, then the area of the flood could well have been limited to the place where people were located. In any case, the Flood was a judgment of God upon the evil of mankind.

Related Extra-Biblical Evidence for the Flood:

Geologically, evidence does exist for a world-wide Flood. (See Whitcomb and Morris, **The Genesis Flood,** Chapter V - *Modern Geology and the Deluge.*) Historically, the Flood account is especially convincing at least insofar as it was ethnologically universal. Stories of a "great flood" are found among all peoples. In general, the accounts tell of a massive flood that liquidates all but a select few. Accounts can be found in such diverse places as among the Indians of the United States, the Aborigines of Australia, the Aryans of India, as well as the ancient Babylonians. The Babylonian (or Chaldean) story is found in the famous Gilgamesh Epic. Many details of the Babylonian account correspond with the Biblical one. In the Gilgamesh Epic the deity Chronos instructs a devotee, Xisuthrus, to build a large vessel 1,100 yards long and 440 yards wide (five furlongs by two). After the boat is built, Xisuthrus takes his wife, children and friends aboard. A flood of indeterminate length ensues. Like Noah, he sends forth birds to locate dry land. At this point, the Babylonian account diverges from the Biblical for Xisuthrus, his wife, daughter, and pilot emerge from the boat. Xisuthrus worships the ground, builds an altar, and sacrifices to the gods. Following this, he and his wife and daughter as well as the pilot disappear. The remaining members of the crew disembark and receive a parting message from Xisuthrus, whom they worship as a god. The message was for them to remain faithful to the gods and to go to Babylon (Sippara) to find a special set of writings that would benefit mankind.

As in the Noahic account, the vessel lands in Armenia, but, in contrast, the Babylonian story is grossly polytheistic. While no attempt is being made to harmonize the two stories, it is pertinent to observe that the similarity of the two accounts does make the Bible description even more credible. Universal accounts of a massive flood in the early history of mankind point to both a great flood and to the Mesopotamian Valley as the area of origin of the human race. Apparently, the flood account was carried all over the world by those who left the Tigris-Euphrates Valley and emigrated into the diverse corners of the earth.

The Results of the Flood: 8:1-9:29

Although the rain and flooding was limited to forty days, the land itself did not return to normal for one year and ten days after the rain began. It is possible that the flood was limited to the area where there were inhabitants and this may well have been the Mesopotamian Tigris-Euphrates River Valley (modern Iraq) although this cannot be absolutely certain. The Flood did accomplish its purpose. It cleansed the earth of the extreme wickedness that had come to dominate its inhabitants. As a faithful remnant, Noah, his sons, and their wives survived along with representatives of the animal kingdom.

Noah's different quality of life was demonstrated by his first act upon leaving the ark. He built an altar and offered a burnt offering thereby expressing his dedication to God. In accepting the offering God declares that He will never again bring a world flood upon the inhabitants of the earth. This promise was established by a covenant with Noah permitting mankind to use the earth and its produce, but forbidding murder. The "rainbow" was set as a sign and guarantee of this covenant. Included in this agreement were Noah's sons and their wives and descendants. From Shem, Ham and Japheth the earth was to be repopulated.

Perhaps the main lesson of the Flood is that God brings judgment upon mankind for sin. No escape from the responsibility for our actions is possible. Whatever is sown must also be reaped. However, God never leaves himself without a faithful remnant. Noah and his family constituted a nucleus from which a new beginning could be made. In due time, the Messiah will come bringing redemption to all humanity who, because of sin, could not save themselves.

Redistribution of Mankind: 10:1-11:9

Genesis ten describes the populating of the earth following the flood. From Noah's sons the various peoples of the world developed. The descendants of Japheth moved out of the Mesopotamian Valley towards the North, Northwest, and East. Those going North became the ancestors of the Scythians and Slavic nations while the Celts, Germans, Greeks, and Romance people developed from those who went Northwest. The descendants of Madai, Japheth's son became the people of the East including the Indian and Iranic nations.

Ham became the progenitor of the nations of the Southwest including the Canaanites, Egyptians, Libyians, and Ethiopians. Shem's descendants, known as Semites, remained in the Near East. The Semites include the Assyrians, Babylonians, Syrians, Arabians and, of course, the Hebrews. From a mixture of these peoples eventually all the nations of the earth emerge.

Genesis 11:1-9 graphically describes the growth of language. The boldness of Noah's offspring is illustrated by their attempt to build a Tower (ziggurat) to heaven. While no physical tower could actually be built to reach heaven, the arrogant attitude of those building it was leading mankind back down the road that led to the Great Flood. In order to diversify the people and prevent easy cooperation in evil enterprises, God intervened and introduced a variety of languages into their speech. The result was a state of confusion since communication became no more than a babble of sounds. Hence the name, Tower of Babel (confusion). This diversity of languages proved to be a blessing in disguise. The descendants of Noah left the Mesopotamian Valley with others of like speech and began to settle the various regions of the earth.

Discussion - Questions to consider:

1. Why did God bring the Flood upon the earth?
2. Who were the "sons of God" and the "daughters of men"?
3. Why does God save Noah and his family from the flood?
4. What is your assessment of Noah's life and character?
5. What historical evidence do we have for a universal flood?
6. What problems are involved in the view that the Flood was a local one? a universal one?
7. What did the Flood accomplish?

8. What lesson can we learn from a study of the Flood story in Genesis?

9. How did the various peoples of the earth develop?

10. Why did God "confuse" the speech of the people at the Tower of Babel?

Resources for additional study:

Gleason Archer, *A Study of Old Testament Introduction* "Noah's Ark and the Flood (Moody) pp. 192-203

W.U. Ault, "Flood," *ZPEB*

Joseph P. Free, *Archaeology and Bible History* (VanKampen)

Alexander, Heidel, *Gilgamesh Epic and Old Testament Parallels* (U. of Chicago Press)

Werner Keller, *The Bible as History* "Digging up the Flood" (Morrow) pp. 25-41

Derek Kidner, *Genesis* (Intervarsity) pp. 83-111

J.H. Marks, *"Flood,"* IDB

T.C. Mitchell, "Flood," NBD

John W. Montgomery, *The Quest for Noah's Ark* (Bethany)

Andre Parrot, *The Flood and Noah's Ark* (Philosophical Library)

A.M. Rhewinkel, *The Flood* (Concordia)

Harry Rimmer, *Harmony of Science and Scripture* (Baker)

Merrill Unger, *Archaeology and the Old Testament* (Zondervan)

John C. Whitcomb & Henry M. Morris, *The Genesis Flood* (Presbyterian and Reformed)

———— . "Flood, Deluge," *ZPBD & WBE*

George F. Wright, "Deluge, of Noah," *ISBE*

CHAPTER IV

Abraham

"Now the Lord said...
'Go from your country and your kindred...
to the land I will show you.' "

Readings: Genesis 11:27-25:10

Faith and a Man of Obedience: 11:27-12:9

Without question, Abraham was a man of faith! Though often repeated, the assertion is a significant one. Hebrew history begins with the patriarch and divine history is affirmed by his life. Abraham was called by God to leave his home in Ur of Chaldea (Old Babylonia) and go to a new and undistinguished land (i.e. Canaan). God would make of Abraham a great nation and, of Canaan, a great land. The call included three promises (12:1-3), each of which became a means of testing his emerging faith. Abraham was promised a "land," but he was a wanderer and stranger there (12:10; 17:8; 20:1; 21:23; 23:4) since the land was occupied by others such as the Canaanites, Hittites, Amorites, and the Jebusites (12:6; 13:7; 15:18-21). He and his family left the land, temporarily, because of a famine (12:10ff) and, later, he had to buy a parcel of ground in which to bury his wife Sarah (23:1-16)! The second promise of a "great nation" (12:2; 13:15; 15:5; 18:18; 22:17) proved to be equally frustrating. Both Abraham and Sarah were beyond the normal child bearing age (11:30). Abraham was, at first, disturbed that Eliezer of Damascus, his chief steward, would be his heir (15:2ff). Later, on the advice of his wife, he tries to obtain an heir by proxy. Through his wife's maid, Hagar, an apparent heir, Ishmael, was born (16:1-15). Although Ishmael was especially blessed by God, he was not to be Abraham's heir. The promised son, Isaac, appeared, at the time, to be an impossibility. Both Abraham (17:17) and Sarah (18:12), who were nearly one hundred years old, laughed at the thought of having a child. Appropriately, as a reminder of their unbelief, the son who was finally born was named Isaac (laughter). Later, the near sacrifice of Isaac on Mt. Moriah appeared almost to negate the promise again (22:12).

The third element of the promise, that of a "universal blessing," was also an area of distress for Abraham. For example, twice Abraham was a source of trouble by misleading Pharaoh (12:10-20), and later, Abimelech, (20:1-18), into thinking Sarah was not his wife. The implications of this action will be discussed later. In addition, disunity arose between Abraham and Lot's servants and they had to separate (13:2-18).

All of these elements of testing proved to be a means of refining the faith of the great patriarch. God's promises, as in the case of Abraham, often find fulfillment through trial and suffering. The value of divine blessing is often enhanced by the purifying power of perseverance and trust.

Faith, Fact or Fiction - Abraham and the Patriarchs: 12:10-20; 16:1-15; 20:1-20

In the early part of the twentieth century it was generally assumed by critical scholars that Abraham, as well as the other patriarchs, were vague traditions with little historical credibility. Wellhausen, for example, argued that Abraham was probably the free creation of the writer's mind. Gunkel regarded Abraham as a legend that was formed into a cycle of Abraham stories. Some, like Winckler and Noeldeke, even went so far as to see Abraham as a deity, perhaps Sin, the moon god of ancient Babylonia. However, modern scholars, with the exception of Noth, accept the essential historicity of Abraham. (For further study see Ignatius Hunt's book, **The World of the Patriarchs** and E.J. Young, **Introduction to the Old Testament.**)

The Old Testament itself presents the account of Abraham and the other patriarchs as straightforward history. Also, the New Testament consistently portrays Abraham as an historical figure (see Mt. 1:1, 8:11; Mk. 12:26; Lu. 13:28; Jn. 8:37; Acts 3:13; Rom. 4; II Cor. 11:22; Heb. 2:16, 11:8-10; James 2:21). In recent years, archaeology has shown that the Biblical account is not only credible, but historically convincing. For example, Wellhausen and others held that there was no writing before 1000 B.C. Now we know, with the discovery of the Ras Shamra texts in 1929, that Canaanite (Ugaritic) writing goes back to the 15th century B.C. In addition, 20,000 Hurrian Cuneiform tablets (dating back to the 19th and 20th centuries B.C.) were discovered at Mari, beginning in 1933, by Andre Parrot. This site (modern Tell Hariri) is located on the Euphrates River in the same area where the patriarchs once lived. Patriarchal names such as Nahor, Serug, and Terah (Abraham's father) occur as place names.

Another Hurrian center, at Nuzi, reflects the cultural environment of the patriarchs. For example, in the past, it was assumed that Abraham lied about Sarah being both his wife and sister (to Pharaoh, Gen. 12 and Abimelech, Gen. 20). In actuality, Abraham did tell part of the truth. According to 20:12, Sarah was his half-sister. In addition, it was the custom of the Hurrians at Nuzi to marry a woman twice, once as a wife and then as a sister. The second marriage ceremony, in which Abraham and Sarah may well have participated, was conducted when a husband was particularly fond of his wife. The same situation applies to Isaac and Rebekah. While no attempt should be made to excuse Abraham for his action, it is clear that he tries to deceive by not reporting the full nature of the "brother-sister" relationship. Perhaps Abraham (and later Isaac) was trying to save himself from death, but his action was wrong nonetheless. While the deception reveals a weakness in the patriarch, yet the action also indicates the humanness of a great man like Abraham. In addition, the archaeological evidence from Nuzi indicates that the wife-sister relationship was a common one among the ancient Hurrians. Another illustration of Hurrian custom is the instance of Sarah obtaining a child through Hagar her handmaiden. This method of securing children, by proxy, was common at Nuzi. The child born from the union belonged to Sarah, although tragically she rejected the child. Another puzzling incident, which will be discussed in the next section, is that of Esau selling his birthright and losing his blessing. The biblical patriarchs reflect the customs that were practiced at Nuzi. Although these archaeological parallels do not prove the Bible accounts, the information does make the patriarchal narratives more believable. As a result, few people today doubt the basic historicity of the accounts.

Faith and the Certainty of God's Promises and Judgment: 13:1-9; 14:17-24; 15:1-20; 17:1-27; 18:1-33; 19:1-36

At Bethel, Abraham and his nephew Lot parted company because of the inability of their servants to get along. Lot's choice of the fertile valley around Sodom and Gomorrah proved to be an unwise one. Shortly after Abraham and his servants had moved to the hill country, Lot and his family are captured, along with some of the citizens of Sodom, by a coalition of kings from Mesopotamia. Abraham, using a crack regiment of 318 men, rescued Lot, his family, and the King of Sodom at Dan (Laish). On his return to Hebron Abraham stops at Mt. Moriah and meets Melchizedek, the priest-king of Salem (later, Jerusalem). Abraham receives bread and wine as well as a blessing from the priest. In turn, the patriarch gives tithes and offerings to the mysterious Melchizedek. In the book of Hebrews Melchizedek becomes a type of the non-Aaronic priesthood of the Messiah (Heb. 7:1-17). Significantly, Abraham's gift of tithes and offerings predates the Mosaic Law where the tithe becomes mandatory.

When Abraham returns to Hebron the original covenant is reaffirmed (15:1-6). Later, God declares that Ishmael is not to be the promised son (16). Then, as a sign of the promise, Abram (lofty father) is circumcised at age 99 and his name is changed to Abraham (father of a multitude). The new name was a prophetic guarantee of the anticipated fulfillment of God's promise of a "great nation." A short time later three men (or angels?) appear to Abraham with two announcements, the coming judgment upon Sodom and Gomorrah and the imminent birth of the promised son. In the case of the first, Abraham intercedes for the city of Sodom asking that it be spared if there are fifty righteous in it, then the request was reduced to forty-five, forty, thirty, and finally to ten. Sarah greets with derision the second announcement that a son would be born within a year. But the promise was fulfilled and the boy was named Isaac (laughter) as a reminder of the lack of faith on the part of the patriarch and his wife. Fifty righteous people were not to be found in the cities of Sodom and Gomorrah, not even ten! In his mercy, God sends two angels to rescue Lot and his family from the impending judgment upon the cities. The degradation of the city of Sodom is seen by the fact that the people of the city had turned to homosexuality (19:4-5), hence the name sodomy. The men of the city, both young and old, sought to abuse the messengers of judgment sent by God! Moral decay and declining civilization are often characterized by sodomy. (See Suetonius, **The Twelve Caesars** for a case in point.) Through divine intervention the men of Sodom were blinded and thus frustrated in their efforts to reach Lot's house.

At dawn the next morning, the angels firmly removed the reluctant Lot, his wife, and daughters from the doomed city. The family was warned to flee for the hills without hesitating to look back. Lot's wife, however, found the enticements of the city too much and looked back (perhaps even started toward the city) and became a pillar of salt. Whether this was a miraculous molecular transformation or that she, in some way, was caught in the destruction of the cities (as in a volcanic eruption) is not important. The key point is that God's judgment is certain and that disobedience of God's will and lack of faith are selfdestructive.

Faith's Final Test: 20:1-22:24; 23:1-25:11

The promised son was born in the South Country of Palestine (21:1-7) when Abraham was one hundred years old and Sarah an unbelievable ninety! A miracle, perhaps, but not an impossibility for God. Even modern medical science recognizes the possibility of late births. As a sign of the covenant between God and himself, Abraham circumcises Isaac at the age of eight days. Afterwards, Abraham reluctantly expels Ishmael and his mother Hagar because of the jealousy of Sarah. God, however, providentially intervenes to take care of both the boy and his mother (21:15-21).

Later, God severely tests the faith of Abraham by calling upon him to offer his son as a burnt offering on Mt. Moriah (22:1-14). Obviously, God never intended that Abraham actually kill his son Isaac. However, the test and the demand were real! The pagan neighbors of Abraham willingly offered their first-born sons to their cherished deities. Abraham was asked to demonstrate an equal loyalty to the One God. The test, however, was really an affirmation of God's total rejection of child sacrifice. God desires dedicated faithful servants, not mutilated sacrificial bodies. From the Mt. Moriah incident the patriarch learned that God neither wants nor approves of human sacrifice.

Even though God's promise to Abraham was conditioned by the continued existence of Isaac, when God commanded that he take his only son and offer him "as a burnt offering," the patriarch obeyed. The demand was a paradox that almost contradicted God's covenant, but the decisive response of Abraham was a clear declaration of his faith. Upon climbing the mountain Isaac notes the wood and fire, but questions the absence of the sacrificial lamb. Abraham's careful response is "God will provide himself the lamb for a burnt offering..." Providentially, at the last moment, God prevents the sacrifice of Isaac and provides a ram as a substitute for the boy. By this act, God permanently rejected human sacrifices for all time. In a dramatic and vital sense the whole scene pointed to the coming of the Messiah (Christ) who would finally, and completely, remove the sin that alienates man from God. Even as God spared the son of Abraham on Mt. Moriah, so God ultimately, through His own Son's death, will restore to all who will accept Him, the position of sonship. (Søren Kierkegaard vividly explores the traumatic psychological tension of Abraham at this supreme moment of testing. (See **Fear and Trembling.**) Through Isaac, the nation of Israel was to come and, in time, the Messiah.

At the age of one hundred and twenty-seven Sarah dies and is buried at the cave of Macpelah, a field purchased from the Hittites for four hundred shekels of silver. (For the approximate value of the shekel and other coins see the appendix.) Later, Isaac marries Rebekah to whom the twins Esau and Jacob are born. After the death of Sarah, Abraham marries Keturah. Finally, at the ripe old age of one hundred seventy-five Abraham dies. Isaac and Ishmael bury him with Sarah at Macpelah.

Abraham's life, although marred by a few misdeeds, was an exemplary one. He was not only a man of faith, but a magnanimous person whose generosity and kindness are well known. When a dispute arose over the territory of Canaan, he graciously gave Lot the better land while taking the less productive hill country for himself. Later, when Lot and his family were captured, he sent his men to rescue them. Abraham refused the spoil of the battle giving his part to Melchizedek the priest of God at Salem. Upon hearing of the impending destruction of the city of Sodom, he immediately interceded in their behalf. Again and again Abraham demonstrates the integrity of his life. Appropriately, it is with Abraham that God made his initial covenant that eventually led to the salvation of mankind through the Messiah, i.e. Jesus Christ.

Discussion - Questions to consider:

1. What is the significance of the promises God made to Abraham? See Gen. 12:1-3.
2. Why was Abraham tested in regard to each of the promises?
3. What evidence do we have for the historical existence of Abraham?

4. What light does archaeology throw on the patriarchal era?
5. Who was Melchizedek? What is his significance for Biblical history?
6. What lesson(s) can we learn from the destruction of Sodom and Gomorrah?
7. Assess both the good and bad points of Abraham's life.
8. Why was it important that Abraham and Sarah have a son?
9. What is the significance of the near sacrifice of Isaac?
10. Why is Abraham known as a "man of faith"?

Resources for additional study:

Steve Barabas, "Abraham," *ZPDB*

J.O. Boyd, "Abraham," *ISBE*

C.C. Crawford, *Genesis, Volume III* (College Press)

F. Davidson, ed., *NBC*, Genesis 12-25

Charles Erdman, *Genesis* (Revell)

Joseph Free, *Archaeology and Bible History*

L. Hicks, "Abraham," *IDB*

I. Hunt, *The World of the Patriarchs* (Prentice-Hall)

Søren Kierkegaard, *Fear and Trembling* (Doubleday)

Andre Parrot, *Abraham and His Times* (Fortress)

D.F. Payne, *Genesis and Exodus,* Scripture Union Bible Study Books (Eerdmans)

Charles Pfeiffer, "Abraham," "Mari," "Nuzi," The Biblical World (Baker)

————. "Patriarch," *ZPEB*

————. *The Patriarchal Age* (Baker)

Samuel Schultz, "Abraham," *ZPEB*

P. Trutza, "Hurrians," *ZPEB*

D.J. Weisman, "Abraham," *NBD*

E.J. Young, "Abraham," *EC*

J.F. Walvoord, "Abraham," *WBE*

CHAPTER V
Jacob
"Your name shall no more be called Jacob, but Israel, for you have striven with God and with men..."

Readings: Genesis 25:19-49:33

Birth and Youth of Jacob at Beersheba: 25:19-28:9

Even before his birth Jacob was destined to over-shadow the lives of his parents, Isaac and Rebekah, as well as his older twin brother, Esau! The conception and the birth of the two boys were in answer to Isaac's prayer for his "barren" wife. As the time neared for the birth of the twins, Rebekah, in physical distress with the impending births, learned from God that the elder of the two boys would serve the younger. This was, of course, in contrast to the normal order in Hebrew families. The firstborn son was named Esau ("hairy") and the second Jacob ("he takes by the heel" or "supplanter"). As Esau grew he matured into a skillful hunter while Jacob remained near the camp. Tragically, Esau became the favorite of his father and Jacob the beloved of his mother. This division of parental affection later proved to be a source of family turmoil.

On one occasion Esau returned from the field ravenously hungry. Esau demanded that Jacob share the soup (pottage) that he was cooking. Jacob immediately seized the opportunity and tricked the hungry Esau into abandoning his seemingly unimportant birthright for an insignificant amount of food. Esau thus forfeited this right of primogeniture (i.e. the privilege of being the prime heir because of age) which, at that moment, had lost its value for him. In our day it certainly appears odd that one would attempt to buy another's "birthright." However, such a practice was common at the time of Jacob among the Hurrians at Nuzi. In one instance a man sold his birthright to his brother for only three sheep! An action almost as ill-advised as was that of Jacob.

A further indication of the arrogance and unbridled ambition of Jacob's early years is the occasion of the "stolen blessing." In Isaac's old age he became blind, apparently due to cataracts on his eyes. Since he was approaching death he requested that Esau hunt game for him and prepare it in order that he might place a final blessing upon his eldest son before he died. Rebekah, overhearing the request, plots to have Jacob receive the blessing. Using goat meat and a disguise, they trick Isaac into thinking that Jacob is Esau. The deception proved successful, although Isaac was suspicious of the success of the rapid kill and especially of the voice that sounded very much like Jacob's. However, following his feelings and not his judgment, he concludes that Esau had indeed returned with the venison. The blessing thus received, though by means of deceit, was valid. In the ancient world a man's word was bond and his oath inviolable. Later, when Esau returns, he discovers the deception but cannot undo the deed. Esau does not request that his father revoke the "blessing" since the very statement of the promise made it irrevocable. Thus, although Esau despised his brother Jacob, he requests and receives another blessing. The whole incident seems strange and foreign to our modern way of thinking, but it does reflect the culture and society of that time. For example, a similar incident occurred at Nuzi where a younger brother protected his inheritance by a death-bed blessing from his father. The "blessing" constituted an oral will that was legally binding. In the case of a dying person the statement or oath had an even higher significance. It was, in fact, a last will and testament. Among the patriarchs of the Bible, as well as at Nuzi, the spoken word was binding and doubly so in the case of a dying man.

These acts of deceit on the part of Jacob reveal a negative side of his character which needed refining. In due time Jacob will become Israel (a Prince of God). The transformation and conversion will take place at Peniel. There, when Jacob meets God "face to face" he becomes a new man. Such a change takes place with every person who meets God on a direct and intimate basis.

The Schemer Continues to Scheme: Gen. 29:1-31:16

Esau's anger over Jacob's deception continues to burn. He anticipates killing his brother upon the death of his father. However, Rebekah learns of his plans and, being anxious to protect her favorite son, convinces Isaac that Jacob should be sent to Haran (Padan-aram) to seek a wife among her kinfolk. Along the way, Jacob sleeps at a spot where he has a vision of a "heavenly ladder." Here God renews the covenant which he had made previously with Abraham and Isaac. Jacob was so impressed with the incident that he named the place Bethel ("House of God"). Even at this most propitious moment Jacob seeks to strike a bargain. And, this time, it is with God! Jacob declares that, if God will take care of him providing food, protection, and guidance, then he would vow to be a faithful servant giving a tenth of all that he receives (28:20-22). While, on the surface, this assertion of Jacob appears to be a statement of faith, in reality, it is more an attempt to bargain or even bribe God for his aid. This level of "faith" is useful as a point of beginning, but obviously it is limited in its value.

Upon reaching Haran, Jacob meets Rachel who later becomes his wife. Rachel then introduces the patriarch to her father, Laban, who proves to be almost an equal to Jacob in deception and deceit. The relationship between Jacob and Laban was, at best, cordial, but proved more often than not to be a matching of wits. Jacob's interest in Rachel became a decided advantage for Laban who maneuvered him into a seven year promissory marriage contract that proved to be invalid. Jacob, unaware of the customs in Haran, did not realize that the older daughter must marry before the younger one could do so. Accordingly, during the marriage ceremony at the end of the seven year contract, Laban substitutes Leah for Rachel. Upon discovering the switch during the light of the next morning, Jacob strongly protests the deception but to no avail since he had no legal recourse. Laban then strikes a second bargain and agrees to permit Jacob to marry Rachel on the condition that he work an additional seven years. Because of his great love for Rachel, Jacob accepts. At this point Laban had outfoxed Jacob and had succeeded in marrying off both of his daughters, who were, at the time, considered to be liabilities. In addition, he received fourteen years of free labor from the hand of Jacob.

From the union of Jacob and Leah six sons were born: Reuben, Simeon, Levi, Judah, and at a later time, Issachar and Zebulun. Bilhah, Rachel's maid gave birth to Dan and Naphtali who were legally Rachel's children. Zilpah, Leah's maid gave her mistress two additional sons, Gad and Asher. Finally, after a long period of barrenness, Rachel gives birth to Joseph. Later, upon her deathbed, Benjamin, the youngest of Jacob's sons is born. Altogether twelve sons are born, each of whom is destined to become a patriarch of the Twelve Tribes of Israel.

Significantly, the children born to Bilhah and Zilpah are proxy children. Legally, the offspring belong to Rachel and Leah. As in the case of Hagar and Sarah, this proxy system reflects the customs of the Hurrian people who lived at Nuzi. (This site was excavated between 1925 and 1931 by Edward Chiera.) Such a method of obtaining children is certainly objectionable on Christian grounds, but the episode does reflect the cultural environment of patriarchal times. While no attempt should be made to exonerate the Biblical patriarchs, it is valuable to know that the Biblical account does reflect real life situations even when they are not praiseworthy. Nowhere does the Bible attempt to hide the faults or shortcomings of the people it describes.

Jacob's Return and his Reformation: Gen. 31:17-33:16

Conflict arose between Jacob and Laban over the cattle contract that was negotiated, apparently, in Laban's favor (30:27-36). Jacob agreed to accept the off-color (speckled and spotted) and black animals which were in the minority in Laban's flock. Jacob was willing to take care of all the animals of Laban for what appeared to be a poor wage. However, through selective breeding, Jacob was able to build a considerable flock of healthy animals. In time Jacob accumulated a large flock and considerable wealth (30:43). Laban's sons were disgruntled about Jacob's success and alienated their father from Jacob. Under these circumstances Jacob finds his status with his employer an uncertain one. Jacob asserts that Laban had cheated him and "changed" his wages "ten times" (31:7). God speaks to the patriarch and tells him to return home.

Jacob left his father-in-law without any farewell since he was convinced that Laban would cheat him again. Rachel, for some reason, stole her father's household gods (teraphim) and this gave Laban a pretext for pursuing his son-in-law. Apparently, Rachel did not take her father's idols because of faith in them. It is more probable that she took them to guarantee her husband's inheritance and possession since the "household gods," according to ancient custom (for example, in Nuzi), would guarantee the possessor a share in the family inheritance. In a sense, they constituted a proof of identity. Although Jacob and his family had a three day head start, Laban pursues them and finally overtakes them in the hill country of Gilead (a 300 mile journey!). However,

God warns Laban in a dream that he is not to harm Jacob. Laban's accusations against Jacob were first, that he had left secretly without a proper farewell for his daughters and grandchildren, and, second, that he had stolen the "household gods." A search of the camp failed to turn up the idols for Rachel was sitting upon them. Jacob and Laban finally make a covenant at Mizpah where Jacob erected a stone of "witness." The covenant "The Lord watch between you and me, when we are absent one from the other" was spoken by Laban and probably implied that he did not trust Jacob and desired that God would keep a watchful eye on him. (See Gen. 31:45-54.)

Jacob's transformation from a "supplanter" to a "saint" took place at Peniel. As Jacob neared his home he was informed that Esau his brother was on his way to meet him. The wily Jacob still feared retribution assuming that his brother's malice continued to smolder. In order to mollify Esau's anger, Jacob attempts to send his brother a series of gifts (bribes?). The night before the meeting he finds himself wrestling with a man (Hos. 12:3-5 says it was an angel) at the ford of the Jabbok river. Exactly what was involved in the incident is uncertain. Perhaps he was wrestling with his conscience, or an angel, or even with Esau. (It may have been a combination of all three.) In any case, the result of the experience is clear. Jacob became a new man! The conversion was so dramatic that he needed a new name--Israel, a prince of God. When Jacob finally does meet his brother, he discovers that Esau no longer hates him. The forgiveness on the part of Esau is as admirable as his earlier hatred was detrimental.

Back Home in Canaan Again: Gen. 33:17-45:28

Temporarily Jacob set up his headquarters at Succoth upon his return. He then moves to Shechem and buys a piece of property from the sons of Hamor. God then tells Jacob to go to Bethel where a covenant had been made with the patriarch. Again, the covenant was renewed and the change of name to Israel was reaffirmed. At Ephrath (later Bethlehem) Benjamin is born at the cost of Rachel's life. Rachel was buried there and the family moves on. Shortly thereafter Isaac dies at the ripe old age of 180 and was buried by his two sons.

From this point on, most of the Genesis account centers in Joseph although there is an account of Jacob's daughter Dinah and her folly (34) as well as a genealogical account of Esau (36).

The story of Joseph will be picked up in the next section. Here it is sufficient to indicate that Joseph's immaturity and pride led to a confrontation with his brothers that culminated in his being sold into slavery in Egypt. After several unfortunate circumstances, Joseph, with the help of God, rises to a high position in Egypt. At this point a famine in Canaan sends his brothers into Egypt to buy grain.

Jacob's Last Days: Gen. 46:1-49:33

After a lot of difficulty and some testing on the part of Joseph, the sons of Jacob are able to purchase the needed grain. In addition, they learn that the administrator of the grain stores in Egypt is their lost brother Joseph. Through the good offices of Joseph, Jacob and his family are invited into Egypt to weather the famine that engulfed the Middle East at that time. At first, Jacob is a little reluctant to leave, but God assures him that the move will be one that is ultimately in the best interests of his family. The patriarch and his family, about seventy in number, settle in Goshen on the eastern edge of Egypt. Joseph is able to provide both land and food for his brethren. As Jacob nears death he calls in his twelve sons and blesses each one (49). Of special interest is the statement that "the scepter shall not depart from Judah" -- a reference to the eventual coming of the Messiah. Jacob makes a special request that he be buried at the family burial ground at Macpelah in Canaan. After the old man's death, his sons return his body to his homeland for burial. The movement of the family of Jacob will later prove to be both a blessing and a curse. In the long run, however, all this serves to achieve God's purpose.

Discussion - Questions to consider:

1. Why did God use Jacob instead of Esau to perpetuate the chosen people?
2. How was Jacob able to obtain Esau's birthright? The death-bed blessing of Issac?
3. What do Jacob's actions say about his character?
4. What parallels can be drawn between the Biblical account and the archaeological discoveries at Nuzi?
5. What is the value in knowing that the actions of the

patriarchs reflect the culture of their time?
6. Assess the strengths and weaknesses of Jacob's career?
7. What role does Esau play in the Biblical account?
8. Why was a death-bed blessing so important?
9. Who were the sons of Jacob? His wives? Why were the children of the maids considered on an equal basis with the other sons?
10. What happened to Jacob at Bethel? Peniel?

Resources for additional study:

James O. Boyd, "Jacob," *ISBE*

Joseph H. Cohn, *I Have Loved Jacob* (American Board of Missions to the Jews)

D. W. Deere, "Jacob," *WBE*

Don Dewelt, *Sacred History and Geography* (Baker)

J.D. Freeman, "Jacob," *ZPBD*

L. Hicks, "Jacob," *IDB*

E.F. Kevan, "Genesis," *NBC*

A.R. Millard, "Jacob," *NBD*

Charles Pfeiffer, *The Patriarchal Age* (Baker)

_____. "Nuzi," "Mari" *BW*

W.T. Purkiser, *Exploring the Old Testament* (Beacon Hill)

Smith's Bible Dictionary "Jacob"

H.W. Tribble, *Old Testament Biographies* (Broadman)

L.L. Walker, "Jacob," *ZPEB*

Kyle M Yates, "Genesis," *WBC*

CHAPTER VI
Joseph
"The Lord was with Joseph and showed him steadfast love, and gave him favor..."

Readings: Genesis 37:1-50:26

Joseph, the Dreamer: 37:1-36

With the exception of Benjamin, Joseph was the youngest of the twelve sons of Jacob. In addition, he was the older of the two sons of his father's favorite, Rachel. Because of Jacob's keen affection for the lad, he bestowed special favors upon him including oversight of his brothers and a garment indicating this favored position. The "long robe with sleeves" (or "coat of many colors") implied that he was a person of authority. However, Joseph's youth, and his brothers' jealousy created an unhealthy situation that culminated in a tragic action on the part of his brothers. Once again we find that preferential treatment of one child in a family can only lead to turmoil and bitterness. Compounding Joseph's favorite son status was his ability to interpret dreams. In particular, his own dreams and their interpretation pointed to a future superiority over his brothers, and even his parents. The dreams of the sheaves and the sun, moon, and stars bowing down to Joseph were more than his brothers could take! Thus, they conspire to kill their brother. Only the intervention of Reuben, the oldest of the twelve, prevented the plot from materializing.

At Dothan, the brothers cast Joseph into a pit at the urging of Reuben who planned to rescue him later. Apparently, Reuben, although he disliked Joseph, felt a responsibility for his younger brother. Stripping Joseph of his special "robe" they cast him into the pit. While Reuben was absent, they decided to rid themselves permanently of an irritating sibling. Hence, when an Ishmaelite (Midianite) caravan passed on their way to Egypt they sold Joseph for twenty shekels of silver thus ridding themselves of a "thorn in the flesh" and making a handsome profit in the process. Reuben's distress, upon his return, was only exceeded by that of his father. The boys contrived a story of Joseph's death by a wild animal. Then they sprinkled blood on the lad's robe as evidence, and lied to their father about his fate. The Ishmaelites took Joseph into Egypt and sold him to Potiphar, a captain of Pharaoh's guard.

Joseph, the Man of Character: 39:1-23

Joseph, as a teen-ager, appeared to be impetuous and, even arrogant, in his pronouncements that his brothers and parents would bow down to him. However, the arrogance of his youth was not a true barometer of his character. Being sold into slavery proved to be a blessing in disguise for Joseph. While no one would want to praise the clearly wrong act of his brothers, God was able to use their wrong intentions for good. The traumatic experience proved that Joseph was a far better person than his brothers would ever have dreamed.

As a servant in the household of Potiphar, Joseph proved to be a valuable asset. Soon, he became the overseer of the property of the Egyptian officer. His success, along with his good looks, interested Potiphar's wife. Her amorous intentions were obvious when she bluntly said to Joseph, "Lie with me" (v. 7). Joseph's integrity and deep religious faith is reflected in his bold reply, "how then can I do this great wickedness, and sin against God?" (v. 9). Not only would such sexual license be a betrayal of trust and an offense to Potiphar, it would be a sin against God! No wonder Joseph fled from her presence. Inadvertently, Joseph lost his coat due to his rapid departure, and this became a pretext for an accusation against him. The wife of Potiphar claimed, falsely, that Joseph had attempted to rape her. Without a fair trial, Joseph is condemned and thrown into prison. Ironically, the man that Potiphar had trusted, he failed to trust when an accusation of sexual misconduct was made. Similarly, people today tend to believe the worst about others even when the evidence is circumstantial or inadequate. Potiphar followed his emotions, not his reason. However, another apparent disaster turns into an opportunity for Joseph. God had more important plans for Joseph than that of being a successful administrator for a minor Egyptian official.*

*In an ancient Egyptian text "The Story of Two Brothers" there is an account of a conscientious young man who avoids a temptation similar to that of Joseph. While the accounts do have parallels, there is no reason to suppose that they are identical. Some have suggested that the Genesis account is based on the Egyptian one, but there is no real evidence to support such a view. Similarity does not prove correspondence or borrowing. (See James B. Pritchard, **Ancient Near Eastern Texts**.)

Joseph, the Interpreter of Dreams: 40:1-23

Joining Joseph in prison were Pharaoh's butler and baker. For some reason the two offended the monarch of Egypt and he had them imprisoned in the same jail as Joseph. While in prison both of Pharaoh's servants had cryptic dreams. The dreams and their meaning troubled them. Joseph, upon hearing of their difficulty, offered to interpret their dreams with the help of God. The chief butler's dream was that of a grapevine with three branches from which the butler took grapes and squeezed the grapes into the cup of Pharaoh. In three days, Joseph said, the butler would be restored to his former position. The patriarch's request of the butler to remember him went unheeded for some time. In the case of the baker the interpretation of the basket of bread was not a happy one. In three days the baker was to be hung and the birds (vultures) would eat his carcass. Both dreams came to pass as Joseph predicted. It was two years later when the butler finally remembered Joseph (41:1-9).

Joseph, the Pharaoh's Counselor: 41:1-57

Two troubled dreams of the king of Egypt become the means of Joseph's advancement in Egypt. Seven skinny cows devour seven fat ones in the first dream and seven plump ears of grain are consumed by an equal number of thin ones in the second. None of the Pharaoh's magicians or wise men could interpret the dreams. Finally, the butler remembers Joseph and his ability to interpret dreams. Pharaoh immediately requests the assistance of Joseph. However, the Hebrew prisoner disclaims ability to interpret dreams on his own. He declares, "It is not in me; God will give Pharaoh a favorable answer" (v. 16). Joseph tells the king that both dreams have the same meaning. There will be seven years of plenty followed by seven years of famine. The twin dreams were meant to reinforce the certainty of the coming cycle of abundance and want. In addition, Joseph suggests that Pharaoh appoint an administrator to assure a preservation of the abundance of the seven years of plenty for the coming years of famine. Convinced of the dreams' interpretation and the wisdom of Joseph's suggestion, the king sought an able administrator. However, since no one of the caliber of Joseph could be found, he appointed the former Hebrew slave to the position of prime minister limited only by the power of Pharaoh himself. To ensure Joseph's acceptance, he took his signet ring from his finger and placed it on the Hebrew's hand. As a further seal of the office, Pharaoh gave him Asenath the daughter of Potiphera, priest of On, as a wife. Later, two sons, Manasseh and Ephraim, were born to them. The offspring of these two sons constituted two very important tribes in the later history of Israel.

Joseph proved to be a very competent administrator. More than adequate grain was stored for the lean years and when the famine did come, though it was severe, there was adequate food for the Egyptians and the peoples of the surrounding countries.

Joseph, the Forgiving Brother: 42:1-45:15

When the famine hit Egypt, it also ravaged Palestine. Jacob learned that there was grain in Egypt and sent his sons there to buy food. All but Benjamin made the trip. As governor of the territory, prospective buyers of grain had to seek Joseph's approval for their purchases. When the brothers arrived with their request, he immediately recognized them. Because of Joseph's clothing and position, they never considered the possibility that he was their brother. Undoubtedly, they assumed that he was either dead or perhaps some menial slave of an Egyptian master. Joseph's accusation that they were spies (44:4-13) was not designed to demonstrate malice on his part, rather he wanted to test them and ascertain what kind of men they had become. In order to prove their innocence of the charge, Joseph demanded that they bring their younger brother Benjamin into Egypt as a sign of their good faith. After a three day detainment, he released all the brothers, except Simeon, requesting that they return with Benjamin.

The incident caused the sons of Jacob to remember their ill-treatment of Joseph although they had no reason to suspect a connection between the Egyptian official and their lost brother. Hearing them discuss their guilt caused Joseph to turn aside and weep. They were unaware that he understood their language since he spoke to them through an interpreter. The released brothers were given the grain they requested and, unknown to them, their money was returned by being placed in the sacks of grain. Upon discovering the money, they were even more distressed.

After the report of the journey was given, the old patriarch refused to permit Benjamin's trip since he was convinced that he had now lost both Joseph and Simeon. However, as the famine continued the grain that was brought back from Egypt was exhausted. Jacob then, reluctantly, agreed to let his sons return under the personal care of Judah. In addition, he requests that they pay double the normal purchase price for the grain. The money that had been placed in the sacks by the governor was taken back along with presents of nuts, honey, and myrrh.

Surprisingly, they found a royal reception when they returned, but the brothers suspected some kind of treachery on the part of the Egyptian official. After trying to return the money for the previous purchases and assured that they did not need to do so, their brother Simeon was released and joined them. When Joseph arrived for the noon meal he inquired of the welfare of his father. Seeing Benjamin, he blessed his younger brother and being deeply moved he left the chamber and wept. To the brothers' amazement they were seated by their ages! The exceptional portion of food given to Benjamin was unusual, but they did not appear to discern anything suspicious in the action. When the sons of Jacob prepared to leave, their money was once again put in their sacks while Joseph's personal cup was placed in Benjamin's bag. Joseph permitted them to leave, but then sent men after them searching for his "stolen" cup. Benjamin was found to be guilty. Judah, true to his promise, offers himself for the life of his younger brother. Judah's earnest plea was that the failure of Benjamin to return would bring his aged father to his death. This series of incidents proved to Joseph that his brothers had indeed reformed. Joseph then sent out his servants and, with deep emotion, reveals that he is the long lost brother.

Joseph does not hold any bitterness toward his brothers for their despicable deed of selling him into slavery. In fact, he makes it clear that their ill-advised act was used by God as a means of preserving the family of Jacob (45:7-8). There is no doubt that Joseph could have sought and applied revenge upon his brothers. However, Joseph was a man of character and integrity. In a sense he did want to teach his brothers a lesson, but it did not originate out of malice, but concern. Joseph's reaction is vividly described - "Then he fell upon his brother Benjamin's neck and wept; and Benjamin wept upon his neck. And he kissed all his brothers and wept upon them..." (45:14-15). Without a doubt, Joseph is one of the outstanding individuals in biblical history. With the exception of his early impetuousness as a teenager, there is little to fault the man.

Joseph, the Benefactor of his Family: Gen. 45:16-47:12

Because of the severe famine in the Middle East at the time, Joseph invites his father, brothers and their families into Egypt so that he could aid them. This arrangement also pleased Pharaoh since he too extended an invitation for the family to move to Egypt. The king offered them the best land in the country for their use. He even provided wagons to transport their wives and children! When the brothers returned to Canaan, they informed their father, Jacob, of the good news. The old patriarch was overjoyed. He declares, "It is enough; Joseph my son is still alive; I will go and see him before I die" (46:28). With his family and possessions Jacob moves to Egypt and is allotted more than adequate territory in the land of Goshen.

Joseph, the Administrator: 47:13-26

Through wise planning and administration, Joseph was able to prepare Egypt for the famine he had predicted. Joseph's able administration made it possible for the Egyptians, and his own family, to survive the raging famine that covered most, if not all, of the Middle East at that time. He was also able to obtain all of the land of Egypt for the Pharaoh, with the exception of the territory controlled by the priests. The result was that Pharaoh now owned the land. The people could then use the land and raise crops. Pharaoh provided the seed and the land, the people provided the labor. Eighty percent of the profits went to the people and twenty percent to the king. Certainly an equitable arrangement for that day and time.

Some have suggested that Joseph's rapid advancement and acceptance by the Egyptian rulers was due to the fact that the country was being ruled by non-Egyptians known as the Hyksos (or Shepherd Kings). However, this is unlikely since the Hyksos invaded Egypt about 1730 B.C., over one hundred years after the time of Joseph. According to Exodus 12:40, the Israelites were in Egypt 430 years. If a date of about 1446 B.C. be accepted for the Exodus, then the period of Joseph must be much earlier than the time of the Hyksos. Undoubtedly, the power of God would accomplish his purpose whether the ruler was Egyptian or not. There is no concrete evidence in the Genesis account to indicate that Pharaoh was non-Egyptian.

Joseph, the last days: 47:27-50:26

Before Jacob dies, he calls for Joseph and makes him solemnly swear that he will return his body to Canaan for burial. Later, Joseph took his two sons, Manasseh and Ephraim, to receive a final blessing from their grandfather. In the ceremony of blessing, Ephraim, although the youngest, receives the prime blessing, for his tribe was destined to be the more important of the two. When the twelve tribes are finally established and territories are allotted in the promised land, both of Joseph's sons receive an inheritance along with the sons of Jacob.

Fulfilling his promise, Joseph with his brothers, took their father back to Canaan and buried him in the cave of Macpelah where earlier Abraham and Isaac had been buried. After the death of Jacob, Joseph continued to show kindness to his brothers and their families. Easily, and with deep emotion, he forgave his brothers for the wrong they had done to him. Joseph lived to be 110 years old and, when he died, he was embalmed and put in a coffin. Later, at the time of Exodus, his body is taken back to Canaan. Significantly, embalming is only mentioned concerning two people in the Old Testament. In the case of both Jacob and Joseph the embalming was done by the Egyptians in order that the body might be returned to Canaan for burial. The Hebrews did not embalm. Burial was immediate after death. The body was wrapped in cloth and anointed with oil, but, beyond that, no effort was made to preserve the body after death.

To sum up the life of a man like Joseph is difficult. From the biblical account we learn that he was a man of great character. Perhaps his two greatest qualities were his honesty and forgiving love. Joseph's admirable life is still an inspiration today.

Discussion - Questions to consider:

1. Why were Joseph's "dreams" an offense to his brothers?
2. How significant a factor was jealousy in the brothers' dislike of Joseph?
3. What is your reaction of Joseph's rejection of the advances of Potiphar's wife?
4. How important are extra-biblical accounts for the understanding of the Bible, especially when they parallel the

Biblical record?

5. Why was Joseph able to interpret dreams? Who else in the Bible had such a talent?
6. Did Joseph have to compromise his convictions to be a counselor of Pharaoh?
7. Why did Joseph "test" his brothers when they came to Egypt for grain?
8. Did the "brothers" learn any lessons from their mistakes?
9. How would you assess the life of Joseph?
10. What was the general attitude of the patriarchs toward death?

Resources for additional study:

Steve Barabas, "Joseph," *ZPBD*

C.C. Crawford, *Genesis-IV* (College Press)

Carl E. DeVries, "Genesis," *WBE*

Charles Erdman, *Genesis* (Revell)

"Hyksos," *ZPBD*

Werner Keller, "Joseph in Egypt," *The Bible as History* (Morrow)

E.F. Kevan, "Genesis," *NBC*

K.A. Kitchen, "Joseph," *NBD*

———. "Hyksos," *ZPEB*

M.G. Kyle, "Joseph," *ISBE*

G.F. Maclear, "History," and "Death of Joseph," *Old Testament History* (Eerdmans)

F.B. Mayer, *Joseph, Beloved-Hated-Exalted* (Zondervan)

Charles F. Pfeiffer, "Hyksos," "Joseph," *BW* (Baker)

———. "Joseph," *ZPEB*

James B. Pritchard, *ANET* (Princeton)

O.S. Wintermute, "Joseph," *IDB*

Leon Wood, *A Survey of Israel's History* (Zondervan)

Kyle M. Yates, "Genesis," *WBC*

CHAPTER VII
Moses
"But Moses said to God, 'Who am I that I should go to Pharaoh, and bring the sons of Israel out of Egypt?'"

Readings: Exodus 1-18

Moses, from Egyptian Prince to Midianite Shepherd: 1-2

Details surrounding the birth of Moses are well known. What started as a limited stay in Egypt to avoid famine at the time of Joseph lengthened into a four hundred year sojourn (Ex. 12:40)! At the time of Moses' birth the rulers of Egypt no longer saw the Israelites as friends but as a threat. The small band of threescore and ten within the territory of Goshen had now grown into a large nation. Fear of revolution and the desire to take economic advantage of these foreigners led the Egyptian Pharaoh to force the Hebrews into slave labor for his building projects in Pithom and Rameses. Ironically, Joseph, who had saved the Egyptians in a time of famine by the forethought of storing grain, was now forgotten and his descendants were building store-cities for the Egyptians. In an attempt to minimize the manpower potential of the Hebrews, the midwives of the Israelites were instructed to kill all the male offspring at birth. Ingeniously, the midwives evaded the directive by asserting that the Hebrew women gave birth to their children before they could answer the call to deliver the baby. Frustrated with this lack of co-operation, the Pharaoh commanded that all the Hebrew infants be tossed into the Nile River. This measure also proved to be insufficient to arrest the population growth of the Israelites.

When Moses was born, his parents, who were of the tribe of Levi, hid him from the Egyptian police. At the age of three months his mother arranged to have the child discovered by Pharaoh's daughter counting, apparently, upon the maternal instinct in the woman. Not only was Moses rescued from his water cradle by the princess, he was also adopted by the girl and through the suggestion of his sister Miriam, his own mother became his nurse.

The child was given an Egyptian name, Moses, meaning "to draw out" (of the water). Undoubtedly the lad was trained in the culture and religion of the Hebrews for, when he reached the age of maturity, he found himself siding with his own people. The incident of killing an Egyptian taskmaster led to his flight from Egypt and the fury of Pharaoh. Providentially, his exile led him to the land of Midian.

Moses, from a Shepherd to the Leader of Israel: 3-4

In the country of Midian Moses met Jethro (Reuel) and married his daughter, Zipporah. Content to stay there, he became a shepherd and a companion of the Midianite priest. In the meantime, the bondage of Israel became increasingly oppressive. God answered his people's plea by calling a reluctant man to their aid. On Mt. Sinai (Horeb) God spoke to Moses from the midst of a burning bush. Intrigued by a bush that continued to burn, he approached and heard God calling his name. He immediately learned that he was standing on "holy ground" for the God of Abraham, Isaac and Jacob spoke to him. God subsequently informs him that he had been chosen to deliver the Israelites from their Egyptian bondage. Due to his previous failure to aid the people, and his absence from their plight, Moses questions the call of God. The objection was based partly on humility, but even more so on his lack of confidence in himself.

Altogether, Moses raised three objections to the call. First, he argued that Israel, as well as Pharaoh, would question his authority for leadership. To this excuse God answers that he should tell them that **"I am"** (Jehovah, or better, Yahweh) has sent you. The word Yahweh ("I am") became the particular and very personal name that Israelites used for God. Moses' authority was from God himself. A second objection that Moses raised was that he lacked credentials to certify his call as authentic. The Lord then showed him that a miraculous change of his shepherd's rod into a serpent and the skin of his hand into leprosy, and back again, would demonstrate his legitimacy. These two miracles coupled with the ten plagues would finally convince the Egyptians. Even with these credentials, Moses questioned his ability. He claimed that he was not eloquent but was "slow of speech and tongue" (4:10). God reprimands Moses for his further hesitancy, but gives him his brother Aaron as his spokesman.

Some criticism could be made of Moses in his unwillingness to immediately accept God's call, but this reluctance arose from his awareness of his own shortcomings and, perhaps, from a lack of faith and trust in God. The hard lesson of faith is difficult for every servant of God.

Moses, from the Confrontation with Pharaoh to the Exodus: 5-11

Aaron is sent by God to meet the now eighty year old Moses in the wilderness. Returning to Egypt both Aaron and Moses report to Israel the words God had communicated on Mt. Sinai. Yahweh had commissioned Moses to lead the Exodus (literally "the going out"). Afterwards, they sent to Pharaoh and requested permission for the Israelites to go into the wilderness to sacrifice to God. Pharaoh responded with a refusal and a declaration that he did not know God. The king was so infuriated by the request that he increased the oppression of the Israelites by making them gather their own straw for the same quota of bricks. The result was that the leaders of Israel were forced into meeting a nearly impossible demand. Now, Israel's anger was turned against Aaron and Moses. Under these circumstances Moses became extremely discouraged. However, Yahweh assures them that the covenant made with his ancestors was still valid! The Lord declares, "I will bring you into the land which I swore to give to Abraham, Isaac, and Jacob; I will give it to you for a possession" (6:8). God tells him to return to Pharaoh, but he must be prepared for opposition. Nevertheless, Moses is to have power over Pharaoh.

Moses again appears before the King of Egypt demanding the release of Israel. In order to demonstrate the power of God in behalf of Israel, Aaron's rod is turned into a serpent. Egyptian magicians duplicate the feat, but Aaron's rod swallowed their serpents. The ensuing refusal of Pharaoh leads to a series of ten plagues. The first three affected Israelites and Egyptians alike. Beginning with the fourth plague the judgments were restricted to the Egyptians. The miracle of the plagues is based on three factors. First, timing; the plagues come and go at the command of Moses. Second, quantity; while all of the plagues had troubled Egypt before, never had they experienced them so severely. Finally, limitation; the area covered was specifically prescribed. Thus, with the fourth plague only the Egyptians fell prey to the judgment. The wonders were designed to demonstrate God's superiority over Pharaoh and the Egyptian gods. For example, the plague of darkness was directed against the sun god, Ra; the plague of frogs against Hecka; the bloody waters against the sacred river Nile; and the death of the first born against the deification of Pharaoh. The ten plagues occur in a series of three triads - blood, frogs, lice, (gnats), flies, Murrain (cattle disease), boils, hail, locust, darkness, and finally, the death of the first born. The plagues lead to a climax in the tenth. Until the third plague, the magicians of Egypt compete with Moses. Beginning with the second series (fourth plague) the Israelites are exempted from the judgments. The third series of three are the most severe since they were designed to remove food, the basic "stuff" of life. In each of the three series the first and second plagues are announced beforehand, but the third comes without warning. The total impact of the ten plagues was that both the Israelites and the Egyptians were to learn the lesson that God is in charge of his creation. Disobedience to his will would not be tolerated. The refusal of Pharaoh in light of these judgments is strange. The Scriptures say that God "hardened" his heart. Apparently, this means that God's permissive will was in force. Pharaoh's own inner desire to preserve an economic status quo with a large number of slaves, and his probable fear that they might become a military threat should they join forces with an enemy, led to the hardening of his heart. The announcement of the impending death of the first born finally led to the conclusion of the confrontation. With the death of the Egyptian first born, including Pharaoh's son, the Hebrews are finally permitted to leave.

Moses, from the Exodus to the Red Sea: 12-13

Before leaving Egypt the Israelites celebrated the Passover. In order to be protected from the death of their first born each Hebrew family was required to kill, or share with a neighbor, an umblemished one-year old male lamb and sprinkle its blood on the doorposts (lintels) of the entrance to their homes. In addition, they were to eat the roasted lamb that night along with unleavened bread and bitter herbs. The meal was to be eaten in haste with staff in hand being prepared to leave at a moment's notice. The Passover, which was to be a perpetual memorial in Israel, commemorated the Exodus from Egypt and the sparing of the first born. Accompanying the passover was a seven day abstinence from leavened bread.

Among the Egyptians, who neither worshipped God nor

prepared the Passover, the death of the first born was a tragic reality. Unable to resist any longer, Pharaoh relents and lets Israel go. According to Exodus 12:37 there were 600,000 men, besides women and children, who left Egypt. It has been argued by some that such a number is an obvious exaggeration since only 70 people went into Egypt. However, allowing only six generations of forty years, when the actual number was probably ten, there would be no difficulty at all. For example, if Jacob's fifty-three grandsons (Gen. 4:6) each had five sons then there would have been over 800, 000 men at the end of just six generations (53X56 = 53X15625 or 828,125). The clear declaration of Exodus 12:40-41 that Israel was in Egypt four hundred and thirty years has also been challenged. Some have suggested that the reference is a general statement and not a specific one. However, there is no concrete evidence to reject the literal interpretation of the statement. Biblical statements should be taken at face value unless there is good reason to do otherwise.

Another problem frequently discussed is the date of the Exodus. In general two views have predominated, one in the 15th century (ca. 1446 B.C.) and the other one in the 13th century (ca. 1280 B.C.). The key biblical clue is I Kings 6:1 which states that the temple was begun in the fourth year of Solomon's reign, the 480th year after the Exodus. If Solomon's rule began ca. 970 B.C., then by subtracting four years we arrive at 966. Adding 480 to 966 places the date of the Exodus at 1446 B.C. (See Gleason Archer, **A Survey of Old Testament Introduction**). Those who hold the 13th century date argue that the 480 years of I Kings 6:1 are not to be taken literally but refer to twelve generations (See John Bright, **A History of Israel**). Without deliberating at length, four telling arguments can be given for the 15th century date. They include, (1) the biblical chronology cited above, (2) the archaeological excavations of Garstang and others at Jericho which point to the early date, (3) the Armarna Letters (ca. 1400 B.C.) which mention the Habiru (Hebrews?), and, (4) the Merneptah Stela (ca. 1229 B.C.) which mentions Israel as an established and significant nation. Accordingly the king of the oppression would be Thutmose III (1504-1450 B.C.), often called the Napoleon of Egypt. The Pharaoh at the time of the Exodus would be Amenhotep II of the 18th dynasty. Some of the above points can be used to defend the late date of the Exodus, but the problem of biblical chronology persists. In addition, it is extremely difficult to incorporate all the events in Joshua and Judges into the 13th century view. Either the events recorded in those books would have to be compressed or else much of the narrative would have to describe simultaneous events. For the purpose of this study the date, of 1446 B.C. will be considered the correct one.

The Exodus began at Rameses (12:37) and the people journeyed to Succoth where Moses taught them the significance of the Passover including the consecration of the first born. At Etham (13:20-22) God gives Israel a "pillar of a cloud" to guide by day and a "pillar of fire" to guide them by night. This cloud represented the glory (or presence) of God.

The next stop at Pihahiroth (14:1-14) proved to be a time of crisis. Pharaoh, having changed his mind, was now pursuing from the rear and an apparently impossible Red Sea crossing faced them. Regardless of the depth of the Red Sea at this time, the possibility of passing through the water appeared to be an insurmountable task.

Moses, from the Crossing of the Red Sea to Mt. Sinai: 14-18

Faced with the pursuit of the Egyptians and what appeared to be a watery grave, the Hebrews complained that Moses had led them into certain death. The moment of distress caused them to forget the oppression of Egypt and volunteer for a return to the dubious status of slaves (14:12). In contrast to their fear, Moses announces the deliverance of God. Yahweh instructs the people to move on toward the Red Sea. Moses stretches out his staff over the sea and the waters part by the power of God. While a strong East wind blows, the children of Israel pass safely to the other side. Meanwhile, the Egyptians are temporarily stopped by a thick fog created by the settling of the "cloud" between them and Israel. Discerning that the Israelites had crossed the water, the Egyptians set out to follow them only to be overwhelmed and drowned by the returning waters. For a short period following the Red Sea events, the Israelites manifested a deeper faith in God.

In commemoration of the nation's deliverance, Moses composes a song (Ex. 15:1-18 - "Song of Moses") which the people sing as a thanksgiving to God. A shorter version, "Miriam's Song" (14:21), was sung by the women. (Note: Technically the name of the Red Sea is a misnomer since the name in the Hebrew text is Yam Suf or Sea of Reeds. However, the common usage Red Sea is preferred to minimize confusion.) From the Red Sea, Israel travelled to Marah where they found undrinkable "bitter water," but God "sweetened" the water for them (15:22-26). In addition, through faith and obedience, the nation was to be exempted from the "diseases" of the Egyptians. The next stop was an oasis at Elim (15:27) where they found 12 springs and 70 palm trees. A cryptic prophecy of the nations' future --12 tribes and 70 elders (later the Sanhedrin).

From Elim, Moses and the Israelites journey through the Wilderness of Sin on their way to Sinai. Forty-five days out of Egypt the people forgot the slavery and oppression of their former residence. Out of their fertile memories they dredged up exaggerated visions of abundance. The oppression in Egypt was now remembered as the "good old days." Against Moses their claim was that he had led them into the wilderness to starve. However, God intervened in behalf of Moses and declared that the food problem would be alleviated by "bread from heaven." This **manna** (literally "what is it?" -- the people's name for the unknown food) was given daily with a double allotment on the sixth day to provide adequate food for the Sabbath when no gathering was to be done. **Manna** is described in Exodus as being "like coriander seed" while the taste of it was like "wafers made with honey" (16:31). Various suggestions have been given as to the nature of this food including a secretion of insects, the sap of the tamarisk tree, and even mushrooms. However, the only certainty is that the **manna** was food provided by God. Later, when the people complain at the lack of meat, God sends quails.

At Rephidim (17:1-17), Israel complained of the lack of water and threatened to stone Moses. God hears Moses' prayer for help and miraculously provides water. Through Yahweh's aid an Amalekite invasion was repulsed. Also, at Rephidim, Moses is visited by Jethro, his father-in-law, who observes Moses' dilemma in serving as judge for a large and a motley group of people. He recommends a series of judges who would have charge of the less pressing matters. The jurisdiction of the judges would range from ten people to a thousand. Obviously these "assignments" would eliminate much unnecessary work for Moses. The people are now near Mt. Sinai and their future is before them.

Discussion - Questions to consider:

1. Why were the Hebrews in Egypt? What was their status at the time of Moses?

2. What advantages did Moses gain from his Egyptian environment? Why did he leave?
3. What is the significance of the "burning bush" incident at Mt. Sinai? (Ex. 3)
4. Why were the Plagues brought upon Egypt? What is their significance?
5. Why was the Egyptian Pharaoh so reluctant to let Israel depart from Egypt?
6. In what way were the Ten Plagues a denunciation of thed religion of Egypt?
7. What is the significance and meaning of the Passover?
8. When should the Exodus be dated? Why?
9. What problems were involved in the journey from Egypt to Sinai?
10. What is the importance of the **manna** in Exodus 16?

Resources for additional study:

J.G. Aalders, "The Book of Exodus"; "Exodus," EC, Vol. IV

O.T. Allis, "Moses," *ZPEB*

Gleason Archer, "Exodus," *A Study of Old Testament Introduction* (Moody)

John Bright, *A History of Israel* (Westminster)

J.C. Connell, "Exodus," *NBC*

Charles Erdman, *Book of Exodus* (Revell)

Phillip J. Johnson, "Exodus," *WBC*

R.F. Johnson, "Moses," *IDB*

Werner Keller, *The Bible as History* (Morrow) pp. 104-103

K.A. Kitchen, "Moses," "Exodus," *NBD*

_____. "Exodus," *ZPEB*

M.G. Kyle, "Moses," *ISBE*

Charles Pfeiffer, *Egypt and the Exodus* (Baker)

_____. "Exodus," *ZPDB*

John Rea, "Exodus, The," *WBE*

S.J. Schultz, "Moses," *ZPDB*

William Taylor, *Moses the Law Giver* (Baker)

J.A. Thompson, *Archaeology and the Old Testament* (Eerdmans)

H.W. Tribble, *Old Testament Biographies* (Broadman)

E.J. Young, "Moses," *WBE*

CHAPTER VIII
Israel At Sinai
"Now therefore if you will obey my voice and keep my covenant, you shall be my own possession among all peoples..."

Readings: Exodus 19-23, 24-29, 30-40; Leviticus 1-27

The Covenant on Mt. Sinai: Exodus 19-20, 24

After nearly three months of travel Israel reached the sacred mountain of Sinai (19:1). Upon ascending the mountain Moses met God who rehearsed his guidance of Israel and reaffirmed the covenant. The nation is given an opportunity to become "a kingdom of priests" and "a holy nation" (19:6). Sadly, this privileged status is rejected with the construction of a "golden calf" a short time later. Instead of priesthood, they chose the false security of an apparently tangible idol. However, the immediate reaction of Israel to the awesome Mount was to declare total allegiance and fidelity to God's commands. Moses, as the representative of God, ascended the sacred mountain and Yahweh communicated the Ten Commandments (Decalogue) to him there. The commands included prohibitions against foreign gods, images of God, misuse and abuse of God's name, profaning the sabbath, dishonor of parents, murder, adultery, theft, false witness, and coveting. Commands one through four establish a basis for a right relationship with God, while the remaining six are concerned with the correct conduct of one person to another. The Commandments became the basis of Hebrew law. The principles involved in these laws are valid for all societies and eras since no nation can survive where lying, stealing, and murder are permitted. Following the Decalogue a series of several laws were given to cover the various needs of the community. Among the laws was the principle of retribution, "an eye for an eye" (21:24). Contrary to popular belief, the purpose of this stringent command was to prevent wrong action, not to encourage retaliation. If one realizes that he will receive a black eye for hitting another person in the eye, then caution and restraint will guide the action and temper of the would-be offender. Altogether, Moses was on Mt. Sinai for forty days.

The Tabernacle: Exodus 25-27, 30-31, 25-40

During Moses' encampment on the Mount, he is instructed by God in the design and function of the tabernacle and priesthood. The sanctuary was to be built with voluntary contributions (25:2). It was to be a work of love dedicated to God. A total of fourteen kinds of material were to be utilized in constructing the tabernacle, including such diverse items as gold and silver, linen, goatskins, acacia wood, spices, and incense (25:3-9).

The outercourt that surrounded the tabernacle (27:9-21) was roughly 150 feet long (east and west) and 75 feet wide (north and south). The entire area was enclosed by a screen of linen curtains 7½ feet high with pillars of the same height serving as the framework for the walls. Cords fastened to bronze pins held the pillars in place. The sanctuary itself was 45 feet long (facing east) and 15 feet wide. The structure was situated on the rear half of the enclosed area. Furniture outside the tabernacle included a laver for ceremonial washing which was located approximately 15 feet in front of the sanctuary's entrance. In the outer court there was also an altar of sacrifice a little over 20 feet in front of the laver. The tabernacle proper was divided into two sections comprising the Holy Place (30'x15'x15') and, in the rear, the Holy of Holies (a 15 foot cube). Three pieces of furniture were located in the Holy Place--the table of showbread on the right, the golden lampstand on the left, and the altar of incense in the center near the veil. Separating the Holy Place and the Holy of Holies was a curtain or veil. Only one article of furniture was placed in the Holy of Holies-the Ark of the Covenant with the over-arching cherubim. Within the ark were the two stones of the Decalogue, Aaron's rod, and a pot of manna.

Each item of furniture carried a significant religious meaning. God's forgiveness of sins was symbolized by the altar of sacrifice, while the laver depicted cleansing from sin. In the Holy Place, the lampstand represented the "light" of God whereas the showbread pointed to God's provision of both daily bread and spiritual food. Prayer was symbolized by the continual burning of incense. The Holy Place represented the assembly of God's people while the veil symbolically separated the kingdom on earth from heaven (Holy of Holies). Finally, the ark of the covenant in the Holy of

Holies was a lesson on God's forgiving love demonstrating his presence (glory) in the midst of the people. (Later, this "glory" is known as the Shekinah.)

The Covenant Repudiated and Reaffirmed: Exodus 32-34

Moses' long stay on Mt. Sinai created an atmosphere of rebellion in Israel. Absence and delay encouraged the wayward leaders of the nation to demand that Aaron construct a god they could celebrate as their deliverer from Egypt. Aaron readily agreed to the project requesting that they collect earrings of gold. From these, he fashioned a golden calf and proclaimed a holy day in behalf of their "god." Meanwhile, Moses received word from God that Israel had constructed the idol and was worshipping it. Yahweh then declares his intention to dispense with Israel and begin anew with Moses. Intervention upon the part of Moses, who reasserts the covenant and its promise of a great nation through Abraham's descendants, prevents the decision. Exodus 32:14 needs clarification. God "repented" of his intended action in the sense that he changed his course of action. The word "evil" implies an unfavorable situation or judgment. When used of God it never carries the connotation of sin. God's actions are neither wrong nor susceptible to error although, at times, they may not be understood. When Moses, accompanied by Joshua, arrived at the camp, he discovered joymaking in the presence of the calf and became incensed, breaking the two tablets containing the Ten Commandments. Without any apparent opposition, he took the molten calf, burned it, and ground it into powder. In order to teach a dramatic and unforgettable lesson he mixed the metal with water and made the people drink it. Confronted by Moses with the wholesale defection of Israel, Aaron blamed the people declaring his own innocence and ludicrously asserting that he simply tossed the gold into the fire and out popped a golden calf.

The moment of truth arrived. Moses fearlessly faced the nation and demanded that they decide on whose side they stood. Three thousand maintained their insolence and were executed. The severity of this action may trouble our modern minds, but the need to prevent further corruption of the nation's religious faith necessitated the judgment. Again, Moses intercedes for Israel. He insists that God give the people another opportunity to prove their faithfulness or else let his name be blotted out of the book of life. Yahweh's response is that he has rejected only those who have rejected him. Moses' offer of himself as an antonement for the sins of Israel is rejected by Yahweh.

Temporarily, God's presence had been removed. Now his glory returned (33:7-11) and Yahweh promised, "My presence will go with you, and I will give you rest" (33:14). With two more tablets of stone Moses reascends the Mount and receives the Decalogue a second time. The Covenant is reaffirmed. From this point on, Moses is the leader, although, at times, there are brief but unsuccessful attempts to wrest the mantle of authority from him.

Even though Moses had earlier questioned his ability and aptitude for leadership, it is obvious that he was the man of the hour. He had an excellent Egyptian education as an adopted son of Pharaoh's family. His assets also included lessons in patience and humility in his period of seasoning in the land of Midian. Finally, he possessed the maturity and experience a competent leader needs. Moses may have doubted the wisdom of God's call, but the validity of the choice is patently obvious. God knows the potential and capability of every person.

Sacrifice: Leviticus 1-5

Exodus describes the call of Moses, the preparations for leaving Egypt including the Passover, and the events from Rameses to Sinai. Then, at the sacred mountain the covenant and the law are established. Leviticus, on the other hand, details Israel's system of worship and outlines guidelines for religious conduct. In general, the book of Leviticus has been either ignored or misunderstood by Bible students. The historicity of the book has been doubted by some who assert that it has only typical significance. The evidence is clear that the manuscript was of prime importance to the ancient Hebrews. The first book of required reading for Jewish boys was Leviticus! The title Leviticus is derived from the name of the priestly tribe Levi. Jews designated the book by its first word in Hebrew-"and he called." Confidence, faith and hope were the immediate benefits of the Levitical law.

Sacrifice, described in detail in chapters one through five, did not begin at Sinai. Cain and Abel offered the original sacrifices although the former's offering was rejected because it was not given in faith. Noah took "clean" animals into the ark in order that some could be used as a burnt offering following the flood. Consistently the Patriarchs offered sacrifices at places such as Bethel and Shechem. Still later, Moses requested of Pharaoh that

Israel be given permission to offer sacrifices in the wilderness. The value of sacrifice for Israel was two-fold. First, there was an immediate need to be aware of sin and God's forgiveness and second, the sacrifice pointed to complete redemption that would come through the death of the Messiah. The immediate need of the people was both psychological and religious. Consciousness of sin and guilt was an ever present factor. Sacrifice brought both an awareness of sin and a realization that sin could be forgiven thereby re-establishing fellowship with God. The five basic sacrifices exhibited dimensions of either forgiveness or fellowship with God.

The Burnt offering (chp. 1) was a voluntary sacrifice of cattle, sheep or fowl. The offerer brought the animal to the priest as a substitute for himself. In the case of the burnt offering the sacrifice was burned in its entirety signifying the complete self-consecration of the believer in God. The Meal ("meat" KJV) offering (chp. two) consisted of flour mixed with oil and incense. Part of the flour was given to the priest. Generally it accompanied other offerings. The meal offering signified thanksgiving on the part of the worshipper. Fellowship between man and God was the key implication of the Peace offering (chp. 3). A bullock, lamb, or goat was used in this sacrifice. The procedure was similar to that of the burnt offering with the exception that only the entrails were burned. Part of the meat was retained by the offerer while the breast and right thigh of the animal belonged to the priest. The offering was intended as a fellowship meal with God present.

Only two sacrifices were compulsory, the Sin (4:1-5:13) and the Trespass (guilt) offerings (5:14-6:17). In the case of the Sin offering, the sacrifice was determined by the economic status of the sinner. A bullock was offered for the whole nation. The ruler was to offer a ram or male goat. If one could afford to do so, an individual was to offer a young female goat. The poor could substitute two doves or pigeons while the very poor were permitted to offer one-tenth of an ephah of very fine flour. A sacrifice did not have to be an animal or "blood" offering. In this instance, the very poor could present a sin offering of flour! In addition, the thank offering was never a "blood" sacrifice. The main difference between the Trespass and Sin sacrifices is that the former not only involved expiation (forgiveness) of sins, but required restitution as well. The Trespass offering required a sacrifice of a ram.

Essentially, the sacrificial system was designed for those who sinned through ignorance and weakness, not for deliberate sin. The offering had to be "without blemish" for two reasons. In the first place, all worship of God needed to be of the highest quality and, secondly, the sacrifice pointed to the coming Messiah who would bring a complete and final atonement for sin (Heb. 10:1-8). (See I Peter 1:8-9 which is an appropriate description of the meaning of sacrifice.)

The Priesthood: Leviticus 8-10 (Exodus 28-29)

God chose the tribe of Levi to maintain and direct the sacrificial system. Ritual and its paraphenalia were under the jurisdiction of the Levites. The tribe was especially chosen for holy service with the family of Aaron as the leaders. Each priest was anointed and consecrated to Yahweh. Due to the demanding nature of the Hebrew ritual, it was necessary to have specialists to maintain and implement it. The entire system was based on symbolism. For example, the high priest was the mediator between God and man. The Ephod (an embroidered linen robe) worn by the high priest contained two precious stones with the names of the twelve sons of Jacob (Israel) engraved on them. A breastpiece contained the two oracle stones, the Urim and Thummim. Literally the words mean "lights and perfections" and apparently were used as "yes" or "no" stones in ascertaining the will of God. The turban featured a plate of gold inscribed with the phrase "Holy to Yahweh (the Lord)," a description of the intended status of Israel. Ordinary priests wore less ostentatious clothing. Like Samuel, they wore a plain linen ephod (robe). Membership in the priestly order was normally determined by birth in the tribe of Levi. Essentially the function of the priests was to be custodians of the law, but they were not intended to be the sole possessors of the law. Israel was supposed to be a nation of priests (Ex. 19:6). Tragically, this privileged position was often neglected.

Laws of Purity: Leviticus 11-16

Distinction between clean and unclean animals carried both a religious and a health significance (chp.11). From a religious point of view the segregation of animals constituted a visible testimony of God's ownership of his creation. The bounds of Israel's choice were set by God as evidence of his sovereignty and concern. At the same time, the restrictions were designed for the benefit of the people. For example, the banning of swine provided protection from potential illness and possible death from improperly cooked pork. Also, the lack of refrigeration made storage of the meat impractical.

Purification of a woman after childbirth likewise contained a double significance. The restriction emphasized the sacred character of childbirth while, at the same time, it gave the mother an opportunity to recuperate from the strenuous birth process. The value of the period of purification following childbirth, and during menstruation, is obvious.

Leprosy (13,14) in biblical times included various skin diseases. It was not limited to what is now called leprosy (i.e. Hansen's disease). The priests functioned as health inspectors. Skin disease was treated by isolating the infected person. If, after seven days of seclusion, the infection cleared or failed to spread, then the disease was declared non-infectious and the individual was released after an additional seven day waiting period. Severe cases that did not heal or stop spreading were kept in permanent isolation to prevent further contamination of the community. Leprosy, perhaps mildew, was also found in garments. Leprosy in houses was probably mold. The restrictions on leprosy were to promote cleanliness and health in both the heart and body.

Day of Atonement (Yom Kippur): Leviticus 16

Yom Kippur is the beginning of the Jewish New Year. The holy day occurs five days before Tabernacles, about October 1. General expiation for the sins of the people was achieved by sacrifice. Before the high priest could offer an atonement for the nation, he had to first cleanse himself and his family by a sin offering. The offering in behalf of the people involved two goats. One was designated for the Lord (Yahweh) and the other for Azazel, the latter one being a "scapegoat" over which the sins of Israel were confessed. The goat was then sent into the wilderness symbolizing the removal of sin from the community. Afterwards, the goat for Yahweh was sacrificed and blood from the animal was sprinkled on the mercy seat in the Holy of Holies, a symbolic cleansing of the nation. This atonement was a temporary covering of Israel's sins in anticipation of the coming Messiah (Hebrews 7:23-28; 9:11-12, 24-27).

Discussion - Questions to consider:

1. What was the significance of the Decalogue (Ten Commandments) for Israel?
2. Compare the Decalogue with the Code of Hammurabi.
3. What implications can be seen in the Golden Calf incident?
4. What is the significance of the tabernacle and its furniture?
5. What is the importance of sacrifice in the Old Testament?
6. Were all Old Testament offerings "blood" sacrifices?
7. Why was the Old Testament priesthood established?
8. What benefits were gained by observing the Laws of Purity?
9. What was the significance of the Day of Atonement (Yom Kippur)?
10. What is the connection between sacrifice and salvation?

Resources for additional study:

J.G. Aalders, "The Tabernacle," *EC*, Volume IV

Steve Barabas, "Sacrifices," *ZPBD*

W. Shaw Caldecott, "Tabernacle," *ISBE*

Charles Erdman, *Book of Leviticus* (Revell)

C.L. Feinberg, "Tabernacle," *ZPEB*

D.W. Gooding, "Tabernacle," *NBD*

I.M. Haldeman, *The Tabernacle, Priesthood and Offerings (Revell)*

R.K. Harrison, "Tabernacle," *ZPBD*

———. "Origin of Sacrifice," *WBE*

Werner Keller, *The Bible as History* (Morrow)

C.F. Maclear, *A Classbook of Old Testament History*

A.F. Rainer, "Sacrifice and Offerings," *ZPEB*

John Rea, "Sacrifice," *WBE*

J.J. Reeve, "Sacrifice" (OT), *ISBE*

S.J. Schultz, *The Old Testament Speaks* (Harper) pp. 65-88

R.J. Thompson, "Sacrifice and Offering," *NBD*

B.K. Waltke, "Leviticus," *ZPEB*

CHAPTER IX
Israel In The Wilderness
"According to the number of days in which you spied out the land, forty days, for every day a year, you shall bear your iniquity, forty years, and you shall know my displeasure."

Readings: Leviticus 25-26; Numbers 1-30; Deuteronomy 1-4, 12-26, 33-34

Preparations for Leaving Sinai:
Sabbatic Year: Leviticus 25

Leviticus 17-26 details the religious and social conduct of Israel. Of particular significance is the Sabbatic year which anticipated the agrarian life of Canaan. The regulation carried a double significance. The religious dimension involved an awareness of God's ownership and Israel's stewardship of the promised land. In addition, the requirement of letting the land lie fallow with sowing, reaping and pruning forbidden was a significant form of crop rotation long before such advanced farming methods were understood. The spontaneous produce of the seventh year was to be reserved for the poor and stranger. Also, all debts were to be forgiven. If Israel kept the Sabbatic year, God promised sufficient produce the sixth year to carry them through the seventh.

Following seven sabbatic years, a year of Jubilee was declared. In effect, Jubilee, occurring every fifty years, was a double Sabbatic year. Jubilee began on the Day of Atonement. Special features of the year included forgiveness of all debts, emancipation of all slaves, and the return of all land to the original owners or their heirs. Obviously, the sale of land amounted to a lease of the land until the year of Jubilee. This requirement was a significant factor in maintaining the balance of wealth, a social feature that was far ahead of its day. Some have questioned whether the Sabbatic and Jubilee years were actually observed as sacred years. That Israel failed to do so in no way minimized the validity of the requirement. A similar statement could be made about many of the nation's obligations. The remainder of

Leviticus (26-27) deals with various laws and vows.

The Census of Israel: Numbers 1-4

The book of Numbers follows the priestly laws of Leviticus. The nation is now ready to resume its journey to the promised land. Before leaving, a census of the tribes is taken, hence the name Numbers. The book begins with a description of the preparations for departure and continues with a narrative of the abortive attempt to enter Canaan along with the ensuing judgment of the wilderness wandering. Finally, forty years after departing Egypt, the nation reaches the border of the promised land ready to begin a new life in Canaan. The actual preparations for departure from Sinai included the numbering and arrangement of the people. The census was taken one month after the erection of the tabernacle. Those numbered were the males twenty years of age and older. Apparently, the total of 603,550 men represented the potential military strength of the nation (1:46). Evidently the population of Israel at this time was well over two million people.

Israel's encampment was arranged so that the tabernacle was at the center of the camp. Immediately in front of the tabernacle (on the east side) Aaron, Moses, and the priests were stationed. Three tribes, including Judah the standard bearer, Issachar and Zebulun were also encamped on the east side. On the south of the tabernacle the tribes of Reuben, Simeon and Gad set up their tents. At the rear (west side) of the tabernacle were Manasseh, Ephraim and Benjamin while Dan, Naphtali and Asher protected the north side of the camp. Immediately surrounding the tabernacle was the priestly tribe of Levi--the Kohathites (south), the Gershonites (west) and the Merarites (north).

In the actual trek through the wilderness, the order of the march was designed to protect the sanctuary and provide an orderly method of re-encampment. Leading the procession was the Ark of the Covenant borne by the Kohathites. Then Judah, Issachar, and Zebulun followed with the Gershonites and Merarites carrying the heavy framework and covering of the tabernacle. The next three tribes, in order, were Reuben, Simeon, and Gad followed by the remainder of the Kohathites bearing the tabernacle furnishings. Ephraim, Manasseh and Benjamin followed the bearers of the sacred furniture. The rear division included the Gershonites and the tribes of Dan, Asher, and Naphtali. The strongest divisions numerically were placed in the front and rear positions of the march. According to Numbers 10:21 the tabernacle was carried so that the work of setting up the sanctuary could be done in an orderly and progressive fashion. The ark led the procession and the length of the journey was determined by the movement of the "cloud."

From Sinai to Hormah: Numbers 10:11-14:45

One year, one month, and twenty days after leaving Egypt, Israel departs from Sinai. The people had been encamped at the mountain for nearly a year. The ark and the cloud were to be the means of guiding Israel. The first stop after Sinai was Taberah (11:1-3) where the people complained about their misfortunes. A judgment of fire broke out in the camp but was abated through an intercessory prayer of Moses. Then, at Hataavah (11:4-34), the complaint was about the continual diet of **manna** and the lack of meat. Again, Moses prayed for the people and God sent quail to satisfy Israel's desire for meat. Because of greed, the people hoard the quails causing the meat to spoil and a plague to break out in the camp. This ill-conceived action proved to be another example of Israel's folly and unbelief. Also, at Hataavah, a senate of 70 elders was chosen to aid Moses. Later, at Hazeroth (11:35-12:16), Aaron and Miriam oppose Moses' leadership. The sedition, which grew out of jealousy was short lived and Miriam, the leader of the rebellion, suffered a temporary attack of leprosy. God did not, nor would he, permit any challenge to Moses' leadership.

Upon reaching Kadesh-barnea (13:1-20) twelve men were sent to spy out the land of Canaan at the direction of God. While the land was found to be a good one, the majority of the spies were convinced that the inhabitants of the territory would prove to be formidable foes. A minority report was given by Caleb and Joshua who insisted that God would grant victory, no matter what the strength of the opposition. God weighs, once again, the possibility of totally rejecting Israel, but Moses' intercession gives the people another opportunity to prove themselves. As a judgment for their lack of belief in him, God places a penalty of wilderness wandering upon the nation. For forty years, including the time elapsed from the departure from Egypt, the people were to wander homeless in the wilderness. Of the men who left Egypt twenty years of age and older, only Joshua and Caleb finally reach the promised land. After consideration of their mistake, Israel, against the advice of Moses, makes an abortive attempt to take the promised land and was defeated at Hormah.

The Wilderness Period: Numbers 15:1-19:22

During the approximate thirty-seven years of wandering a series of laws were given anticipating the coming life in Canaan. Korah, with some of his friends, made an unsuccessful attempt to wrest the power of leadership from Moses. The severe judgment meted out to them, and their families, appears unduly harsh in our day and time, but it must be remembered that Moses' authority was constantly being challenged and all attempts at rebellion had to be quelled immediately. Even the people of Israel complained at the severity of the judgment. Nevertheless, God in his sovereignty and all prevailing knowledge acted in accord with his own purposes. Ultimately, the judgment benefited the nation. Various laws for the priests and sacrificial system were given and clarified during the wilderness period. The wandering was a time of testing and maturation for Israel.

From Kadesh-barnea to Moab: 20:1-21:35

Returning to Kadesh-barnea, following the period of wandering, the people begin their final odyssey toward the promised land. While encamped at Kadesh, Miriam died and was buried. When no water was found, the people again complained wearying Moses to the point that he brought forth water from a rock without giving due credit to God for the miracle. As a judgment for his error, God excludes Moses from entrance into the promised land (20:10-13).

An attempt to gain passage through Edom on the way to Canaan was denied by the inhabitants. Israel therefore detoured by Mt. Hor where Aaron died. Eleazar, Aaron's son, succeeded him to the high priest's office. At Hormah (21:1-3), the Israelites became engaged in battle a second time, but, with the help of God, they win the second encounter. Soon thereafter the people once more murmur against Moses and challenge his leadership. This time a judgment of fiery serpents was sent upon the camp. Through intercession, Moses is instructed to make a bronze serpent which, when looked upon after being bitten by a snake, would prevent death. God's power did the actual healing, but the bronze serpent was a reminder of the people's lack of faith. Israel continues moving northward where they encounter and defeat the kings of Sihon and Og.

In Moab, on the Border of Canaan: Numbers 22-36

As Israel encamped in the plains of Moab ready to enter Canaan, they found strong opposition from Balak, the king of Moab. However, in order to defeat Israel Balak attempts to obtain the services of the prophet Balaam (22-24). Although Balaam is not an Israelite, he is warned by Yahweh not to speak against the chosen people. At first, Balaam refuses to go with the princes of Moab since God had warned him not to curse Israel. Later, God permits Balaam to go, but only to bless the sons of Jacob. Apparently, Balaam had intended to double-cross God for Yahweh sent an angel to block his way. Unable to see the angel, Balaam blamed his donkey (ass) for the difficulty. Miraculously, God permits the animal to speak and rebuke its master. Through this incident Balaam learns that he must carry out God's will to the letter. At the request of Balak, Balaam prophesies, however it is a blessing, not a curse on Israel. Four times Balaam blesses Israel, each time kindling the anger of Balak who had hired him. However, Balaam's consistent response was that he had to speak the message God gave him. Balak tried changing locations for Balaam in hope that he would curse Israel, but to no avail. Finally, after the fourth blessing, unable to curse Israel, Balak gives up and goes home. The key point in this narrative is that the message of God is inviolable. The prophet had to speak God's word, not his own. From the context, it appears that Balaam would have cursed Israel for the money Balak offered him, but could not do so since he was a prophet.

On the border of the land of Canaan, a second census is taken. The total number of men was roughly the same as at the beginning of the wandering, slightly over 600,000 men (a net loss of 1,820). Significantly, a whole new generation of men and leaders had arisen. With the exception of Joshua and Caleb, all men over twenty years of age at the first census had died. God used the wilderness bondage as both a judgment against the older unfaithful generation and as an opportunity to develop a new nation. As a symbol of Israel's judgment, circumcision was not practiced during the wilderness period. Upon entering the promised land, the covenant is renewed by the act of circumcision (Joshua 5:2-8).

Before entering the promised territory several laws were given to aid the people in their service of God. One of the most interesting is the Nazirite law (Numbers 6:1-21). A Nazirite was a person who took a vow of consecration to God for a specific period of time. The vow included abstinence from wine (or grapes in any form), haircutting, and the touching of anything dead. Normally, the vow was for a short time (a few weeks or months). At the conclusion of the vow, the Nazirite was to offer a burnt offering and shave his head. The purpose of this vow was to develop spiritual maturity. Other vows were usually made to indicate integrity of life in everyday affairs, although some did have specific religious intent. (See Leviticus 27 and Numbers 30.)

In Numbers 28-29 regulations are given for the various holy days. The five main feast days were Passover, First Fruits, Trumpets, Atonement, and Tabernacles. The latter part of the book of Numbers describes the coming distribution of the promised land along with the establishment of special cities for the Levites and the six cities of refuge. (These matters will be discussed in the next chapter.) The book closes with the settlement of the claim of Zelophehad's daughters. In this instance there were no male heirs and so arrangements were made to maintain the family name and inheritance by marrying within the same family and tribe.

Deuteronomy 1-34:

The last book of the Pentateuch (or Torah) is designated Deuteronomy not to imply a second law, but rather the repetition (or restatement) of the law. As a nation faced with a new life, Israel needed to be reminded of God's laws and provisions for their welfare. The laws given at Sinai and during the wilderness march needed to be applied to the new institutions that would develop in the settled life of Palestine. It was especially necessary that they be warned of the detrimental influences that awaited them in Canaan. In addition, the mantle of leadership was now to pass from Moses to Joshua and so this was an occasion for the prophet to give his final admonitions to his people. The book is a series of four messages repeating much of the information and events found in Exodus, Leviticus, and Numbers. The first message is a historical review of God's leadership and Israel's lack of faith. In the second discourse, an exposition of the Ten Commandments is given. The third address is a reaffirmation of the covenant, while the final message is a farewell declaration of faith in God. The theme of the Book of Deuteronomy is succinctly stated in 6:4-5:

"Hear, O Israel: The Lord our God is one Lord, and you shall love the Lord your God with all your heart, and with all your soul, and with all your might."

Apparently, the final chapter (34) detailing the death and burial of Moses was penned by his successor, Joshua, although it would not have been impossible for Moses to have written his own obituary.

Discussion - Questions to consider:

1. What was the economic and social importance of the Sabbatical and Jubilee years?
2. What is the purpose of the book of Numbers?
3. What was the significance of the order of march for the tribes of Israel during the Wilderness Wandering?
4. What important factors are involved in the Nazirite law? Vows?
5. Assess the importance of the mission of the twelve spies and its results.
6. Discuss the significance of the numerous murmurings during the wilderness period?
7. Discuss the problem of sedition during the Wilderness Wanderings. Why was Moses' leadership challenged so often?
8. What lessons can we learn from Balaam and his prophecies?
9. What are the three chief festivals of the Hebrews?
10. What is the significance and value of the book of Deuteronomy?

Resources for additional study:

Steve Barabas, "Jubliee," "Vow," *ZPBD*

R.O. Coleman, "Vows," *WBE*

E.E. Ellis, "Vow," *NBD*

H.F. Freeman, "Festivals," *WBE*

Charles Erdman, *Book of Numbers: Book of Deuteronomy* (Revell)
Werner Keller, *The Bible as History* (Morrow)
K.A. Kitchen, "Wilderness Wandering," *NBD*
Meredith G. Kline, "Deuteronomy," *WBC*
Paul Levertoff, "Vows," *ISBE*
J. Lilley, "Jubilee Year," *ZPEB*
A.A. MacRae, "Numbers," *NBC*
G.F. Maclear, *A Classbook of Old Testament History* (Eerdmans) pp. 142-199
G.T. Manley, "Deuteronomy," *NBC*
J. Morgenstern, "Jubilee Year," "Sabbatical Year," *NBC*
NBC - Numbers, Deuteronomy
J.B. Payne, "Nazirite," *ZPEB*
John Rea, "Wilderness Wandering," *WBE*
J.C. Rylaarsdam, "Nazirite," *IDB*
S.J. Schultz, *The Old Testament Speaks* (Harper)
Elmer Smick, "Numbers," *NBC*
M.N. Tod, "Nazirite," *ISBE*
G.H. Waterman, "Sabbatic Year," ZPEB

CHAPTER X
Joshua
"...the Lord said to Joshua the son of Nun, ...as I was with Moses, so I will be with you; I will not fail you or forsake you."

Readings: *Joshua 1-24*

Entrance into the Promised Land: 1:1-5:12

The book of Joshua begins with the commissioning of Joshua as Moses' successor and God's assurances to him that, as in the case of Moses, he will have the same guidance and authority, especially through the "book of the law." Preparations for crossing the Jordan included a reminder to the two and a half tribes (Reuben, Gad, and the half-tribe of Manasseh) that they were obligated to help the other tribes subdue the land of Canaan. To this they readily acceded. Before the actual invasion, two spies were sent to survey the situation in Jericho. Word of their presence reached the king of Jericho who sought to arrest them at the house of innkeeper Rahab. The soldiers, upon being erroneously informed that the spies had left, pursued them to the Jordan River. After hiding the spies on the roof of her house, Rahab requested that they guarantee safety to her and her family. (Obviously, Rahab experienced a reformation of life for the New Testament (Heb. 11:31, Ja. 2:25) describes her as a woman of faith.) The spies agreed to her condition and she placed a scarlet cord in her window to designate her house. The deliberate lie of Rahab concerning the spies is not commended in the Scripture. The New Testament references to her faith speak of her trust in God, not of the deception. After three days of hiding in the nearby hills, the men return and report to Joshua. The decision was then made to enter the promised land.

Crossing the Jordan was a spectacular sight! Leading the way were the Levitical priests bearing the ark of the covenant. As soon as the feet of the priests bearing the ark stepped into the Jordan the waters parted, just as they had done previously at the Red Sea. Even though the river was at flood stage, the priests miraculously were able to stand on dry ground in the midst of the Jordan while the people of Israel passed over safely. In thanksgiving for God's miraculous intervention two sets of twelve stones were set up as a memorial to the event. One was placed in the middle of the stream where the priests stood, and the other on the east bank of Gilgal. In addition to the memorial stones, four other significant events occurred at Gilgal. Circumcision was reinstituted after the wilderness hiatus. All the males were circumcised for the first time since Israel left Egypt. Then, the Passover was celebrated for the first time on the soil of the promised land. The following day **manna** ceased and the people ate the "produce of the land." Grain from Palestine replaced the miraculous food of the wilderness. Finally, an angel of Yahweh appeared affirming Joshua's leadership and confirming the presence of God. The celebration of the Passover, the harvesting of grain, and the flooding of the Jordan all indicate that the entrance into Canaan took place in the spring of the year, probably April.

Capture of Jericho: 5:13-6:27

Jericho's conquest was unusual. The actual date for the fall of the city has been debated since Jericho has been destroyed numerous times in its long history. In this instance, the date is probably 1406 B.C. The military tactics used by Joshua were strange. Each day for six days the people were to march around the city following the priests who were blowing ram's horns and carrying the ark. On the seventh day, the city was to be circled seven times. Other than the sound of the trumpets the people were to make no noise until the thirteenth trip when a loud shout was to be given. Clearly, the fall of Jericho was not dependent upon the military strength of Israel. The collapse of the walls and the victory were a result of faith in God, not a demonstration of ability on their part. The city's conquest was a lesson in God's power and Israel's need to trust their Lord. As promised, Rahab and her family were spared. She became a convert and an ancestress of the Messiah. A ban (**herem**) was placed on the city of Jericho. This ban meant that the city and its contents belonged to God. Because of Achan's failure to observe the ban, Ai was a difficult conquest.

Trouble at Ai: 7:1-9:27

Achan's theft of the objects devoted to God prevented the capture of the city of Ai. The **herem** (ban) meant that none of the spoil of a conquered city could be taken for personal use. Failure to capture Ai after the success at Jericho distressed Joshua. God reveals to him that the problem arose because someone broke faith by stealing devoted objects from Jericho. By means of lots, probably the Urim and Thummim (yes/no stones), the guilty culprit was found. Achan confesses that he had stolen a Babylonian garment, 200 shekels of silver, and a fifty shekel bar of gold - an extremely large sum of money for that day and time. Achan and his accomplices were stoned at Achor. Clearly it was a severe, but at that time a needed judgment. The second attempt to take the city of Ai was not marred by defeat. Joshua and his men prepare a well-devised strategy. Two groups of soldiers were deployed in ambush. A large contingent of 30,000 were sent the night before the battle to encamp on the north (or back) side of the city, while a smaller force of 5,000 were set in hiding on the west. When the Israelite army approached the city of Ai, they pretended to flee in defeat as in the previous encounter. The soldiers of Ai unsuccessfully pursued them. It was relatively easy for the two deployed divisions to take the unprotected city. Following the battle, an altar was erected at Mt. Ebal. Peace and burnt offerings were sacrificed upon it. Then, the law of Moses was read and reaffirmed. The name Ai means "ruins" and some hold that the reference is to the city of Bethel. Perhaps Ai was a military garrison belonging to Bethel.

News of the conquest of Jericho and Ai spread rapidly. Some of the tribes in Palestine prepared to defend themselves, but the Gibeonites chose another stratagem. They approached Joshua giving him the false impression that they had traveled a great distance as evidenced by their apparently well used torn clothing and moldy food. Under the guise of a distant tribe they made a covenant with Joshua. Later, upon reaching the cities of the Palestinian Gibeonites the Israelites were obligated to keep their treaty of peace even though it was obtained under false pretenses. However, as punishment for the deception, Joshua makes them "hewers of wood and drawers of water" for Israel. In the ancient world the spoken word was inviolable, thus Joshua kept his word even though it was given to people who were dishonest with him.

The Conquest of Southern Palestine: 10:1-43

Under the leadership of Adonizedek, king of Jerusalem, a southern coalition sought to stop the advance of Israel. The coalition attacked Gibeon because they had made an alliance with

Joshua. Gibeon appealed to Israel for help. Joshua and his men marched all night from Gilgal to Gibeon meeting and defeating, with the help of God, the army of Adonizedek. In the battle, God helped Israel by raining down hailstones. To aid Israel God also made the sun and moon "stand still" (10:12-14). The exact meaning of this incident is unclear. Obviously, the sun would not actually stand still. Some have suggested that the earth stopped on its axis and ceased rotation but continued in orbit. Perhaps, but such an action would have created as many problems as it solved. There is a good possibility that we have a mistranslation here. The Hebrew word (**dom**) can mean to be dumb, silent, or "to be darkened." Possibly the storm that brought the hailstones also created a cloud cover so that the battle could be fought without the oppressive heat of the sun. (See John Rea's discussion in the **Wycliffe Bible Commentary**.) In any case, the point of the intervention is clear. God aided Israel and the battle was won. At the cave of Makkedah Joshua found the five rebellious kings of the southern coalition and executed them. Afterwards, several smaller battles ensued and most (but not all) of the southern territory was secured.

The Conquest of Northern Palestine: 11:1-12:24

Jabin, king of Hazor, headed the confederacy that attempted to prevent the expansion of Israel into northern Canaan. The northern coalition assembled a very large army of soldiers and chariots. With God's assistance, Israel meets Jabin and his armies at the waters of Merom and defeats them. After the defeat of Jabin's coalition, most of the other major cities fell without too much opposition.

The conquest of Canaan is troubling in light of Jesus' statement that we should love our enemies. However, the account in Joshua must be understood in light of the situation at the time. In the first place, God was using Israel as a means of judgment upon a wicked people, just as he later used Assyria and Babylon to bring judgment upon the evil of first Israel, and then Judah. Secondly, God in his sovereignty and justice was seeking to do what would be best for Israel and ultimately all people. This is particularly obvious in the area of moral influence. The lower ethical standards of Canaan were to prove to be detrimental to Israel's national health. Finally, it should be observed that Israel's besetting sin, idolatry, was rampant in Canaan. Israel's failure to completely rid Palestine of these negative influences proves, finally, to be her undoing, especially in the wholesale adoption of the Baal fertility cult. The conquest of Canaan should not be used as a pretext for war. The situation at the time of Joshua is a special one. Nevertheless, Israel never really carried out the judgment and the disastrous results are evident in the nation's history.

Tribal Divisions of the Promised Land: 13:1-19:51

As Joshua approached old age the conquest of Canaan was still incomplete. Areas such as Philistia, Phoenicia and Lebanon still belonged to non-Israelites. The actual apportionment of the land began with the territory assigned to the eastern tribes of Reuben, Gad and the half-tribe of Manasseh. All of the land assigned to the two and one-half tribes was on the east side of the Jordan River. On the west side both Caleb and Joshua were given cities in appreciation for their faithfulness. Hebron was assigned to Caleb (14:13-15) and Timnath-serah (19:49-50) to Joshua. The actual method of division was by casting lots (perhaps with the use of Urim and Thummim). The order of allotment began with Judah (15:1-63) then passed to the sons of Joseph, Ephraim (16:1-10) and Manasseh (17:1-18), on the west side of the Jordan.

At Shiloh, in the central section of Palestine (Ephraim's territory), the tabernacle was set up (18:1). In order to distribute the rest of the land to the remaining seven tribes, a survey crew was sent out to draw up an accurate description of the remaining area. Beginning with Benjamin (18:10-28) the rest of the territory was allotted. Immediately south of Judah, Simeon was to settle (19:1-9). Zebulun, Issachar, Asher and Naphtali all received territory north of Manasseh (19:10-39). Dan was assigned a small territority along the Mediterranean Sea and directly east of Benjamin. Later, Dan acquires additional land in the northern extremity of Palestine (Judges 18).

The Cities of Refuge and Priestly Lands: 21:1-22:34 (See also Numbers 35)

The tribe of Levi did not receive a specific territory but rather was given forty-eight cities scattered throughout the other tribes. Apparently, one of the reasons for this arrangement was to keep a close contact between the priestly tribe and all the other tribes of Israel. In addition, Joseph was promised a double inheritance through his two sons, Ephraim and Manasseh. Thus, if Levi had received a special territory there would have been thirteen tribes. Of particular interest is the fact that six of the forty-eight Levitical cities were designated as "cities of refuge." The purpose of these cities was to prevent injustice through "blood revenge" or vendetta. Sanctuary was given only to those who committed an unpremeditated crime. Such a person could present his case at the gate (council chamber) of the refuge city and, if the elders judged the individual innocent of premeditation, then he would be given the protection of the city (20:2-5; Num. 35). Sanctuary was given until the death of the high priest when the offender was set free. The cities of refuge included Kedesh in Naphtali, Shechem in Ephraim, Hebron in Judah, Bezer in Reuben, Ramoth in Gad, and Golan in the eastern half of Manasseh. Undoubtedly, the system worked very well since there was a greater respect for law among the ancient Hebrews than is evident in modern societies. Following the distribution of the territory, the two and one-half tribes on the eastern side of the Jordan were sent home.

Farewell Message of Joshua and Covenant Renewal at Shechem: 23:1-24:33

As Joshua neared the time of his death, he assembled the people at Shechem and admonished them to remain faithful to God. If the covenant were kept, then God would guide and bless them. On the other hand, if they failed to observe God's law, then judgment would come swiftly (23:14-16). It is evident from Joshua 23-24 that the covenant was conditional. Israel had to remain faithful to Yahweh in order to receive the blessings and privileges of the covenant. At Shechem, Joshua set forth a challenge to the people. They were faced with a choice. Either they would serve the One God as did Abraham, Isaac, and Moses, or else they could choose to follow the gods of the land in which they were now dwelling. For Joshua the decision was clear, "as for me and my house, we will serve the Lord" (24:15). Israel's response was equally affirmative. They declared that God's past deliverance and blessings were overwhelming. Like Joshua, Israel says, "we also will serve the Lord, for he is our God" (24:18). The people pledge that they would obey God. At Shechem, the covenant between Yahweh and Israel was renewed and written in "the book of the law of God." A stone of witness was set up there to remind Israel of her commitment to Yahweh.

Shortly thereafter, Joshua died and was buried in his city at

Timnath-serah. Throughout the days of Joshua, and the elders who outlived him, the nation was faithful to God. However, when a new generation arose major problems developed. These matters will be discussed in the next chapters.

In summary, it should be said that Joshua had the qualifications of a great leader and Israel had the potential to become a great nation. In the case of Joshua, he demonstrated his faith and obedience to God through his actions. Israel, on the other hand, proved to be another story. Joshua served as an able successor to Moses. With the death of Joshua and his associates, the theocracy began to fall apart. Many of the commands of God were either neglected or outright disobeyed. The consequences of Israel's unfaithfulness during the period of the Judges will be considered in the next chapter.

Discussion - Questions to consider:

1. Why was Joshua chosen by God to succeed Moses as the leader of Israel?
2. Why was it necessary to remove the Canaanites from Palestine?
3. What archaeological information do we have concerning the city of Jericho?
4. What significant events took place at Gilgal?
5. Discuss the problems involved in Achan's sin and the capture of Ai.
6. Discuss the question of tribal allotments. Why were the Levites omitted?
7. What was the purpose and significance of the "cities of refuge"?
8. What significant developments took place in the Northern and Southern campaigns?
9. What is the importance of the covenant renewal at Shechem?
10. Evaluate the contributions of Joshua. How does he compare with Moses?

Resources for additional study:

W.F. Albright, *The Archaeology of Palestine* (Pelican)

Hugh J. Blair, "Joshua," *NBC*

A.S. Geden, "The Book of Joshua," *ISBE*

John B. Graybill, "Jericho," *ZPBD*

H. Jamieson, "Jericho," *ZPEB*

Werner Keller, *The Bible as History* (Morrow) pp. 150-159

Kathleen M. Kenyon, *Archaeology in the Holy Land* (Praeger)

K.A. Kitchen, "Jericho," *NBD*

J.P.V. Lilly, "Joshua," *NBD*

G.F. Maclear, *A Classbook of Old Testament History* (Eerdmans) pp. 200-223

J. Rea, "Joshua, Book of," *ZPEB;* also *WBE, WBC*

David F. Roberts, "Joshua," *ISBE*

S.J. Schultz, *The Old Testament Speaks* (Harper) pp. 89-102

E.B. Smick, "Jericho," *WBE*

J.A. Thompson, *Archaeology* (Eerdmans)

H.W. Tribble, *Old Testament Biographies* (Broadman)

H.F. Vos, "Archaeology," *WBE*

W.W. Winter, *Studies in Joshua, Judges, and Ruth* (College Press)

CHAPTER XI
The Era Of The Judges
"In those days there was no king in Israel and every man did what was right in his own eyes."

Readings: Judges 1-21

The Political and Religious Situation at the Time of the Judges: 1:1-3:6

The name "judge" is slightly misleading. Actually, the Hebrew word (**shophet**) would be better translated "leader", "deliverer" or "defender." On occasion, the "judges" did function as judicial authorities, but most of the time they were divinely sent deliverers who helped Israel to extricate herself when oppressed by a neighboring nation. Normally they were military leaders, but this function was usually expanded to that of a **de facto** governor or ruler. Although the author of Judges is unknown, the book was probably written around 1000 B.C. during the reign of Saul or in the early days of David. Tradition holds that Samuel was the author. Historically, the book of Judges continues the events in Israel from the death of Joshua (ca. 1380 B.C.) to the time of Samuel (ca. 1050 B.C.).

During the era of the Judges, the land of Canaan was still not fully under the political control of Israel. Canaanites, Perizzites, Jebusites, Philistines, and others were occupying large segments of the land. Most of the tribes had not secured their designated territories. This failure proved to be a "thorn" in the side of Israel as the book of Judges so graphically describes. A generation after the death of Joshua found the people backsliding on their commitment to Yahweh. Pointedly the writer of Judges delcares "And the people of Israel did what was evil in the sight of the Lord and served the Baals; and they forsook the Lord, the God of their fathers..." (2:11-12). The result of this apostasy was the loss of God's blessing and protection.

The prevailing situation in Israel during the period of the Judges was an arrogant individualism. Nearly everyone sought to do what was "right in his own eyes." This rejection of God, and his law, left no standards of conduct. Religiously and morally the nation became corrupt. Surrounding pagan nations moved into this vacuum and dominated the territory. Even so, when the people cried to God for assistance, he sent a deliverer (judge).

Throughout the era of the Judges there is a discernible historical cycle. The first phase of the cycle was a time of faithfulness and blessing followed by a period of disobedience. The result of this second period was a season of oppression and judgment. When this bondage became unbearable, the people would call on God for help. This third stage led to a final one where God sent a "judge" to deliver them from an oppressing nation. Then, an Indian summer period followed when the nation was once more faithful for awhile. However, after a time of peace and prosperity, the people would turn from God and find themselves, once again, in bondage, and so the cycle would repeat itself. This routine continued through no less than seven cycles.

Certain lessons can be gained from a study of this period. In the first place, God expects faithfulness from his covenant people. Failure to maintain commitment, meant discipline. Discipline for Israel was a means of restoring them to their rightful position as God's people. Secondly, events of the era are a clear demonstration that human beings need God. On his own, an individual will only come to ruin - politically, economically, socially, and morally. A third observation is that Israel's besetting sin of idolatry was a futile attempt to be like everyone else. In turning to the Baals, the nation invalidated their covenant with Yahweh. As God's chosen people, they were supposed to be distinctive, and therefore different. Finally, the history of this period teaches that the real strength of a nation is not its military power, but its moral fiber. While Israel could not save herself from political enemies, God could provide the protection needed. Faith and obedience to God and the covenant were the answer. Such lessons are significant for Christians today. God is always displeased with sin, but he will provide mercy for those who are willing to repent. This is a valid principle for all time.

The rest of this chapter will deal with the judges and their contributions to Israel's religious and political life.

Judges of Israel
Othniel: 3:7-11   1375-1336 B.C.

Very little is said about Othniel, Caleb's nephew. Soon after the death of Joshua the people of Israel forgot Yahweh their God and turned to a worship of Baal. As a consequence, God brought judgment on the nation by permitting them to be conquered by Cushan-rishathaim, the King of Mesopotamia. Israel's cry for help was heard and God raised up Othniel as a judge. Through his leadership the Mesopotamians were ousted and a forty year period of peace followed.

Ehud and Shamgar: 3:12-30, 3:31 1319-1240 B.C.

From about 1336 to 1319 B.C. Israel was once again under foreign domination with Eglon, King of Moab, in control. After eighteen years of oppression the people cry to God for assistance. In this instance, the deliverer (judge) was a left-handed Benjamite by the name of Ehud. Ehud was sent by Israel to deliver the tribute, (tax) money to the extremely obese Eglon. After presenting the tribute Ehud informs Eglon that he has a secret message for him. Whatever the "message," the Moabite king was intrigued by it, and arrangements were made for the two of them to meet in the king's private chamber. At the appointed time, Ehud arrived at the apartment carrying a concealed dagger which he used to stab the king. Apparently, the king did not suspect foul play since normally the right hand is the sword and dagger hand. The "judge" slipped out through the doors of the roof chamber locking them behind him. Eglon's servants were reluctant to bother him since the door to his private rooms were locked. By the time they worked up the courage to open the door, Ehud had escaped. Under Ehud's leadership the Moabites were forced out of Palestine and an eighty year era of peace followed. Sometime during this period, Shamgar was able to defeat a strong contingent of Philistines in the southern part of Canaan. The Judges account says of Shamgar, "He too delivered Israel" (3:31).

Deborah and Barak: 4:1-5:31 1240-1201 B.C.

Beginning in about 1260 B.C. the central part of Palestine, in particular the tribe of Ephraim, was under the domination of Jabin, king of Hazor. (This Jabin was probably the son or grandson of the Jabin that opposed Joshua. Also, it should be kept in mind that there are some overlapping periods in the era of the Judges. Usually the oppression was limited to a particular area and did not extend to the whole nation of Israel.) Due to the people's neglect of God, the north central territory was overrun by the Canaanites. After twenty years of subjection the people call on God for help. Interestingly, the leader or "judge" in Ephraim at this time was a prophetess by the name of Deborah. She summons Barak, a military commander of Naphtali, to come down and lead an army against Sisera, the commanding general of Jabin's forces. However, Barak refuses to fight unless Deborah accompanies him. Popular belief usually holds that women had very little status in the ancient world. Such was not universally the case as is evident in this account.

Under Deborah's leadership, Israel attacks the army of Sisera near Mt. Tabor. With God's assistance, the Canaanites are routed. Apparently, God intervened with a rainstorm and flood that incapacitated the army of Sisera (5:20-21). Sisera, himself, escaped on foot and sought refuge with the Kenites. Jael, the wife of Heber, invites the general into her tent. Instead of the water Sisera requested, she gave him warm milk and he quickly fell asleep, assuming that he was with friends. However, Jael took the opportunity to assassinate an enemy of her people. With a tent peg and hammer she killed him fulfilling Deborah's prophecy that a woman would bring the final victory over Sisera (4:9) since Barak refused to lead Israel without Deborah's help. The Song of Deborah in chapter five is an old poem that recounts the battle and the fall of the Canaanites and their leader Sisera. It is a beautiful poem expressing faith in God. Lack of faith in God epitomizes several of the tribes of Israel in the Song. A good illustration of this is the fact that many of the north central tribes refused to come to the aid of Ephraim when Deborah summoned them. Of Reuben it is said, "there were great searchings of heart" (5:15b). Dan stayed with his ships, while Asher "sat still at the coast of the sea" (5:17). Only Zebulun and Naphtali came to the aid of Ephraim. This general lack of cooperation is probably an appropriate commentary on the loose confederation of the twelve tribes at the time of the Judges.

Gideon: 6:1-8:35   1194-1155 B.C.

Midian controlled much of Israel from 1201 to 1194 B.C. Nomads from Midian joined with the Amalekites to prevent the agrarian development of Palestine. Constant raids not only decimated the crops of the Hebrews but also resulted in the loss of herd animals. This time, when the people cried to God, he first sent a prophet to remind them of the covenant and their failure to keep it. Finally, Yahweh sent an angel to Gideon who was threshing wheat hidden in a wine press. Like Moses, Gideon was unwilling to accept the call. He objected saying that he was unworthy of the leadership offered him. As proof that the messenger was from God an offering of meat and unleavened bread was consumed by a miraculous fire. Later that night, the Lord speaks and tells him to tear down his father's altar to Baal and the Asherah. In its place, he was to build an altar to Yahweh and offer a burnt offering upon it. When the townspeople learned of Gideon's action, they sought to kill him. However, Joash, his father, who was apparently in charge of the altar to Baal, defended his son's action arguing that, if Baal is God, he will take care of the matter himself.

Shortly after, the Midianites and Amalekites assemble in the Valley of Jezreel to battle Israel. God's Spirit takes hold of Gideon and he calls for Manasseh, Asher, Zebulun, and Naphtali to gather with him to defend their territory. In order to know for certain that God was with them Gideon applies the "fleece" test. First, he wanted the wool to be wet and the ground about it dry, then he asked just the opposite. The confirmation of these signs gave the "judge" the confidence he needed. Yahweh informs Gideon that his army of 32,000 men was too large, and self-confident. When the fearful and trembling were asked to leave, 22,000 went home. Still the army of 10,000 was too large for the people to understand that God would give the victory. Then the drinking test eliminated another 9,700. With a meagre contingent of 300 men Gideon was to face the enemy. Being assured of God that victory would come, Gideon divided this small army into three groups of 100 men. Stationed around the Midianite camp their weapons were trumpets, and empty jars with torches inside. At the signal of Gideon the men blew the three hundred trumpets, broke the same number of jars, and then waved their torches. In the dark the Midianites, assuming they were being attacked by a large army of Israelites, panicked and began fighting each other. Those that were not killed in the melee, fled. The battle was won through the intervention of God. Today, we would classify the battle as one of psychological warfare. Following the conflict some of the people wanted to make Gideon king, but he wisely refused the offer. A forty year period of "rest" followed the battle in the Valley of Jezreel. From the Midianite victory the people of Israel should have learned a permanent lesson. However, with the death of Gideon (or Jerubbaal, as he was also known for opposing Baal) the people turn from Yahweh and begin worshipping the Baals once more. One of the excuses for worshipping Baal was that he was supposed, according to the Canaanites, to provide fertility of crops. Lack of trust in the One God caused them to turn to a non-existent god for aid.

Episode of Abimelech: 9:1-57   1155-1152 B.C.

In a sense, Abimelech was not really a judge. Although he was a son of Gideon, it would be better to classify him as a usurper of power. Abimelech was able to convince the men of Shechem that he would make a good leader. With the money they gave him, he hired a group of scoundrels who sought out and killed all his brothers but one. Of the seventy sons of Gideon only Jotham, the youngest, escaped Abimelech's massacre. Later, Jotham presents a parable of the bramble bush to the men of Shechem challenging them as to whether they had acted in good faith and honor in choosing Abimelech. Jotham then goes on to predict the downfall of both Abimelech and Shechem. Soon thereafter discord arose between the men of Shechem and Abimelech. A series of tragic events led to the destruction of Shechem and the death of Abimelech. The usurper was mortally wounded by a millstone that a woman dropped on his head. His death, at the hand of a young aide, was a fitting judgment for the evil he perpetrated. The significance of this account is that only tragedy can ensue when people seek to ignore God's will and guidance.

Tola and Jair 10:1-5   1152-1129; 1129-1107 B.C.

Little is said about these two "judges." Both were instrumental in saving the nation following the episode of Abimelech. Tola was from the tribe of Issachar, but lived in Ephraim. He "judged" the nation for 23 years. Jair lived in Gilead, a territory of Manasseh. He had 30 sons that ruled over 30 cities. He was a "judge" for 22 years.

The Tragedy of Jephthah: 10:6-12:7   1089-1083 B.C.

From about 1107 to 1089 B.C. Israel was under the control of the Ammonites. The eighteen year oppression centered in Judah, Ephraim, and Benjamin (10:9). Israel's preference for the Baals, and the gods of her neighbors, only compounded her woes. When

Gilead was attacked, they sought a leader. Because of his ability, Jephthah is called upon to lead even though he was the son of a harlot. In the heat of the battle Jephthah made a rash vow to sacrifice the first thing that came out of his house, if he returned victorious in battle. There is no indication that God either accepted or approved of his obviously foolish vow. Returning from the successful battle he meets his daughter coming out of his house. Considerable debate has gone on about the result of this vow. Some say that Jephthah sacrificed his daughter to God while others suggest that he simply placed her in a convent the rest of her life. On the balance, the latter view appears more probable since she asked for two months to bewail her virginity. In addition, the text does not explicitly state that he killed his daughter. In any case, neither the vow nor its fulfillment is condoned. Jephthah acted without God's direction, or approval, in the matter. The judgeships of Ibzan (1083-1076), Elon (1076-1066), and Abdon (1066-1058) are relatively short and do not merit much attention in the Biblical account (12:8-15).

Samson: 13:1-16:31   1071-1051 B.C.

(This account overlaps with that of Elon and Abdon who were northern contemporaries of Samson.)

The story of Samson is a familiar one. His birth is announced ahead of time to his mother by an angel. From birth Samson was to be a Nazirite. As the lad grew, he managed to break all three of the Nazirite vows. Contrary to his calling he touched the dead, drank wine, and finally, in his folly, permitted his hair to be cut. Samson's amorous escapades are indicative of his unwillingness to follow God's direction in his life. In spite of his mistakes, God was able to use Samson to bring about a release from the Philistine oppression that held the southern and eastern parts of Israel. Samson fell in love with several Philistine women who only created trouble for him. In the case of the last one, Delilah, he was so blinded by what he considered to be his affection for her that he did not realize she was wresting his secret of power. When he awakes to find his hair cut, it is too late. Nevertheless, God was still able to use Samson in all of his folly. Samson was arrested and blinded, but the Philistines failed to realize that, as his hair grew, his strength returned. Thus, when they brought him into the temple of Dagon for sport, they did not discern his potential danger to them. By collapsing the main pillars of the temple, he was able to eliminate three thousand Philistine leaders at once. In many respects Samson was not really a judge, but God used him to accomplish his purpose. In no way could Samson be considered one of the better judges. Yet one can learn from his mistakes realizing that God's purposes are never thwarted.

Illustrations of a People who Fail to Trust God: 17:1-21:25

The appendix of the book of Judges gives three dramatic descriptions of what happens to a nation that turns its back on God. In the first example an Israelite, Micah the Ephraimite, was so weak in his belief in God that he broke the second commandment and made a graven image. In addition, he had no difficulty in encouraging a Levite to become priest at his shrine. He simply offered him a good salary with excellent fringe benefits. Ten pieces of silver, a new suit of clothes each year, along with room and board quickly converted the Levite to a new religion! Later, the Danites envy Micah's setup and steal his idols and priest. The story of the Levite who permits his concubine to be ravaged by the sodomites of Gibeah is so bad that the account is almost unbelievable (19). Nevertheless, these stories illustrate the moral degradation of Israel who turned from God and worshipped at the feet of idols. The internecine war between Benjamin and the rest of Israel (20-21) nearly destroyed the tribe of Benjamin.

In contrast, the book of Ruth which describes events at roughly the same time shows the beneficent results of faith in God. Although Ruth was a Moabitess, she accepted the One God, which Israel should have been worshipping, and she was able to find both purpose and meaning in life. Through her marriage to Boaz she became an ancestress of David, and eventually the Messiah himself. The story of Ruth is a refreshing account in a tragic era.

Discussion - Questions to consider:

1. What is the distinctiveness of the Old Testament office of a "judge."
2. How do they compare with modern judges?
3. Describe and discuss the lone woman judge in Israel.
4. What problems do you see with the actions of Ehud and Jephthah?

5. What contributions did Gideon make?
6. Assess the weaknesses and strengths of Samson.
7. Discuss the implication of the philosophy "every man did what was right in his own eyes." (17:6.)
8. How do the incidents of Micah and the Levite illustrate the moral and religious conditions of the time of the Judges?
9. What commendable features are reflected in Ruth's actions?
10. Why was Ruth different?

Resources for additional study:

Steve Barabas, "Jephthah," "Samson," *ZPBD*

F.F. Bruce, "Judges," *NBC*

A.E. Cundall, "Judges, Book of," "Judges, Period of," *ZPEB, TOTC*

John D. Freeman, "Gideon," *ZPBD*

A.S. Geden, "Book of Judges," *ISBE*

H.E. Jacobs, "Period of Judges," *ISBE*

Werner Keller, *The Bible as History* (Morrow) pp. 160-164

G.F. Maclear, *A Classbook of Old Testament History* (Eerdmans) pp. 224-266

Max L. Margolis, "Deborah," *ISBE*

J.B. Payne, "Deborah," *ZPBD*; "Judges," *NBD*

Charles F. Pfeiffer, "Judges," "Ruth," *WBC*

John Rea, "Samson," *NBD, WBE;* "Gideon," *WBE*

G.L. Robinson, "Samson," *ISBE*

S.J. Schultz, *The Old Testament Speaks* (Harper); "Judges," *WBE*

CHAPTER XII
Samuel and Saul
"And the Lord said to Samuel, 'Hearken to the voice of the people in all that they say to you; for they have not rejected you, but they have rejected me from being king over them...'"

Readings: *I Samuel 1-31*

Birth and Early Life of Samuel: 1-2   ca. 1100 B.C.

I and II Samuel are so named because he is the principal character in I Samuel and, as a prophet, priest, and judge, he anointed the first two kings of Israel. Although the Talmud indicates that Samuel was the author of both books (Baba-Bathra 14b), it is clear that he could not be the writer of all of the material since his death is recorded in I Samuel 25:1. No one knows for certain who the author of the material was. Abiathar, the priest, is a good possibility since he would have had access to the sources and was a close companion of David.

Samuel's birth came at a time when the judges' era was coming to an end. Often Samuel is described as being the last "judge," although some suggest Saul. Eli, the then current high priest, was old and nearly blind and his sons were unfit to succeed him. Individualism had become so rampant that the Mosaic law was ignored and the priesthood, in general, had become corrupt. God was not being considered nor consulted, even by the priests. Samuel's parents, Elkanah and Hannah, were of the minority that still considered the obligations of the law a central part of their lives. Yearly the family made a trip to the tabernacle at Shiloh to worship and sacrifice. It was on such occasion that Hannah, who was barren, prayed that God might give her a son whom she would gladly dedicate to God's service. In due time God answered her request. The son that was born was named Samuel or "asked of God." Even though Elkanah continued to make the yearly sacrifice at Shiloh, Hannah remained at home with the boy until he was weaned.

At about six or seven years of age, Hannah takes Samuel to Shiloh so that he might be brought up by Eli in the environs of the tabernacle. Such an act may seem odd to us since she wanted a son so badly. However, as a woman of faith, she kept her promise and brought the boy to Eli in order that he might be dedicated to God. Later, she has three more sons and two daughters (2:21). Hannah's Song of Praise (2:1-10) is not only an affirmation of trust in God, it is also a statement of God's sovereignty and power. The scripture says of Samuel, he "continued to grow both in stature and in favor with the Lord and with men" (2:26). In contrast, the sons of Eli were "worthless men" who abused the privileges of the priestly office. Eli attempted to rebuke them, but to no avail. The situation becomes so intolerable that God finally sends a prophet to announce the downfall of the house of Eli.

Call and Judgeship of Samuel: 3-7

Samuel's call to be a judge, and a prophet, came at a time when there was little communication between Yahweh and his people. When Samuel was about thirteen years old, he was in the tabernacle keeping the lampstand burning. Eli was old and nearly blind. Evidently his sons had no interest in the affairs of the tabernacle. Four times in one night Yahweh calls Samuel. The first three times the boy went to Eli assuming that the old priest was calling him. After the third trip, Eli finally discerned that it was God who was calling. Samuel is instructed to return to his place and when the call would come again he was to answer, "Speak, for thy servant hears." The message God gave to the young boy was not a pleasant one. Reluctantly, Samuel informs Eli that God had spoken of an imminent judgment upon the house of the high priest. As Eli and his sons diminished in importance, Samuel's distinctive contributions increased. From Dan to Beersheba, Samuel was known as a prophet of God.

As Israel weakened religiously, they also developed social and moral instability. Under these circumstances, the Philistines easily routed the Israelite army at Aphek. In desperation, the people requested the presence of the ark of the covenant. Without God's direction, Hophni and Phinehas take the ark into battle. The thunderous ovation Israel gave the ark chilled the Philistines. However, instead of creating an atmosphere of despair, the Philistines resolved to fight even harder in order that they might avoid slavery at the hands of the Hebrews. The result was that the

Philistines fought with valor and determination killing 30,000 Israelite soldiers. In addition, the ark was captured and Hophni and Phinehas, Eli's sons, were slain. A man of Benjamin escaped and reported the tragic news to Eli who fell backward and broke his neck. Perhaps the fall, and death, of the old man was due to a heart attack. At almost the same moment, the wife of Phinehas heard the sad news. As she neared death, after giving birth to a son, she insisted that the child be named Ichabod "the glory has departed."

For a time, the ark of the covenant was in the hands of the Philistines, but they soon found that it was no asset at all. Upon placing the ark in the temple of Dagon, they discovered that the idol had fallen on the ground in obeisance to the ark. The next day the situation was worse, the hands of Dagon were separated and only the torso remained. Concurrently the people of Ashdod were afflicted with tumors. Immediately they decided that Israel had planted the ark to bring harm to them. They became more than anxious to rid themselves of the menace. After some debate, it was decided to return the ark on a cart with a guilt offering of five golden tumors and mice. Obviously, they associated the plague with mice. In returning the ark, they placed it on a new cart pulled by two cows with calves. They assumed that, if the ark were the source of their trouble, the cows would go directly into Israelite territory, regardless of their calves. The cart stopped in the border area of Bethshemesh in the field of a man named Joshua. Later, some men touched the ark and died. It was then generally assumed that the ark was taboo. However, Abinadab and his son Eleazar agreed to take care of the ark. Meanwhile, Samuel led the Israelites in battle against the Philistines and, with the help of God, they won a resounding victory. The site of the victory was called Ebenezer or "Rock of Help."

Beginning of the Monarchy: 8-12

For a while, following the Battle of Ebenezer, there was peace in the country and Samuel was the recognized leader. He judged the people following a circuit from Bethel to Gilgal and Mizpah then returning home at Ramah (7:16-17). However, as Samuel became an old man, the people began to clamor for a more glamorous leader. They wanted a king like everyone else. Their immediate excuse was that Samuel's sons lacked his integrity since they readily took bribes and perverted justice. While undoubtedly there was truth in the assertion, there is no doubt that the people wanted the apparent prestige of a king. The whole matter disturbed Samuel since by virtue of the covenant, they were a theocracy, i.e. ruled by God. To a degree, Samuel saw the request as a rejection of himself, but God assured him "they have not rejected you, but they have rejected me from being king over them" (8:7). With the covenant they did not need a king, but because the covenant was not a vital force in their lives they opted for a monarchy. Even when Samuel rehearses the obligations and restrictions that a king would bring (8:11-18), they still insist upon a monarch to lead them in battle. This shortsighted decision was to prove to be extremely detrimental to Israel. Nevertheless, God, in his mercy, would still be able to use them.

The selection of Saul, the son of Kish, a Benjaminite, was an obvious one. God revealed the choice ahead of time to Samuel who met, and anointed, Saul when he was looking for some lost animals of his father. Later, when all the people assembled at Mizpah, Saul was the clear choice. He was tall and apparently handsome. By acclamation Saul was proclaimed king following his presentation to the people. At first, Saul demonstrated excellent qualities. He was humble, forgiving, and a leader engendering respect. When the Ammonites attacked Jabesh-gilead, he was able to muster a considerable army by dramatically cutting up a yoke of oxen and sending the pieces throughout Israel. For those who would not heed his summons, he threatened to do the same to their oxen. They came! Obviously, Saul was a born leader. After defeating the Ammonites some suggested that those who rejected Saul's authority should be punished, but he graciously forgave them. Certainly, this was a good start.

Since Israel now has a king, Samuel offers to step down from his position of judge. Samuel's life as a judge was one of utmost integrity. As he passed the mantle of leadership to Saul he challenged them to be faithful to God.

> If you will fear the Lord and serve him and hearken to his voice and not rebel against the commandment of the Lord, and if both you and the king who reigns over you will follow the Lord your God, it will be well; but if you will not hearken to the voice of the Lord, but rebel against the commandment of the Lord, then the hand of the Lord will be against you and your king (I Samuel 12:14-15).

Israel could still be God's people, with a monarch, but they must follow God's direction! Sadly, most of the history of the nation is a commentary on their failure and unfaithfulness.

Saul's Early Years as King: 13-20   ca. 1043-1011 B.C.

Following Samuel's farewell address Saul's influence and popularity come to the fore. However, Samuel does not go into complete retirement for he continues to play a significant role in Israel's history. Sporadic confrontations with the Philistines had continued since the Battle of Ebenezer. In addition, since the Philistines controlled the smelting and manufacture of iron, the Israelites were faced with a considerable armament gap. Saul attempted an all out offensive at Gilgal, but a strong Philistine army weakened their morale. While waiting for Samuel to come and offer a sacrifice in behalf of the people, Saul became impatient and offered a burnt offering on his own. Shortly after concluding the sacrifice Samuel arrives and reprimands him for offering an unauthorized sacrifice. Because the act, though out of desperation, was done in violation of God's command and reflected Saul's lack of faith, Samuel announces that Yahweh has rejected Saul as king and another will be given the kingdom.

At Michmash, Saul's son, Jonathan, decides on a bold and direct attack against the Philistine garrison. Through courage and the conviction that God was directing them, Jonathan and his armor bearer were able to take the garrison outpost. At the same time, an earthquake occurred and the Philistines, fled in panic. The noise of the tumult reached the ears of Saul and the army of Israel who also joined in the rout of the Philistines. During the course of the battle Saul, out of arrogance, utters a foolish oath. He declares, "Cursed be the man who eats food until it is evening and I am avenged on my enemies" (14:24). Jonathan, who was in the front battle lines, was unaware of his father's curse. So, being hungry, he ate some honey and was refreshed. Upon hearing of the restriction of his father, Jonathan realized that the command was for the personal benefit of Saul. He then predicted that the battle against the enemy would not be conclusive, since the people had to fight on an empty stomach. Later, when Saul learns that someone had eaten food during the battle, he discovers, by use of the Urim and Thummim, that Jonathan was guilty. Even though the fault was with his own son, Saul was determined to enforce the penalty. However, the people intervened in behalf of Jonathan preventing his execution.

Samuel again appears on the scene (15:1ff) and instructs Saul to carry out God's judgment upon Amalek. The command was for a complete destruction of the Amalekites, including their property. Nevertheless, Saul decided to save the spoils and at least one hostage, Agag the king. God informs Samuel that Saul's disobedience invalidated his right to the throne. While these judgments appear to be unnecessarily severe to us, it must be remembered that God was making decisions that were in the best interests of all. Saul's excuse that the spoils were brought back as an offering for God was unacceptable. Samuel responds by saying, "Behold, to obey is better than sacrifice, and to hearken than the fat of rams" (15:22b). Saul's immediate reaction was to repent of his misdeed, but Samuel informs him that it is too late. Saul's life to this point already demonstrated a history of disobedience and unfaithfulness.

Yahweh's rejection of Saul grieved Samuel, but God had a more than adequate replacement. Samuel is sent to Bethlehem to the house of Jesse to find Saul's successor. When Samuel meets Jesse's oldest son, Eliab, he is certain that he had found the new king, but God rejected Eliab and six of his brothers. In desperation, Samuel asks if there are any other sons. When David, the shepherd boy, is ushered into the old man's presence, Yahweh's immediate command was to anoint him as the next king. Subsequently, when Saul suffered moments of deep depression and despair, David, who was an accomplished musician, was brought to Saul's court to soothe the savage beast in him. Apparently, this "evil spirit" sent upon Saul refers to the fact that God withdrew his Spirit from the disobedient monarch. Thus, through God's permissive will the "evil spirit" came.

Sometime later the Philistines gathered for another battle at Soco. Israel found themselves being challenged by a supersize champion. The Philistines were willing to reduce the battle down to one man, Goliath of Gath. But, there were no challengers. During this stalemate David was sent, by his father Jesse, to take food to his brothers and ascertain the situation at the battlefield. Upon arriving, David was disturbed to learn that no one had the courage to face Goliath. Words of David's criticism reached the king who summoned him to an audience. David readily agreed to face what appeared to be a certain death. Rejecting Saul's cumbersome armor, he took only a staff, five smooth stones, and a sling. Seeing the young lad, the Philistine giant was enraged and threatened to feed him to the dogs. With great faith and trust in

God, David felled the champion with the throw of a single stone. At first, Saul was grateful for David's help but this attitude was soon to be spoiled by jealousy. Following the battle, David received more praise than Saul. From that moment on, Saul was determined to kill David. On one occasion he failed to pin David to the wall with a spear, so he sent him into battle hoping that he would be killed, but David not only succeeded, he grew in popularity. Saul even offered his daughter's hand in marriage confident that, if David would go out and fight the Philistines, he would fall in battle. However, David was not so easily eliminated and Saul's jealousy continued to grow.

In contrast to their father, Saul's children liked David. Jonathan, for example, made a covenant of friendship with him and looked forward to David becoming the next king. Michal, Saul's daughter, loved David and became his wife. As Saul's envy and hatred of David grew, he accused his son, Jonathan, of siding with his enemy. Even Michal found it necessary to aid David in escaping her father's wrath. On several occasions Jonathan attempted to bring a reconciliation between his father and David, but failed to do so.

David's Years as an Exile Leader: 21-26

Since Saul would settle only for David's life, the latter had no choice but to go into exile to prevent further confrontation. On his way, David stopped at Nob, the city of the priests, obtaining food and the sword of Goliath. From there he sought, but was unable to find, asylum with Achish, the king of Gath, who suspected him of being a spy for Saul. David then set up headquarters at the cave of Adullam. The stop at Nob proved to bring tragedy upon the priests for Doeg the Edomite reported their friendship with David to Saul. Under Saul's direction all the priests, with the exception of Abiathar who escaped, were slain. At En-gedi, Saul attempted to locate and kill David, but the option was David's, and he refused to assassinate the king. When Saul discovered David's kindness, he had a temporary siege of repentance. For a time, Saul gave up his obsession. Shortly thereafter, Samuel died and was buried at Ramah (25:1).

While an exile, David befriended Nabal, a rich herdsman and rancher, who refused to reciprocate. David's anger flared and he sought to kill him, but was stopped by the kind and wise action of Nabal's wife, Abigail. Later, after a drunken feast, Nabal dies of a heart attack. In due time David marries the widow.

Saul's Later Years: 27-31

Apparently, God's removal of his guiding light from Saul created a mental and emotional condition in Saul somewhat akin to that of a maniac depressive. Faced with another battle against the Philistines he sought, but did not receive, direction from God. In an act of desperation, he seeks the aid of a medium at Endor. Disguised so that he could not be recognized, he asked the woman to bring up Samuel from the dead. Evidently she intended to resort to her normal bag of tricks, but when Samuel actually appeared she was in a state of shock and fear. Samuel reprimanded Saul for disturbing him, and then dramatically announces that Saul, and his sons, would be killed in battle the next day. Meanwhile, David had attempted to aid the Philistines, but they rejected his services. At the battle of Mt. Gilboa Saul's sons were killed, and he was mortally wounded. Not wishing to die by the hand of a Philistine, he requests that his armor-bearer kill him. When he refused to do so, Saul fell on his own sword. Consequently, the lad took his own life. Saul's death, while tragic, was not the result of suicide, but an attempt to die gallantly in battle. So ended the life of a potentially great man.

Discussion - Questions to consider:

1. Assess the life and contributions of Samuel.
2. What role did Samuel play in the establishment of the Monarchy?
3. What qualities did Saul possess that made him appealing as a king?
4. What are some of the positive contributions of Saul's reign? Weaknesses?
5. Contrast and compare Saul and his son Jonathan.
6. Why was Saul's jealousy of David so great?
7. What factors are involved in Saul's visit to the medium at Endor?
8. Why was David unwilling to harm Saul even though the latter sought to kill him?

9. What kind of sickness did Saul have that brought moments of madness upon him?
10. What happened at the Battle of Mt. Gilboa?

Resources for additional study:

Carl E. DeVries, "Samuel," "Saul," *ZPBD*

A.S. Geden, "Samuel," "Samuel, Books of," *ISBE*

Werner Keller, *The Bible as History* (Morrow) pp. 171-179

P.C. Johnson, "Saul," *WBE*

T.H. Jones, "Saul," *NBD*

G.H. Livingston, "Saul," *ZPEB*

W.J. Martin, "Samuel," "Books of Samuel," *NBD*

G.F. Maclear, *A Classbook of Old Testament History* (Eerdmans), pp. 267-291

A.M. Renwick, "I Samuel," *NBC*

S.J. Schultz, *The Old Testament Speaks* (Harper) pp. 115-126; "Samuel," *ZPEB*

E.B. Smick, "Samuel," *WBE*

H.W. Tribble, *Old Testament Biographies* (Broadman)

T.H. Weir, "Saul," *ISBE*

Fred E. Young, "I Samuel," *WBC*

CHAPTER XIII
David
"The Lord of hosts is God over Israel, and the house of thy servant David will be established before thee."

Readings: II Samuel 1-24

David, Established as King: 1-5   ca. 1011-971 B.C.

At the outset, the choice of David as king and successor to Saul seemed to be inappropriate. He was the youngest of Jesse's sons and, at the time of his anointing, was only a shepherd lad. In consequence, God had forewarned Samuel not to "look on his appearance or on the height of stature" (Sam. 16:7). Furthermore, he was a musician and a poet, hardly king material! But, God knew the potential and capability of an unpolished stone. On the whole, David was the best king of the United Kingdom. It is true that he made some very serious mistakes, yet the Lord did not lightly say that David was a man "after his own heart" (I Sam. 13:14). While David's great military and political accomplishments are obvious, it is equally clear that he was a man of religious faith. When faced with his sin, he readily admitted his guilt and sought God's forgiveness. In this regard, he differed from Saul whose humility had turned to pride. For the most part, Saul would not repent of his sins.

Although David was anointed king while Saul was still on the throne, the future king never attempted to take over the monarchy. David always had a high regard for Saul, and the office he held. On several occasions the son of Jesse could easily have killed Saul, but he refused to do so. When the Amalekite arrived at David's camp with the news of Saul's death on Mt. Gilboa, the soldier assumed that he was bringing good news. He foolishly claimed that he had killed Saul at the king's request. Since it was general knowledge that Saul, on several occasions, had attempted to kill David, the Amalekite assumed that he would be rewarded for eliminating a dangerous enemy. However, the lie only brought about his demise. The judgment is a severe illustration of the disaster of dishonesty. Perhaps the man protested his innocence, but it was too late.

In memory of Saul and Jonathan, David penned a poem of praise in their behalf. In the song, David speaks highly of both Saul and Jonathan. Special consideration is given to his close friend Jonathan. Such a statement as "your love to me was wonderful, passing the love of women" has been taken by some to imply an unnatural relationship. Nothing could be further from the truth! The statement simply indicates a close bond of friendship. The poem, along with several others mentioned in the Old Testament, comprise a poetic collection known as the Book of Jashar which is no longer extant.

Following the death of Saul, the tribe of Judah anointed David king at Hebron. Most of the northern tribes continued, for a time, to favor a successor from the family of Saul. Abner, Saul's commander in chief, attempted to take advantage of this situation and anointed Ishbosheth, a surviving son of Saul, as king at Mahanaim. Later, Abner and his army challenge a contingent of David's soldiers under the leadership of Joab. Initially twelve champions were chosen from both sides but, when no decisive advantage was gained, a full scale battle broke out. Abner and his soldiers were routed. Asahel, a brother of Joab, pursued Abner only to be killed by the older more experienced man. Although Joab reluctantly calls a truce, he continued to harbor hatred towards Abner for his deed. Later, Abner and Ishbosheth quarrel and Abner decides to cast his lot with David and thus heal the breach between the tribes. Joab, however, was unwilling to accept reconciliation with his brother's murderer, so he treacherously slays him near the entrance to the gate of Hebron. David was genuinely grieved over the action of Joab, but because of the latter's military skill, he keeps him on his staff. This decision later proves to be unwise.

Ishbosheth's assassination followed shortly after Abner's death. Although David did not desire the death of Saul's son, the act did become a means of solidifying his throne since all the tribes of Israel now agreed to accept him as king (5:1-5). David was 37 years old when he became the sole king of Israel. His first act was to capture the fortress city of Jebus and make it his capital. Jerusalem, as it was renamed, was ideally located on the border of Benjamin (Saul's tribe) and Judah (David's tribe). Upon hearing that David was established as king over Israel the Philistines attempt to challenge him, but are defeated in a battle in the valley of Rephaim.

David's Religious Concern: 6-7

Firmly established upon the throne, David sets out to strengthen the religious dimension of Israel's national life. The ark of the covenant is obtained from the house of Abinadab for the purpose of housing it in the new capital. On the way, the ark being moved on a cart, contrary to the levitical requirement of carrying it by poles, began to tip and Uzzah put forth his hand to steady it, and died. David was so upset by the swift judgment of God that he placed the ark at the house of Obededom instead of taking it to Jerusalem, as he planned. After three months, David learned that the ark had brought only blessing to the house of the Gittite, so with great rejoicing he brought the ark into Jerusalem. His wife, Michal, saw the king's joy and exuberance at the return of the ark and privately reprimanded him for such an emotional display before his servants. The king's response was that he did it as an expression of praise to God. From that time on, David and Michal lived separate lives.

With the ark safely in Jerusalem, and a general condition of peace in Israel, David sought to build a temple to house the ark of the covenant. The king consulted with the prophet Nathan who, at first, favored the undertaking. However, later that very night God spoke to the prophet and informed him that since David was a man of war, he should not build the temple. David's disappointment was assuaged by God's assuring him that the temple would be built by his son, and by permitting him to gather materials for the construction of the temple.

David's Military Victories: 8-10

During David's reign as king he encountered in battle, and defeated, the Philistines, Moabites, Syrians, Edomites, and Ammonites. Under David's administration Israel reached its zenith in terms of military might and territory controlled. Later, Solomon did little to secure the land and, during his reign, the country began to shrink in size. Under David's rule the territory of Israel extended from the Negev in the south to Damascus in the north.

The quality of David's character is shown in his concern to

befriend Mephibosheth, the crippled son of Jonathan. The house of Saul was placed under Mephibosheth's control and Ziba, a former servant of Saul, administered the property. Jonathan's son was brought to the king's house and was welcomed as one of the family.

David's Double Sin: 11-12

Unquestionably, the low point of David's religious and moral life occurred when he committed the sin of adultery and attempted to hide it with murder. Perhaps Bathsheba was partly at fault for bathing so openly, and she was certainly wrong in answering David's invitation without any apparent protest. Regardless of Bathsheba's guilt, David cannot be excused for his wanton act of passion and his deliberate injustice to Uriah.

David attempted to cover his sin by encouraging Uriah to come home from battle for a visit with his wife. But, being a good soldier, he refused the comforts of home while his fellow soldiers were still in battle. Failing to cover his guilt by this method, David sends Uriah back to the battlefield with his own death warrant. David simply suggests that Uriah be placed in the front of the battle and, when the enemy attacked, the other soldiers were to drop back leaving Bathsheba's husband in a death trap. Joab followed the orders of David without question, and Uriah was killed. How David could have committed such direct and deliberate acts of wrong is difficult to comprehend. While David was not a perfect man, the Biblical record consistently describes him as a man of integrity. If David had been about his normal affairs or had been following his better judgment, he would never have committed such despicable acts. Clearly the power of temptation is real, even for the best of men. David's marriage to Bathsheba following Uriah's death may have been an attempt to partially atone for his wrong. However, God's judgment was due and David was soon to experience it.

Yahweh sent Nathan to David with a parable of two men, one rich and the other poor. When David heard the story of how the rich man forcibly took the poor man's pet lamb, he was enraged and declared that such a man should be shown no pity. He had judged himself. When Nathan pointed the finger and said "you are the man," the message was clear and loud. To David's credit it must be said that when faced with his sin, he confessed his guilt without any attempt to rationalize his actions. It is the element of repentance that differentiated David from Saul. Yet in no way can David be exonerated for his wrong.

Nathan informed David that God would forgive him of his sin, but the child that would be born to Bathsheba would die. When the child became ill, soon after birth, David prayed hoping that God might spare him. Fasting and regret could not change the announced judgment of God. David knew that he was the one who had brought about this tragedy. Nevertheless, when the child died, David rose from his fasting and praying, washed himself, and ate. This latter act was soundly criticized by his servants for they saw it as improper and sacrilegious. David's response is most revealing. He says,

> While the child was still alive, I fasted and wept; for I said, 'Who knows whether the Lord will be gracious to me, that the child may live?' But now he is dead; why should I fast? Can I bring him back again? I shall go to him, but he will not return to me. (12:22-23)

One must credit David with a healthy attitude toward death! Later, God gave him another son, Solomon, who was destined to follow his father on the throne of Israel.

David's Problems with his Children: 13-14

Here we meet one of the supreme lessons of life. The sins of the parents **do** affect and influence the children. In the case of David his adultery was far more disastrous than he could possibly have believed at the time of his passion. Parents who assume that their wrongs are a private matter are simply being dishonest. Obviously, Amnon's lust for his half-sister, Tamar, cannot be blamed directly on his father, but the negative influence was there. Compounding the problem was polygamy. Nowhere does the Bible approve or advocate a plural marriage. The ideal marriage from the beginning of human creation was monogamous (Gen. 2:23-24). It is true that God used men who were polygamous, but this does not mean that he endorsed the arrangement. As one traces polygamous marriages through the Scriptures it is obvious that such life styles breed trouble. (Consider the problems of Abraham and Jacob at this point.) Amnon's incest with his sister led to his death at the hands of her full-brother, Absalom. After the act, Amnon's so-called love for Tamar quickly turned into hate, an appropriate commentary on illicit sexual relationships. Absalom's murder of his half-brother forced him to flee from the rest of the family. Later, Joab tricks David into bringing Absalom back into Jerusalem, but it proves to be a disastrous mistake. The whole business could probably have been avoided, if David had set the right example.

David's Abdication of the Throne; Absalom's Rebellion: 15-18

Absalom's return created almost immediate trouble for David. By no stretch of the imagination could Absalom be described as a humble or considerate man. He was handsome, articulate, and self-centered. After some difficulty, and a considerable amount of intrigue, Absalom was reinstated as a prince by his father. Once Absalom had been restored to favor he immediately began a concerted effort to usurp the throne. Among the tactics he used was that of playing the role of king by riding a chariot with fifty men running in front of him. In addition, he would go down to the court of judgment at the city gate and sympathize with the cause of both sides in a dispute. Since Absalom did not have to make the judgment he could infer that both disputants were right. In this way he gained friends whether a cause was won or lost. By using various devious tactics he "stole the hearts of the men of Israel" (15:6).

As Absalom's cause continued to build momentum, he set up a center of operations at Hebron inviting those who favored his claim to join him. Included in the defectors was Ahithophel, a close friend and counselor of David. Opposition grew to the point where David found it necessary to abdicate the throne. Among the friends that chose to stay with David were Ittai the Gittite, the priests Abiathar and Zadok, and Hushai. Since Abiathar and Zadok were carrying the ark of the covenant, they were sent back to Jerusalem with the ark to try to maintain the religious life of the people. Hushai was also sent back as an undercover agent to keep David informed of Absalom's plans. Others, such as Shimei of the house of Saul, gloated over David's predicament.

With David's abdication Absalom became the **de facto** king of Israel. Ahithophel counsels that they should immediately pursue David while he is weak and disorganized. Hushai, however, anxious to give David time to establish himself, appealed to Absalom's vanity. He suggested that a large army be gathered from all over Israel and then, like a great monarch, Absalom could lead his men to victory. The grandiose scheme was favored by Absalom against the protest of Ahithophel that delay would be dangerous. Finding himself no longer the chief advisor, Ahithophel went home, set his affairs in order, and then committed suicide to save face. Hushai sends word to David that he will have time to prepare a defense against Absalom. In the battle that ensues Absalom is routed and attempts to escape on his mule, but, because of his long hair, his head is caught in the thick foilage and he finds himself suspended and helpless. Contrary to the expressed command of David, Joab comes upon the erring son of David and has him killed.

David's Re-establishment as King: 19-24

David's restoration to power was not a happy one since he lost a son in the process. Joab rebukes David for his maudlin display in behalf of a renegade son while ignoring the needs of the nation of Israel. Returning to the throne, David does not seek vengeance. He forgives Shimei for his insults. Mephibosheth is restored to his rightful inheritance since Ziba had acquired it by deceit. Later, another Benjaminite, Sheba, revolted and tried to wrest the power of the throne from David. Through Joab's efforts, the revolt was quelled. This was followed by several other minor rebellions and battles, but David's power held secure. A list of David's soldiers and supporters is found in chapter twenty-three. The final event recorded in the book of II Samuel is the census of Israel and a resulting judgment by God. Evidently, David had come to rely too much upon his own ability and not enough on God. In any case, a judgment by pestilence broke out and was finally stopped by an offering on a make-shift altar at the threshing floor of Araunah. Later, the Temple was built on the same spot. The last days and death of David are recorded in I Kings 1:1-2:12.

Discussion - Questions to consider:

1. Why was David chosen to replace Saul as king?
2. What were some of the significant events during David's exile life?
3. Assess the value of David's military career.
4. How would you regard the friendship between David and Jonathan?
5. Why did David treat Saul with such great kindness and consideration?

6. Discuss the problem of David's double sin of adultery and murder.
7. Why was David called a man after the Lord's "own heart"?
8. What were some of the strong points of David's reign? Weak?
9. What factors lead to Absalom's rebellion?
10. Assess both the problems and the benefits of the monarchy in Israel.

Resources for additional study:

Steve Barabas, "Joab," *ZPBD*
Henry Buis, "David," *EC*
W.W. Davies, "Absalom," *ISBE*
J.D. Douglas, "Joab," *NBD*
A.S. Geden, "Books of Samuel," *ISBE*
C.P. Gray, "Joab," *ZPEB*
T.H. Jones, "Absalom," "David," *NBD*
W.C. Kaiser, "Absalom," *ZPEB*
Werner Keller, "David, a Great King," *The Bible as History* (Morrow)
F.C. Kuehner, "Absalom," *EC*
G.F. Maclear, *A Classbook of Old Testament History* (Eerdmans) pp. 291-351
J.M. Meyers, "David," *IDB*
J. Barton Payne, "David," *ZPBD*
A.M. Renwick, "II Samuel," *NBC*
George L. Robinson, "David," *ISBE*
S.J. Schultz, *The Old Testament Speaks* (Harper) pp. 127-140
J.B. Scott, "David," *ZPEB*
W.M. Taylor, *David, King of Israel* (Baker)
Fred E. Young, "David," *WBE;* "II Samuel" *WBC*

CHAPTER XIV

Solomon

"And as for you, if you walk before me as David your father walked, with integrity of heart and uprightness, doing according to all that I have commanded you, and keeping my statutes and my ordinances, then I will establish your royal throne over Israel for ever..."

Readings: I Kings 1-11; I Chronicles 28-29; II Chronicles 1-9

The Final Days of David's Reign: I Kings 1:1-2:11; I Chronicles 28-29; Date ca. 971 B.C.

As David approached old age, senility set in. The question of a successor to the throne was left unanswered. For some unexplained reason David had not designated an heir. Earlier, God informed David that Solomon was to be his successor (see II Samuel 7; I Chronicles 22:9-10, 28:5-7).

David's reluctance to clearly declare Solomon as his heir encouraged Adonijah to make a bid for the throne. Adonijah, the son of Haggith and David, did have some arguments in favor of his contention. He was the oldest living son. He was a "handsome" man. He had played the role of king by putting on a display of chariots, horsemen, and a contingent of royal runners. In addition, Joab, David's general, and Abiathar, the chief priest, favored Adonijah's pretension. Furthermore, David failed to indicate any displeasure with Adonijah's attempt to assert his claim to the throne. In fact, David did not even inform Adonijah that he was not to be the successor (see I Kings 2:15).

Adonijah, assuming that he was the legitimate heir to the throne, set about to consolidate his position. In order to do so, he called a meeting at Enrogel of his followers including all of his brothers, except Solomon. Most of the royal officials in Judah were invited. Excluded were Nathan, the prophet; Bathsheba; Zadok, the priest; Benaiah; and, of course, David. Hearing of the assembly and its intended purpose, Nathan urged Bathsheba to secure David's open endorsement of Solomon as king. Nathan agreed to back the request. Upon learning of Adonijah's intended coup, David delcares that Solomon, his son by Bathsheba, was to reign in his stead. In order to effect an immediate transfer to kingly authority, David requests that Zadok and Nathan take Solomon to Gihon and straightway anoint him king.

Adonijah's claim to the throne was severely weakened by the nation's ready and enthusiastic acceptance of Solomon. Most of the pretender's followers deserted him and he himself, in fear of Solomon, went to the temple to find sanctuary by laying hold on the horns of the altar. Adonijah demanded and received clemency on the grounds that he would be co-operative and acquiescent.

As David approached the last moments of his life, he placed a charge upon Solomon to remain faithful to God and to the "law of Moses." In addition, David warned his son of the treachery and unpredictability of Joab. In contrast, he commends Barzillai who had been a faithful servant. Shimei, a source of irritation and trouble for David, was to be spared, if possible. Shortly after these final words David died and was buried in Jerusalem. Altogether he had been king for forty years (1010-970 B.C.). Solomon also reigned forty years (971-931 B.C.).

The reign of David was a time of joy and sadness in Israel. In many ways David was one of the greatest kings in the nation's history. Under David, the wars of conquest ceased and general prosperity followed. Israel had become a world power! The thrust of Israel's influence was felt all over the Middle East at that time. The kingdom that was bequeathed to Solomon extended from the Euphrates to Egypt. David's personal shortcomings are obvious, but he was aptly described as "a man after God's own heart" since he was willing to repent of his wrongs and accept the consequences of his mistakes. Although Solomon is known as a great builder, it was David who was the architect. Not only did David plan the Temple, but he also provided much of the material and skill to build it.

The Establishment of Solomon's Reign: I Kings 2:12-3:2

The early days of Solomon's rule were marred by the need to establish his throne firmly. Adonijah's continued attempts to gain authority and power led to his death sentence. Abiathar the priest, who had earlier befriended David, preferred Adonijah over Solomon and had to be exiled and defrocked. Joab, David's general, had proven himself to be both a valuable servant and a prime source of anguish. Against David's wishes he had killed

Saul's general, Abner, and ordered the death of the king's rebellious son, Absalom. Now he sided with Adonijah against Solomon. Reluctantly, Solomon had him executed. Finally, Shimei who favored the claims of Saul's dynasty, had to be put to death for his seditious activities. While no attempt needs to be made to justify these severe measures, it is obvious that no consolidation of Solomon's reign could be attained until the major opposition was removed. In Solomon's favor is the fact that he preferred peaceful settlement with his enemies, but they would not co-operate.

A significant tactical mistake occurred in the early days of Solomon's rule when he arranged a "marriage alliance" with the Pharaoh of Egypt. This unwise decision, and apparent lack of trust in God, was later to prove disastrous for both the king and the nation.

The Nature of Solomon's Wisdom: I Kings 3:3-38; 4:29-34; II Chronicles 1

At Gibeon Yahweh appeared to Solomon in a dream and offered him the opportunity of requesting a special gift. Wisely he chose wisdom rather than wealth, prestige, or power. The wisdom Solomon received consisted basically of an understanding mind. This gift was one of discernment and judgment. A case in point is the account of the two women who both claimed the same child (3:6-28). Solomon easily discovered that the real mother would never permit the dismemberment of her own child. Today such a man as Solomon would be considered a keen psychologist. The king was also famous for his composition and collection of 3,000 proverbs and 1,000 songs. People from all over the world came to seek and hear his wisdom (4:29-34).

With all of his renown as a man of wisdom, the question persists as to why the king failed to measure up to his potential. Often he showed a lack of wisdom. Solomon's foreign policy was too ambitious and clearly indicated a lack of trust in God. Tolerance of the foreign religions of his wives proved to be both a personal and national disaster. The point is that the king failed to act wisely in his own behalf. Possession of wisdom is no guarantee that it will be utilized. Many a physician has helped a patient while ignoring his own medical problems.

The Erection of the Temple: I Kings 5:1-7:51; II Chronicles 3-4 (967-960 B.C.)

The Solomonic Temple, though dedicated to God, proved to be primarily a monument to Solomon. Although not large in size, the building was ornate and unusually expensive. While the building was a magnificent work of art, the glory of the Temple centered more in physical beauty than spiritual quality. Built on Mt. Moriah, the dimensions of the Temple were roughly twice those of the tabernacle. The site of the Temple was the "threshing floor" of Araunah purchased by David for the purpose of erecting an altar to Yahweh. The actual building of the temple began in 967 B.C. four years after Solomon came to the throne and took seven years of forced labor to complete. For nearly 400 years, until the fall of Judah in 586 B.C., the Temple brought glory and prestige to Jerusalem.

Preliminary preparation for the building of the Temple was done by David including the provision of silver, gold, lumber, stone, and the necessary materials as well as the basic plans for the structure (see I Chronicles 22:2-16, 28:9-21). Most of the timber and some of the craftsmanship for the Temple was provided by Hiram, King of Tyre. Thirty thousand Israelites were conscripted to cut and prepare trees in Lebanon. These men were worked in relays of ten thousand a month. Stone was quarried locally with eighty thousand men involved in the cutting and another seventy thousand transported the finished blocks. This massive undertaking had an administrative force of over three thousand. The actual cost was astronomical. Translated into modern terms a billion dollars would not be unrealistic. All the materials were prefabricated and assembled without hammer or tool at the site (6:7). The building was stone masonry lined with cedarwood, overlaid with gold.

Most of the dimensions for the Temple were double those of the tabernacle. For example, the Holy of Holies was a 30 foot cube with cedar floors, walls and ceilings completely overlaid with gold. The general floor plan was that of the tabernacle. In addition to the Holy of Holies, the front portion of the temple known as the Holy Place was 30 feet wide, 45 feet high and 60 feet long. In front of the Holy Place was a porch with two bronze pillars 27 feet high (7:15-22). Inside the Holy Place were to be found ten golden lampstands as well as ten tables of showbread (II Chronicles 4:8). However, only one table was used for the twelve loaves representing the tribes of Israel. As in the tabernacle, an altar of incense was placed in the Holy Place with a veil separating the Holy of Holies. The only piece of furniture that survived from the earlier Tabernacle was the Ark of the Covenant with its guarding cherubim. The Ark was placed in the inner sanctuary of the Holy of Holies. In the front Temple courtyard stood the altar of sacrifice and the "molten sea" which, cast of bronze, held 10,000 gallons of water. In addition, ten smaller lavers were used for ceremonial washings.

Near the Temple, Solomon built his own palace and a number of other buildings. During the four hundred year life of the structure many changes took place. On occasion, idolatry was introduced (II Kings 16: 10-18, 21:4-9; Ezek. 8:3-18). At other times, pious kings such as Hezekiah and Josiah refurbished and rededicated it. Although the Temple was sacked several times by foreign invaders, (I Kings 14; II Kings 12, 14, 18) the building stood until it was destroyed by Nebuchadnezzar in 586 B.C. (II Kings 25:8-17).

The Dedication of the Temple: I Kings 8; II Chronicles 5-6 (ca. 960 B.C.)

Nearly a year elapsed from the time of the Temple's completion and its dedication (cf. I Kings 6:38 with 8:2). Apparently, the consecration service took place during the Feast of Tabernacles which commemorated the wilderness wandering and marked the beginning of the new year. At this time, the "ark of the covenant" and other sacred vessels from the tabernacle were placed in the Temple. Only the two tablets of stone containing the Ten Commandments remained in the Ark (8:9). Immediately following the installation of the ark, the "glory" of Yahweh filled the Temple.

Solomon's dedicatory speech in I Kings 8 affirmed the fulfillment of God's promise to David that his son would build the Temple. Solomon's dedicatory prayer was a reaffirmation of God's covenant and love toward Israel. Two significant declarations are embodied in the prayer. The first stresses the infinitude of God (vs. 27), and the second the finiteness of humans (vs. 46). In the former, Solomon declares that God is not limited nor confined to the Temple which was recently completed. The latter emphasized the human predicament of sin which can only be alleviated through God's mercy in response to repentance and faithfulness (vs. 47-52).

The benediction concluding the Temple dedication service was a plea for divine assistance and guidance.

> Blessed be the Lord who has given rest to his people Israel, according to all that he promised; not one word has failed of all his good promise, which he uttered by Moses his servant. The Lord our God be with us, as he was with our fathers; may he not leave us or forsake us;... I Kings 8:56-57

Following the closing prayer a massive peace offering of 22,000 oxen and 120,000 sheep completed the service. This sacrifice constituted a fellowship meal between Yahweh and his people.

Yahweh's Conditional Covenant with Solomon: I Kings 9:1-9; II Chronicles 7

After Solomon completed his extensive building projects, Yahweh appears again, as at Gibeon, and confirms the consecration of the Temple. With Solomon, the Davidic covenant was renewed on the condition that the monarch walk "with integrity of heart and uprightness, doing according to all that I have commanded you" (vs. 4). However, failure to maintain the commitment by Solomon, or his children, would invalidate the covenant. Accordingly, Israel would be "cut off" and become a "heap of ruins." Tragically, neither Solomon nor his descendants consistently maintained the covenant. The judgment that ensued from this disobedience was corrective, not vindictive.

Solomon's Prosperity and Fame: I Kings 9:10-10:29; II Chronicles 8:1-9:27

Wealth, prestige and power became more dominant than wisdom, prayer, and penitence in the life of Solomon. Twenty apparently worthless cities in Galilee were sold to Hiram at a handsome profit. The people of Israel were pressed with heavy taxation and work conscription. Native Canaanites were forced into slavery. A large fleet of boats were built at Eziongeber. Utilizing Phoenician and Israelite seamen, a lucrative sea trade was developed.

The illustrious Queen of Sheba, who ruled a territory in southwestern Arabia, was amazed at the wealth, fame, and power of Solomon declaring that not even "the half" of his prosperity had been told. She brought him handsome gifts of gold, spices and gems. Solomon's income from trade and taxation was enormous. He had an ivory throne overlaid with gold. He was even a "horse trader," against the specific injunction of the law (Dt. 17:16), importing and selling horses at a significant profit. Along with his stables, he kept 1,400 chariots and 12,000 horsemen. Silver became "as common in Jerusalem as stone" (10:27).

The Demise of Solomon: I Kings 11:1-43

Solomon's wealth and wisdom became a legend in his own day, yet he failed to use either wisely. In order to strengthen and consolidate his reign as well as maintain his power as a potentate, he contracted, against the express command of God, a large number of marriage alliances with neighboring countries. Altogether, he acquired 700 wives and 300 concubines who were instrumental in leading him into a tacit acceptance of idolatry. His "heart" was not true to Yahweh as was his father David. Not only did the king become enamored with idolatry, he also built worship centers for Molech and Chemosh. Because of Solomon's unfaithfulness, Yahweh declared that the kingdom would be divided and only one tribe (Judah) would be left to continue the dynasty of David. Following the death of Solomon, the Northern tribes withdrew from the tribal alliance and set up Jeroboam as their first king. Solomon's son, Rehoboam succeeded his father to the throne but foolishly alienated the northern ten tribes.

Solomon's reign lasted forty years (971-931) but was marred by greed and lust. Granted that his early years were a time of prosperity and religious vitality, yet the overall evaluation of the Solomonic era is not a good one. While Solomon was a man who could dispense wisdom to others, he frequently failed to follow his own good advice. If he had been less ambitious, controlled his amorous nature, and maintained a strong faith in God, then Solomon would undoubtedly have become one of the really great men in Israel's history. As the evidence now stands, his end was a tragic one. Tradition suggests that in his latter years the king wrote Ecclesiastes repenting of all his wrongs. If this be true, then the penitence came too late to avert the tragedy of the Divided Kingdom. Appropriately the "Preacher" concludes his sermon:

> The end of the matter; all has been heard. Fear God, and keep his commandments; for this is the whole duty of man. For God will bring every deed into judgment, with every secret thing, whether good or evil. Ecclesiastes 12:13-14

Discussion - Questions to consider:

1. Discuss the key factors in the final days of David's reign.
2. Compare the claims of Adonijah and Solomon as successors to David's throne.
3. What was the nature of Solomon's wisdom?
4. Discuss the preparations involved in the building of the Temple.
5. Compare and contrast the Tabernacle (in Exodus) with Solomon's Temple.
6. What were the key features of the Temple dedication service?
7. Discuss Yahweh's covenant with Solomon. Why was it conditional?
8. Evaluate the quality of Solomon's prosperity and fame.
9. In what respects did Solomon's reign prove to be a weak one?
10. Compare the reign of Solomon with that of David.

Resources for additional study:

D.W. Deere, "Solomon," *WBE*

Carl E. DeVries, "Solomon," *ZPBD*

H.L. Drumwright, "Temple," *WBE*

H.L. Ellison, "I Kings," *NBC*

J.T. Gates, "I Kings," *WBC*

D.A. Hubbard, "Solomon," *NBD*

Werner Keller, "Solomon the Copper King," *The Bible as History* (Morrow) pp. 191-216

J.K. Kuntz, *The People of Ancient Israel* (Harper) pp. 198-229

G.H. Livingston, "Solomon," *ZPEB*

G.F. Maclear, *A Classbook of Old Testament History* (Eerdmans) pp. 350-367

J.M. Meyers, "Solomon," *IDB*

W.T. Purkiser, ed., *Exploring the Old Testament* (Beacon Hill) pp. 196-217

George L. Robinson, "Solomon," *ISBE*

S.J. Schultz, *The Old Testament Speaks* (Harper) pp. 141-153

H.G. Stigers, "Temple, Jerusalem," *ZPEB*

G. Ernest Wright, "The Golden Age," *Biblical Archaeology* (Westminster) pp. 121-146

CHAPTER XV

The Divided Kingdom*

"...I will take the kingdom out of his son's hand, and will give it to you, ten tribes. Yet to this son I will give one tribe, that David my servant may always have a lamp before me in Jerusalem..."

Readings: *I Kings 12 - II Kings 25, II Chronicles 10-36*

Introduction:

Division, discord, and distrust were the fruits of Solomon's unjust rule over Israel. God clearly forewarned Solomon that his death would mark the beginning of the end of the United Kingdom of David. When Solomon's son, Rehoboam, ascended to the throne in 931 B.C., the seeds of division between the North and the South had already been sown. Several secondary factors helped to precipitate the split. The history of Israel was one of instability and jealousy among the various tribes. In particular, Judah's favored position was resented. During the wilderness period Judah was the leading tribe. Later, the choice of David to replace Saul of Benjamin alienated another large element in the North (II Samuel 20). In addition, the rapid economic development of Judah and Jerusalem under David and Solomon brought a greater portion of the wealth into Judah. The northern tribes very much resented the payment of taxes to maintain and develop the ambitious building programs of David, and especially Solomon.

Rehoboam's Rash Reaction: I Kings 12:1-14:20

The primary cause of the split was Rehoboam's unwillingness to negotiate a tax reduction with the emissaries of the North. The appeal for a tax adjustment was made through Jeroboam, the leader of the northern delegation. Rehoboam declared a three day recess to deliberate on the request. Counsel was sought from two sources. The elders in Judah recommended that Rehoboam agree to the North's appeal and lower taxes. On the other hand, the

*See Divided Kingdom: An Analytical Outline-Appendix

young men urged him to rebuke the delegation and levy a heavier tax. This latter suggestion appealed to Rehoboam's vanity and arrogance. The novice king gleefully declared "My father made your yoke heavy, but I will add to your yoke; my father chastised you with whips, but I will chastise you with scorpions" (I Kings 12:14). Secession of the northern ten tribes resulted from this deliberate and wanton act of an inexperienced and insensible king. Dramatically the tribal representatives of the North said, "What portion have we in David? ... To your tents, O Israel!" (I Kings 12:16).

Earlier, foreseeing the split, God sent the prophet Ahijah to Jeroboam appointing him king of the northern confederacy. God's continued blessing and direction was conditionally promised if Jeroboam, and the northern kingdom, would display faithfulness and obedience to the covenant. Jeroboam, however, sought to sever completely the ties with the South. As a declaration of the North's independence, two centers of worship were set up; one at Bethel and the other at Dan. In order to make the religious centers distinctive and independent of the temple in Jerusalem, Jeroboam instituted Calf worship at both centers. Ostensibly, the purpose of these cult objects was to remind the people of Yahweh since he was supposed to sit upon the bulls. However, instead of simply symbolic reminders of Yahweh, the calves themselves became objects of devotion. Thus, the reign of Jeroboam became one of reproach for the succeeding kings of Israel and set the general tone for their reigns.

The Northern Kingdom's Dismal History (931-722 B.C.)

Israel's Early Instability: I Kings 15:25-16:22

Nadab, the son of Jeroboam, succeeded his father to the throne in 910 B.C. Nadab's reign was an abortive one. After two years, he was assassinated by Baasha. By killing the family of Jeroboam, Baasha was able to establish the second dynasty in Israel. Although Baasha reigned twenty-four years (909-886 B.C.), Jehu, the prophet, announced the imminent end of his dynasty. Elah, the son of Baasha, ruled two years (886-885) and was slain in a drunken stupor by Zimri who instituted the short lived third dynasty. Rejected by the people, Zimri set fire to the king's house dying in the flames, an apparent suicide. Zimri's death concluded the shortest reign and dynasty in Israel, only seven days.

The Omrid Dynasty: I Kings 16:23-II Kings 8:15

Probably the most significant dynasty in the history of Israel was that of Omri. Omri began his reign as the people's choice. Politically, the reign was a success but religiously it was a failure. While his reign lasted only twelve years (885-874), his rule determined the direction of the ensuing political history of the Northern Kingdom. Of particular significance is the fact that he moved the capital from Tirzah to the hill of Samaria. Here he built the fortified city of Samaria and established Israel as a political power. The Assyrians knew Israel as the land of Omri. On the other hand, the auther of I Kings sees the king's religious life as even worse than that of Jeroboam. Omri preferred idolatry to the worship of Yahweh.

Ahab's reign is, by far, more notorious than that of his father Omri. Not only was his reign ten years longer (874-853), but he made the mistake of marrying one of the most infamous women in history--Jezebel, the daughter of Ethbaal, King of Sidon. Under Jezebel's guidance, an insidious form of idolatry was introduced into Israel. Phoenician Baalism was imposed on the nation under the influence of Jezebel's religious fervor. Although Ahab and the people of Israel maintained a nominal faith in Yahweh, it was Baal who became dominant in the religious life of the people. The famous contest on Mount Carmel (I Kings 18) clearly indicates that the prophets of Baal, and his consort Ashteroth, received official sanction while the prophets of Yahweh were either killed or forced into hiding.

Elijah's successful confrontation with the prophets of Baal on Mount Carmel (I Kings 18) proved to be dramatic but short lived. It is true that the people did affirm the supremacy of Yahweh at Carmel, however they soon returned to the worship of Baal. The whole incident serves to illustrate the fickle character of Israel in her covenant with Yahweh. An example of this point is Ahab's reluctance to take the vineyard of Naboth against his will. Although Ahab coveted the vineyard, he would not seize it since the property was an inheritance of Naboth's family and had the sanction of Yahweh. Jezebel had no such scruples; she trumped up false charges against Naboth accusing him of cursing both God and the king. The result was that an innocent man was stoned to death, while a characterless king received an unjust possession.

Later, at Elijah's rebuke, Ahab does show signs of repentance. Ahab's political ambitions included the annexation of Syrian territory. At first, his forays were successful, but his early successes caused him to become overconfident. In alliance with Jehoshaphat, King of Judah, he decides to attack Ramoth-gilead. At Jehoshaphat's insistence the prophet Micaiah is consulted, but Ahab refuses to heed his prophecy. In order to circumvent Yahweh's judgment, Ahab disguises himself as a common soldier, but he was mortally wounded anyway. For the most part, Ahab's reign was a disaster. Later, Jezebel was assassinated when her servants threw her out of a window during Jehu's massacre of Ahab's descendants.

Two sons of Ahab succeeded him to the throne. The first, Ahaziah, had a short reign of two years (853-852). Under Jezebel's influence he worshipped Baal. When he fell sick, he asked for the aid of Baal-zebub, the god of Ekron, rather than Yahweh, the God of Israel. Nevertheless, Yahweh sent Elijah to reprimand him and announce that he would die on his sickbed.

Jehoram, another son of Ahab and Jezebel, succeeded his brother to the throne and reigned twelve years (852-841). Although Jehoram was not a devotee of Baal, he did not actively seek to serve Yahweh either. During his reign the Israelites were able to successfully contain the political ambitions of Mesha, King of Moab. Later, when Benhadad laid siege to Samaria the nation experienced extreme suffering and famine (II King 6). In due time, the city was saved by the intervention of Yahweh through the prophet Elisha. Jehoram's rule proved to be the last one of the Omrid dynasty. He was killed in a confrontation with Jehu at Jezreel (II Kings 9:14-26).

The Dynasty of Jehu: II Kings 9:1-10:36; 13:10-25; 14:23-29; 15:8-12

Jehu the son of Nimshi founded the fifth and longest dynasty in Israel. He ruled for twenty-eight years (841-814). He was swept into office as a reformer and quickly exterminated the house of Ahab. Not only did he kill seventy princes in the line of Ahab, he also slew over forty innocent princes of Judah whom he considered to be his enemies. Later, he assembled the leaders of the Baal cult under the pretense of allegiance. While they were gathered for sacrifice, he ordered his soldiers to kill them all. Though the action was politically motivated, it did rid Israel of

Baalism temporarily. Elisha annointed Jehu king in order to bring Yahweh's judgment on the house of Ahab, but Jehu did not really institute any significant reform. The Black Obelisk of Shalmaneser III (ca. 842 B.C.) shows Israel's subjection to Assyria. Jehu is depicted as kneeling before the Assyrian monarch.

With the death of Jehu, Jehoahaz his son, succeeded him to the throne and reigned for seventeen years (814-798). Jehoahaz permitted idolatry to flourish. Yahweh brought judgment on him, and Israel, through the invasions of the Syrian kings, Hazael and Benhadad. Under this oppression, Jehoahaz repents but the nation as a whole refused to do so. This changed attitude on the part of the king resulted in a temporary reprieve for Israel, but the nation was reduced to a weak military position.

Jehoahaz's death brought his son Joash (Jehoash) into prominence with a sixteen year rule (798-782). From a political point of view, Joash was a relatively good king and many of the cities that were lost to the Syrians were recovered. Samaria became an independent state. Religiously, the writer of II Kings gives him a bad grade declaring him to be a follower of the "sins of Jeroboam," a characteristic description of all of the kings of Israel. When Joash dies he is succeeded by his son, Jeroboam II, who proved to be an able and aggressive ruler, but not a religious reformer. Jeroboam II's reign of forty-one years (793-753) was the longest and most prosperous period in the Northern Kingdom's history. However, the economic stability of the country was marred by the social, moral, and religious abuses which the prophets Amos and Hosea forcibly, and dramatically, denounce. For the most part, Jeroboam II's rule proved to be an "Indian summer" before the final collapse and destruction of the Northern Kingdom of Israel. The twin problems of religious idolatry and social injustice led to the demise of both the economic and political prosperity of the nation. Zachariah, his son and successor lasted only six months. He was assassinated by Shallum, thus terminating the dynasty of Jehu in 753 B.C.

The Northern Kingdom's Last Days: II Kings 15:13-31; 17:1-41

Shallum reigned only one month. He had gained power by assassination and was, in turn, assassinated by his successor Menahem. The sixth dynasty was a brief one. Menahem's seventh dynasty was similar to that of Jeroboam. During his ten year rule (752-742), Israel was conquered by Assyria and became a vassal state paying tribute to Tiglath-pileser (Pul). Pekahiah, the son of Menahem, reigned two years and was assassinated by Pekah, thus ending the seventh dynasty.

Pekah's reign was a little longer than that of his predecessors. He remained on the throne twenty years (752-732). However, the Assyrian conquest continued. Many Israelites were taken captive to Assyria because of Tiglath-pileser's relocation policy. Pekah's reign ended when he was assassinated by Hoshea.

The ninth, and final dynasty, was established by Hoshea. It lasted nine years. Shalmaneser, who succeeded Tiglath-pileser, placed Hoshea under his rule but the king plotted against him causing the Assyrians to attack Samaria. The city finally fell in 722 B.C. to Sargon. The leadership of the ten northern tribes was deported and relocated by the Assyrians. This action gave rise to the myth of the so-called lost Ten Tribes. Actually the northern tribes were never totally lost, only relocated. Those who remained behind intermarried and, the resulting mixed population, became known as the Samaritans.

Thus, the Northern Kingdom of Israel came to a tragic and final end. Because the people rejected God's direction, they found themselves captives of their enemies. As a nation, the Northern Kingdom was never to exist again, although individual members of the ten tribes did survive.

The Southern Kingdom of Judah (931-586 B.C.)

The Tenth Century B.C. - The Reigns of Rehoboam, Abijah, Asa: I Kings 14:21-15:24; II Chronicles 10-16

Solomon's son and successor, Rehoboam, began his reign with indiscretion and indecision. Instead of accepting the advice of his older and wiser counselors, he chose to ignore the pleas of the Northern tribes for tax relief. The nation split in two with Rehoboam controlling only the tribes of Judah and Simeon in the South. Essentially, he was a failure. The writer of Kings describes him as one who "did evil in the sight of the Lord." During his seventeen year reign (931-913) the city of Jerusalem was attacked by Shishak, the King of Egypt, who also looted the Temple. Much of his reign was given over to war with Jeroboam, king of the newly formed northern kingdom. Abijah, the son of Rehoboam, had a short reign of three years (913-910). He was able, however, to win back a few cities that had been lost to Israel.

Abijah's son and successor, Asa, had a long and basically good reign. He was on the throne for forty-one years from 910-869. His action of hiring Benhadad of Syria to attack the Northern Kingdom of Israel was denounced as ill-advised by the prophet Hanani. The action displayed a lack of trust in Yahweh and his covenant. However, Asa did rid the country of sodomy. While he refused to compromise on idolatry, he did not clear the land of all of the "high places" (i.e. cult centers of Baal).

Ninth Century B.C. - The Reigns of Jehoshaphat, Jehoram, Ahaziah, Athaliah and Joash: I Kings 22:41-51; II Kings 8:16-29; 11:1-12:21; II Chronicles 17-24

Jehoshaphat, the son of Asa, was a faithful worshipper of Yahweh as was his father. His reign extended from 872 to 848 (25 years). Contrary to his father's policy, Jehoshaphat made an alliance with King Ahab of Israel and permitted his son Jehoram to marry Athaliah, the daughter of Ahab and Jezebel. The prophet Jehu spoke strongly against this pact. On the whole, however, Jehoshaphat proved to be an able administrator and a good king. Jehoram's reign was relatively short (848-842 - eight years). His greatest mistake was his marriage to Jezebel's daughter, Athaliah. With the encouragement of his wife, Jehoram openly practiced idolatry. Because of this, when he died, he was not buried with the other kings of Judah. Ahaziah, the son of Jehoram, reigned only one year. During that time he carried on the policies of his father. He was wounded by Jehu at Jezreel. Later, he died at Megiddo and was returned to Jerusalem for burial.

The reign of Athaliah was not really a legitimate one. She usurped the throne by killing all the royal family including her own children, except Joash, who was saved by Jehosheba the sister of Ahaziah. Athaliah was the only woman to rule in Judah, but her reign was never officially recognized by the people. Like Jezebel, Athaliah was a dedicated proponent of Baalism. She even built a temple in honor of Baal. Jehoiada, the priest, led in her overthrow and the establishment of Joash as the legitimate heir.

Joash's reign was a long one. He became king at the age of seven and ruled for forty years (835-796). During his early years the guiding hand behind the throne was Jehoiada. After the priest died, the young Joash lost his religious fervor. He even had Jehoiada's son, Zechariah, murdered. God brought a judgment on Joash and Judah by permitting the Syrians, under Hazael, to attack Judah. Jerusalem was delivered only after paying a ransom from the temple. Joash's reign ended with his assassination in 796 B.C.

Eighth Century B.C. - The Reigns of Amaziah, Uzziah, Jotham, Ahaz and Hezekiah: II Kings 14: 1-22; 15:1-7, 32-38; 16:1-20; 18:1-20:24; II Chronicles 25-32 Prophets - Amos, Hosea, Isaiah, and Micah

Amaziah succeeded his father Joash to the throne in 796 B.C. and ruled until 767, a reign of twenty-nine years. He killed those who were responsible for his father's death. In general his reign was a stable one, but he did permit the "high places" to remain. In a war against Israel he was defeated and taken captive. Later, Joash, King of Israel, released him. Upon returning home he became the victim of an assassination plot.

Uzziah, also known as Azariah, became the ninth king of Judah upon the death of his father. He was only sixteen years old when he began his fifty-two year reign (790-739). Politically, he was a good administrator. He rebuilt the defenses of Jerusalem and reopened a trade route to the Red Sea. Religiously he served Yahweh but, like his father, he permitted the "high places" to continue. In his pride, he presumed to be a priest and God smote him with leprosy as a judgment for his disobedience. As a leper he was ineligible to rule, thus his son became co-regent with him in 751 B.C. Jotham's independent reign began in 739 B.C. Altogether Jotham ruled sixteen years (751-736), but he did little to raise the moral and religious level of the nation.

During the latter years of Jotham's reign his son, Ahaz, became co-regent with him. Like his father, Ahaz' reign lasted sixteen years (743-728) overlapping the rule of both his grandfather and his father. For the most part, Ahaz proved to be a wicked king. He chose to reject the guidance of Yahweh and the prophet Isaiah. He offered one of his sons as a sacrifice and built a pagan altar similar to one he had seen in Damascus. He made an alliance with Tiglath-pileser of Assyria against the express command of Yahweh (Isaiah 7).

From almost every vantage point Hezekiah, Ahaz' son, proved

to be one of the ablest kings in the history of the Southern Kingdom. Hezekiah was co-regent with his father from 728-725 B.C. and was the only king in Judah from 725-696 B.C. Without a doubt, his rule was a good one. He did away with idolatry and repaired the Temple in Jerusalem. During his tenure, the law of Moses was reaffirmed, the Passover was reinstituted, and the city of Jerusalem was refortified. The prophets Isaiah and Micah were a positive influence on his rule, especially the former. In 701 B.C. the city of Jerusalem was surrounded and sieged by Sennacherib. However, through the intervention of Yahweh, the city was spared. The Assyrian army was attacked by a plague carried perhaps, as the Greek historian Herodotus says, by rats. With a decimated force Sennacherib retreated to Assyria and gave up the siege of Jerusalem. Later, because of prayer, Hezekiah was miraculously granted a fifteen-year extension of life.

Seventh Century B.C. - The Reigns of Manasseh, Amon, Josiah, Jehoahaz and Jehoiakim: II Kings 21:1-24:6; II Chronicles 33:1-36:8 - Prophets - Zephaniah, Nahum, Habakkuk, and Jeremiah

Manasseh, the son of Hezekiah, rejected his father's religious faith and turned to idolatry, especially Baalism. His long reign (55 years - 696-641) was a wicked one. Tradition says that he killed the prophet Isaiah. According to II Chronicles 33:14-20 the king repented of his evil ways in his latter years. Amon, the next in line, was very much like his father. After a two-year reign (641-640) Amon was assassinated by his servants, and his eight year old son Josiah was placed on the throne.

In many respects Josiah's reign of thirty-one years (639-609) was one of the best in the history of the Southern Kingdom of Judah. There is a great deal of similarity between Josiah and his great grandfather Hezekiah. Both were religious reformers and devoted followers of Yahweh. Through the guidance and influence of Hilkiah the Priest, Josiah set out to rebuild and refurbish the Temple. In the process of repairing the Temple a copy of the Book of the Law of Moses was found. Some hold that this copy of the "law" was the book of Deuteronomy, although it may well have been the entire Pentateuch. In any case, the discovery led to the famous reforms of 621 B.C. In addition to the reaffirmation of the law, the land was cleansed of idolatrous priests and pagan altars. Once again, as in the days of Hezekiah, the covenant was reaffirmed and the Passover was reinstituted. During his reign Josiah was very much influenced by the advice of the prophet Jeremiah as well as the prophets Zephaniah, Habakkuk and Nahum. The only serious mistake of Josiah's rule was his foolish and unexplained attempt to stop the northward movement of the army of Pharaoh Necho of Egypt. The young king was killed in the Battle of Megiddo in 609 B.C. After the death of his father, the anti-Egyptian Jehoahaz became king of Judah but three months later he was deposed by Pharaoh Necho and taken captive to Egypt. Necho then placed Josiah's oldest son Jehoiakim on the throne.

Jehoiakim began as a puppet of Egypt but, after three years, he became the servant of Nebuchadnezzar of Babylon. His eleven year rule (605-597) was characterized by a disdain for God and the people of Judah. He even destroyed the first edition of Jeremiah's book of prophecy. In contrast to his father, he refused to accept the guidance of God or the prophets. In the early part of his reign (605) the Southern Kingdom suffered its first deportation. Included among those taken to Babylon was Daniel. For the most part, Jehoiakim proved to be a poor king.

The Sixth Century B.C. - The Reigns of Jehoiachin and Zedekiah: II Kings 24:8-25:7; II Chronicles 36:9-21 - Prophets - Jeremiah, Obadiah

Jehoiachin's abortive rule lasted three months. In 597 B.C. Nebuchadnezzar's army surrounded Jerusalem and took over control of the city. Jehoiachin the son of Jehoiakim and others, including Ezekiel, were taken captive and deported to Babylon. Finally, Zedekiah the third and last son of Josiah was permitted to rule. He served as king during the last eleven years (597-586) of the Southern Kingdom's existence. Zedekiah was a vacillating and incompetent ruler. He refused to heed the guidance of Jeremiah, although he sought it. Apparently, he did not have the courage to follow his own convictions. He attempted, against the advice of Jeremiah, to resist the power of Babylon. This act simply brought about the final siege and destruction of Jerusalem. In 586 B.C. the city fell, and the Temple was destroyed. The king was blinded and taken captive to Babylon. Thus began a seventy year exile for the nation.

Discussion - Questions to consider:
1. What precipitated the division between the Northern and Southern tribes of Israel?
2. Why could the history of the Northern Kingdom be characterized as dismal?
3. Describe the key features of the Omrid dynasty.
4. Characterize the strengths and weaknesses of the Jehu dynasty.
5. Describe the problems Israel faced leading to the Northern Kingdom's downfall in 722 B.C.
6. Why did Rehoboam's reign give the Southern Kingdom of Judah a poor beginning?
7. Which kings would you consider to be the best rulers in Judah? Why?
8. Which kings would you consider to be the worst? Why?
9. Why did the Southern Kingdom of Judah last over one hundred and thirty-six years longer than the Northern one?
10. What features would you consider essential for a good king?

Resources for additional study:

G.L. Archer, "Israel, Kingdom," *WBE*

John Bright, *A History of Israel* (Westminster) pp. 209-320

F.F. Bruce, "Israel," *NBD*

Alfred Edersheim, *The History of Israel and Judah* (Revell)

H.L. Ellison, "Judah," *NBD*

John B. Graybill, "Judah, Kingdom of," *ZPBD*

Werner Keller, "Two Kings--Two Kingdoms: From Rehoboam to Jehoiachin," *The Bible as History* (Morrow) pp. 225-293

Eugene H. Merrill, *An Historical Survey of the Old Testament* (Craig) pp. 243-291

E.W.K. Mould, *Essentials of Bible History* (Ronald) pp. 217-270

C. von Orelli, "Israel, History of," *ISBE*

J. Barton Payne, "Israel-Divided Kingdom," *ZPBD*

Charles Pfeiffer, *Old Testament History* (Baker) pp. 305-397

W.T. Purkiser, ed., *Exploring the Old Testament* (Beacon Hill) pp. 305-397

H.H. Rowley, "Israel, History of," *IDB*

A.C. Schultz, "Judah, Kingdom of," *ZPEB*

S.J. Schultz, *The Old Testament Speaks* (Harper) pp. 155-228

E.B. Smick, "Judah, Kingdom of," *WBE*

Edwin R. Thiele, *The Mysterious Numbers of the Hebrew Kings* (Eerdmans)

J.A. Thompson, "Israel, Kingdom of," *ZPEB*

Thomas H. Weir, "Israel, Kingdom of," *ISBE*

CHAPTER XVI
The Prophets Of The Ninth Century B.C.
*"...for the law shall not perish from the priest,
nor counsel from the wise, nor the word
from the prophet."*

Readings: I Kings 17 - II Kings 13, Joel 1-3, Jonah 1-4

Significant portions of the Old Testament are largely an undiscovered land to many Bible students. This is especially true of the prophets who comprise one-fourth of the Old Testament and nearly one-fifth of the entire Bible. The Old Testament prophets are an extremely inviting study. The prophets arose in a small and obscure country of approximately 150 miles in length and 50 miles in width, roughly the size of Vermont. Israel's glory lay not in its size but in the character of her people. Palestine was uniquely situated as the main North-South caravan route in the ancient Middle East. The country was an oasis surrounded by desert and the Mediterranean Sea on the west. The land and the religious faith of Israel were inseparably associated in the minds of the Hebrew people. The people of Israel, as well as the prophets, considered themselves chosen by God for a great destiny. In fact, the prophets were really super-patriots with a deep religious faith in Yahweh.

Israel was surrounded by countries who fluctuated between being friends and enemies. On the South, lay Edom a people descendant from Esau, Jacob's brother. To the Southeast along the Dead Sea was Moab. On the North was Syria with its ancient capital, Damascus. Phoenicia was immediately Northwest, while Philistia was located in the Southwest coastal area of Palestine. Beyond the immediate borders of Israel were the two great empires of the ancient world -- Egypt and Assyria (later, Babylon and Persia). The land lay in a strategic position as a bridge between Asia and Africa. Both military and commerical interests used that bridge.

Introduction to the Prophets:

The prophets were men of their time who sought to deal with

the problems of their immediate era. In this respect, they were not so much foretellers of the future as they were forthtellers, i.e. preachers of righteousness. While at times, they did predict the future, especially in reference to the coming Messiah and his kingdom, prediction was not their primary task. The most distinctive term for prophet in the Old Testament is **nabi**. Essentially, the word refers to a person who is called by God and speaks in his behalf. Appropriately, the prophet has been called a "Spokesman" for God. The prophet stood firmly for Yahweh, as T.H. Robinson says, "he was first and foremost an enthusiast for his God." It was to Yahweh that he owed his allegiance and it was to him he dedicated his life. Although the prophet was a social reformer, his special function was that of a spiritual leader. He sought to call Israel from idolatry to the living God. Prophets were directly called of God for a special mission. Reform and revival of morality and the true religion of Yahweh was his aim.

Prophets existed early in Hebrew history. The first specific reference is in Exodus 7:1 where Aaron is said to be a prophet (spokesman) for Moses. The first reference to the prophetic function is in Numbers 11 where Eldad and Medad are said to have prophesied in the camp during the wilderness period. However, the prophetic office did not arise until later. Apparently, Samuel organized the first "school" of the prophets. Individuals who are not normally thought to be prophets are so designated in Scripture. For example, Enoch is called a prophet (Jude 14), so are Abraham (Gen. 20:7), Moses (Deut. 18:15, 34:10) and Miriam (Ex. 15:20). The prophet mediated between God and man.

Old Testament prophets may be divided into roughly two classes, i.e. those who wrote down their prophecies, and those who did not. Among the latter would be Deborah, Samuel, Nathan, Gad, Ahijah, Micaiah, and especially Elijah and Elisha. Sixteen prophets are listed in the Old Testament as having placed their prophecies in literary form. Sometimes they have been designated as the major and minor prophets, but such a designation is misleading. The terms major and minor simply refer to the length of the writing, not to its importance. The messages of Amos, Hosea, and Micah are just as significant as are those of the longer books of Isaiah, Jeremiah, and Ezekiel.

One further distinction should be made. In addition to the great prophets, there was an organized group known as the "school" or "band" of the prophets. This group played a significant role in the religious life of Israel. They probably functioned much as ministers and teachers do today. These guilds cultivated and developed religious literature and music. Obviously there were both true and false prophets in these guilds. The temptation was to use the office for selfish ends. Many undoubtedly fell into a false professionalism. Often they would prophesy for pay (see I Kings 22, Amos 7:12-14; Micah 3:5-8). The true prophets denounced this misuse of the prophetic office. Sadly, as in this case, a good ministry is too often distorted and produces a bad image for all. As the kings of Israel turned from God, so did many of the religious leaders. In contrast, the true prophets of Yahweh often became unpopular since they refused to be "yes" men.

For the most part, all of the great prophets found themselves speaking out against the "status quo." They sought to call the people back to Yahweh and the covenant which he had made with them. The true credential of a prophet was not merely his ability to predict the future. It was the spiritual quality of life that determined the real status of the true prophet of God. Prophetic predictions were always conditional. H.L. Ellison has stated an important principle when he declares, "a prophecy of good may be annulled or delayed if men do not obey, while repentance may suspend or reverse a prophecy of evil." Perhaps the best illustration of this point is the case of Jonah's prediction concerning Nineveh. Although the prophet announced the impending doom of the city within "forty days," the prediction was never fulfilled because the whole city repented and God spared them.

Whenever the future is foretold, it is for a purpose. Normally, the prophet spoke to the immediate needs of the people of his day. For this reason, the student must know something of the historical and social background of each prophet in order to understand adequately his message. The prophet emphatically declared that his message was from God. Frequently he would say, "thus says the Lord" or "the Lord spoke to me." Since the prophetic message was from God, it has a timeless application. The message is relevant for every age.

Prophets, Priests, and Wise Men:

In a very real sense the "learned" professions among the ancient Hebrews were the prophets, priests, and wise men. The people sought instruction and guidance from these leaders in both the private and public areas. In addition, these men constituted the primary channels through which Yahweh revealed himself to Israel. It is important to understand the function and contributions of each group.

Essentially the work of the "wise men" was to give counsel, especially in practical every day affairs. Apparently, the "wise men" were not organized, but functioned mainly as teachers of moral admonitions, particularly for the young. The first mention of these counselors as a distinct group is found in Jeremiah 18:18. In general, the prerequisite for admission to this class was natural ability enhanced by experience and education. The first two "wise men" mentioned in the Scriptures were women (II Samuel 14: 1-24, 20:16-22). Clearly, the office was not limited to men although most of the "wise" were male. Usually the "wise man" was a person of mature age. Solomon, of course, is an outstanding example of this group. The "wise" were primarily concerned with the practical and common dimensions of life but, even these, were understood in terms of divine providence. Proverbs and Ecclesiastes give us specific insight into the nature and work of the wise men.

Much of the history and religious life of Israel centered in the work of the "priests." The contributions of the priests to the life of Israel are more evident than that of the wise men. Their history and influence range from the time of Moses to the close of the Old Testament canon. Basically the function of the priest was to declare and interpret the Torah or law of Moses. These laws covered both the civil and religious dimensions of national life. The primary duties of the priests were judicial and sacrificial. Decisions were rendered according to the teachings of Moses. From the wilderness period on, the priesthood was limited to the tribe of Levi, particularly the house of Aaron. Earlier, the heads of the family functioned as the priests as in the cases of Abraham and Jacob. Birth then became the primary prerequisite for admission to the priestly class. In view of this hereditary character of the priestly office, its members tended to be very conservative, especially in the preservation of traditional customs and rituals. Even with this conservative bias, the priests often found themselves compromising with the pagan cults about them. They were particularly susceptible to the enticements of Baalism. When reprimanded by the prophets, they often reacted negatively with strong opposition to the reforms advocated by the prophets. On the whole, however, the priests represented well the traditional and nationalistic values of Israel.

If the distinctive function of the wise men was to give "counsel" and that of the priest to interpret the "law," then the basic work of the prophet was to proclaim the "word" of God. As discussed previously, the primary function of the prophet was to serve as a spokesman for Yahweh his God. In this respect, the prophets would be better characterized as preachers than simply predicters of future events. This very function distinguished the Hebrew prophets from their pagan neighbors. In contrast to the priests and wise men who received their office by birth and ability respectively, the prophets were called by God without regard to social, economic, or educational status.

The priests and wise men were "traditionalists." They did not seek to introduce new or innovative ideas. Without the prophets, who spoke with the direct authority of God, the religion of Israel would have stagnated into rigid custom. The prophet wanted to transform Israel into a redeemed nation that would usher in the Kingdom of God. The prophet did not seek his office, he was called by Yahweh. The prophetic role was open to all. The message of the prophet, whether one of judgment or promise, came from God. The prophet declared the deity's word, not his own.

The Prophets of the Ninth Century B.C.
Elijah: I Kings 17 - II Kings 2:12a

One of the greatest of the early prophets in the Northern Kingdom was Elijah, the Tishbite. He was a powerful and aggressive servant of Yahweh. During most of his prophetic ministry he was attempting to stem the tide of the rampant growth of idolatry. In particular, he opposed the development of Baalism under the tutelage of Jezebel and her weak willed husband Ahab. Jezebel, a Phoenician princess, was a strong supporter of Baal *(see note at end of chapter).

A most dramatic and decisive confrontation occurred between Elijah and Ahab on Mt. Carmel (I Kings 18). Ahab and Jezebel had been supporting a large contingent of 450 prophets of Baal and 400 prophets of Asherah. At Mt. Carmel Elijah challenges the Baal prophet-priests to a contest as to who was really God. The prophets of Baal were asked to erect an altar and place a sacrifice upon it calling upon their god to consume the offering by fire. By noon no response had come! Elijah teased them by suggesting that their god was on vacation or asleep. Their prayers and ritual blood-letting proved to be ineffective. Toward evening, Elijah repaired the altar of Yahweh using twelve stones representing the twelve tribes of Israel. After placing the sacrificial bull on the altar, he requested that the people thoroughly soak the sacrifice and altar with water. This was done three times. Then he called upon Yahweh the God of Abraham, Isaac, and Jacob to accept the sacrifice. Fire fell from heaven and completely consumed not only the animal, but the altar as well. The immediate reaction of the people was to cry out "The Lord, he is God; the Lord, he is God" (I Kings 18:39).

With the return of the people to a trust in Yahweh, a long standing drought was ended (I Kings 18:41-46). Following Elijah's magnificent demonstration of faith on Mt. Carmel, he waivered in his trust of Yahweh and fled to the wilderness in response to Jezebel's threat to kill him. There, in a cave, he learned that the power of God is not always present in the dramatic and dynamic events of life but is more often to be found in the Lord's "still small voice." Elijah erroneously assumed that he was the only faithful follower of Yahweh. He learned that seven thousand in Israel had not "bowed to Baal" (I Kings 19:18). Later, Elijah reprimanded Ahab and Jezebel for illegally seizing the vineyard of Naboth. The prophet pronounced God's judgment on them for the dual crimes of stealing and murder. Ahab was mortally wounded in a battle against the Syrians while his wife Jezebel was assassinated by her own servants.

Elijah proved to be a powerful influence for Yahweh in Israel. Although he did not stem the tide of idolatry, he did present an effective witness for the worship of Yahweh. Like Enoch, Elijah never suffered death but was miraculously "translated" directly to heaven (II Kings 2:11-12).

The importance of Elijah in Israel's religious life is clear. Before the advent of the Messiah the prophet Elijah was to reappear (Malachi 4:5). At the transfiguration it was Elijah who represented the Old Testament prophets (Matthew 17:1-13; Mark 9:1-7: Luke 9:28-36).

Elisha: II Kings 2:12b-13:21

Elijah's successor and heir was Elisha, the son of Shaphat. Elisha took up the mantle and ministry of Elijah at the time of the latter's "translation." Immediately, Elisha became the leader of the "sons of the prophets" who had previously followed Elijah. Like his mentor, Elisha performed many miracles. At Jericho, he purified the water with salt. During Jehoram's campaign against Mesha, king of Moab, a dry stream-bed was filled with water without the appearance of wind or rain. Both Elijah and Elisha were befriended by widows whom they repaid by a miraculous continuation of their oil supply. Both restore to life a dead boy (I Kings 17:17ff and II Kings 4:18ff). Perhaps the most well known miracle of Elisha was the healing of the leper Naaman (II Kings 5). On another occasion a prophet lost an axe head in the Jordan River while cutting a log. Elisha caused the axe head to float and it was restored to its owner. During the Syrian siege of Samaria the city fell upon hard times and a severe famine developed. Through the intervention of Elisha the siege was lifted, and food became available once again. Later, he instigated the revolution of Jehu which put an end to the dynasty of Ahab. On his death bed, the prophet predicted the victory of Joash over the Syrian army at Aphek (II Kings 13:14-21).

In some respects Elisha was much more a miracle worker than his predecessor. Both prophets however were firmly committed to the work of Yahweh. While the primary area of interest for the two was a restoration of pure Yahwism, they did not limit themselves to the religious arena. In particular, Elisha was involved in the overthrow of the house of Ahab.

Joel: 1-3

The name Joel means "Yahweh is God." He was the son of Pethuel and prophesied in Judah and Jerusalem. He may have been a priest since a number of his addresses are directed to the priests. Very little is known about the prophet beyond the name of his father and the content of his book.

The date of both the prophet and his writing are uncertain. Suggested dates for the book range from the division of the Kingdom (ca. 931 B.C.) to the time of Malachi (ca. 400 B.C.). However, the best date for the book is pre-exilic, probably during the reign of Joash of Judah (ca. 835-796 B.C.). Reasons for this conjecture include: its position between the books of Hosea and Amos suggesting an early date coupled with its similarity in style and content to the two books, especially Amos. In addition, there is no mention of a king in the book, only priests and elders. While this situation would fit the circumstances following the Exile, it also describes the period when Joash ruled Judah under the guardianship of Jehoiada the high priest. Joash was only seven years old when he began to reign (II Kings 11:21). For a number of years Judah did not really have a king but a caretaker government under Jehoiada. Some have objected that the mention of Greeks (Jevonim or Ionians) in 3:6 implies a later date. Greek involvement in Palestine, however, had a long history and may well have extended back to this early period. Assyrian records mention the Greeks as early as the 8th century B.C.

The purpose of this short book is to emphasize that the nation of Judah needs repentance and a reaffirmation of its faith in Yahweh. The plague of locusts served as a declaration not only of God's immediate judgment on the nation's sins but it is a portent of even greater judgment, if they fail to repent. At the same time, Joel seeks to remind the people that their coming salvation from their enemies is dependent upon their faithfulness.

Joel's prophecy was precipitated by a severe invasion of locusts which served as a dramatic declaration of Yahweh's displeasure with the nation's disobedience. Some scholars, such as Pusey, suggest that the locust plague is only figurative and represents an invading army. However, there is no reason to make such an assumption. The description is realistic and accurately describes the ravages of locusts. Admittedly it would be unusual for locusts to arrive from the north (2:20), but it is certainly not impossible. Natural events and catastrophes often become a declaration of God's judgment which lead to a call for repentance.

The locust plague was so severe that no one could recall a similar disaster (1:2). Joel 1:4 describes either four types of locusts, or four stages in the development of the insect. The plague is followed by a drought. Both would be judgments of God calling the people to repent and return to Yahweh. This judgment could be reversed by a clear repentance on the part of the people (2:12-14). National penitence would remove the stigma of judgment and repentance would guarantee that Yahweh would bless them once again and restore what was lost during the locust invasion (2:23-25).

Characteristically, the prophets describe the judgments of God as the "day of the Lord." Israel saw the "day" of Yahweh as a time when their enemies were to be judged. Yet, Joel, and later Amos, declared that this "day" of the Lord would be judgment on all the wicked including unfaithful Israelites. The locust plague pointed to an even greater day of judgment which was to take place in the future (2:28-31). On the day of Pentecost (Acts 2:14-21) Peter quotes this passage and declares its fulfillment, at least, in part. In particular, the day of Pentecost was a time of reckoning as in Joel's day. Those who repented and accepted God's offer of redemption in Jesus Christ were saved. Those who refused were under the judgment of God.

Chapter three of Joel promises a future restoration of Judah accompanied by a judgment of Yahweh upon the nation's enemies. Ultimately, the "day" of the Lord will bring salvation, happiness, and peace to the faithful. Those who refuse to repent will find themselves accountable to God for their sins.

Jonah: 1-4

The son of Amittai was a reluctant prophet! Although his name means "dove," there was little of the peaceful dimension in him. Presumably, he is the same Jonah who is mentioned in II Kings 14:25 as a prophet from Gath-hepher in Zebulun during the reign of Jeroboam II (793-753 B.C.) of Israel. If this identification is correct, then the events recorded in the book should be dated in the early part of the eighth century B.C. Some have argued that this book is fictional. However, the book clearly purports to be historical. The general form and structure of the book is historical. Jesus refers to Jonah's experience as a real one (Matthew 12:39-41; Luke 11:29-32). While the experiences of Jonah are unusual, they are not impossible for God.

Events recorded in Jonah coincide with the historical conditions in Nineveh, at the beginning of the eighth century B.C. Under Semiramis, queen regent, and her son Adad Nirari III (810-782 B.C.), a religious revival took place in Assyria. There was an approach to monotheism similar to that of Ikhnaton in Egypt earlier. Jonah may well have appeared in Nineveh during the closing years of Adad-Nirari or early in the reign of Assurdan III (771-754 B.C.). If the book is autobiographical, a date of about 775 B.C. would be possible. However, it may well be that someone other than Jonah wrote the book. In that case, a later date is probable.

It has been suggested by a number of scholars that Jonah is a personification of the nation of Israel. In many respects this is true, but such an assertion need not be a denial of the historicity of

Jonah. Israel was certainly unwilling to be a "light" to the nations. Jonah's narrow attitude does portray the general view of Israel. For Jonah, as well as Israel, salvation was for the seed of Abraham only. Jonah was reluctant to go to Nineveh and pronounce judgment for he feared that the city might repent and Yahweh would have to accept them (see 4:1-4). To save a non-Hebrew was unthinkable! Yet, this was exactly what happened. The repentance of the city saved it from destruction. Significantly, Jonah offered no encouragement to the city, only a declaration that in "40 days" the city would be destroyed. Nevertheless, the citizens repented and the city was spared!

There are some problems with the book. That Jonah could be swallowed by a whale seems far fetched to many (1:17, cf Matthew 12:40). However, the animal was a large fish or sea monster, not a whale. (This is true of the original Hebrew word and its Greek translation.) The clue to the account is found in 1:17 where the text says that Yahweh "prepared" a great fish to swallow Jonah. While such a feat is extraordinary, it is not necessarily a physical impossibility. Certainly God could create such a fish. Jesus refers to Jonah's three days and nights in the "belly of the whale" and compares it to his own coming burial and resurrection (Mt. 12:40).

Another problem that has bothered some students of the Bible is the size and population of Nineveh. In 3:3-4 the writer says that Nineveh was a great city of three days journey. Obviously a city of about forty-five miles or more in width would be highly improbable in the ancient world. Archaeological investigation indicates that the city proper was much smaller. However, if one included the suburbs and the villages as a part of Nineveh, then such a distance is not unrealistic. Diodorus Siculus, an ancient geographer, held that greater Nineveh had a perimeter of about sixty miles. More recently archaeologists Henry Layard and Andre' Parrot have advocated a similar view. It has been estimated that the total population of greater Nineveh could have been about 600,000. Thus the possible reference to 120,000 children in 4:11 is not unreasonable. On the other hand it may well be that the number refers to the total population of the city whose moral sensitivity was so low that they did not know their right hand from their left.

The book of Jonah clearly demonstrates that God's love and providence includes his whole creation. Yahweh was not just Lord over Israel. Contrary to Jonah (and Israel's) belief, God's salvation is open to all. Israel, like Jonah, was chosen by God to be a servant and especially to give knowledge of God to all the world. Through Jonah's experience, the people of Israel were to learn the true meaning of God's love and mercy. It was not possible for Jonah, or Israel, to run away from God. The privileges of being Yahweh's people carried the responsibility of being a "light" and "blessing" to the nations. Neither Jonah nor Israel could ignore the command of God.

*Note from page 127: Baalism was a fertility cult based on the belief that the god Baal was the owner of the land. When he was beneficent he provided rain and sunshine for good crops. When angry he was destructive either by means of excessive rain or drought. This subject will be discussed more fully in the next chapter.

Discussion - Questions to consider:

1. What was the nature and function of the prophetic office in the O.T.?
2. Compare and contrast the prophet, priest, and wise man.
3. Discuss the problem of Baalism in Israel.
4. Discuss the "contest" between Elijah and the Prophets of Baal on Mt. Carmel.
5. What contributions did Elijah make to the religious life of Israel?
6. Compare and contrast the ministries of Elijah and Elisha.
7. Discuss the meaning and significance of the "locust plague" during the time of Joel.
8. Describe the impact of the phrase "the Day of the Lord."
9. Compare the life and ministry of Jonah with the religious thought of Israel.
10. What is the basic message of the book of Jonah?

Resources for additional study:

W.A. Alcorn, "Joel, Book of," "Jonah Book of," *WBE*

Leslie C. Allen, *The Books of Joel, Obadiah, Jonah and Micah* (Eerdmans)

Steve Barabas, "Jonah," "Jonah, Book of," *ZPBD*

M.J. Buss, "Prophecy in Ancient Israel," *IDB* - Supplement

B.T. Dahlberg, "Joel," *IDB*

C.C. DeVries, "Elijah," *ZPEB*

H.L. Ellison, *The Old Testament Prophets* (Zondervan)

F.K. Fair, "Elijah," *ISBE*

John B. Graybill, "Joel," *ZPDB*

James Iverach, "Jonah," *ISBE*

A.A. MacRae, "Prophets and Prophecy," *ZPEB*

T.E. McComisky, "Elisha," *ZPEB*

J.A. Motyer, "Prophecy, Prophets," *NBD*

B.D. Napier, "Prophet, Prophetism," *IBD*

William Neil, "Joel, Book of," "Jonah, Book of," *IDB*

C. Von Orelli, "Prophecy, Prophets," *ISBE*

D.C.F. Payne, "Jonah," *NBD*

W.T. Purkiser, ed., *Exploring the Old Testament* (Beacon Hill) pp. 274-281

John Rea, "Elisha," *WBE*

J.J. Reeve, "Elisha," *ISBE*

James Robertson, "Joel," *ISBE*

Emmett Russell, "Elijah," "Elisha," *ZPDB*

Samuel J. Schultz, *The Old Testament Speaks* (Harper) pp. 173-182, 379-381, 393, 395; "Elijah," *WBE*

B.L. Smith, "Elijah," "Elisha," *NBD*

R.A. Stewart, "Joel," *NBD*

S. Szikszai, "Elijah the Prophet," *IDB*

E.J. Young, "Prophets," *ZPDB*, "Prophet," *WBE*

CHAPTER XVII
The Hebrew Prophets of the Eighth Century B.C. in Israel - Amos, Hosea

"For thus says the Lord to the house of Israel: 'Seek me and live...'"

Readings: *Amos 1-9, Hosea 1-14*

The Book of Amos:
The Shepherd of Tekoa:

In the middle of the eighth century B.C. near the small town of Tekoa, about ten miles south of Jerusalem, God called a most unusual man to be a prophet. Amos, whose name means "burden," was a shepherd and a "dresser of sycamore trees" when God called him to prophesy. The latter occupation was seasonal. Amos' job was to puncture the figlike fruit of the "sycamore" tree releasing the insects inside, thus hastening the ripening process. Amos, who had very little formal education, was not a member of either the priestly or prophetic families although he may have been a member of the "wise men" community. The lack of any mention of his father indicates that his origin was humble and obscure. Amos strongly denied that he was a professional prophet (7:14). The shepherd of Tekoa was a prophet only because Yahweh called him to be one!

All of Amos' prophetic ministry was concentrated in the Northern Kingdom of Israel. Although he was from the Southern Kingdom of Judah, God's call was for Amos to be a prophet to the North (7:15). Most of his preaching was done at Samaria (3:9-12, 4:1-3), Bethel (7:10) and Gilgal (4:4, 5:4,5). All were important religious centers in the North. Amos' denunciation of sin, and his prophecy of the coming judgment of God which would lead to the destruction of the Northern Kingdom, triggered considerable opposition in Israel. Amaziah, priest at Bethel, denounced Amos as a traitor to Jeroboam II, king of Israel (7:10-12). Shortly thereafter, the prophet was deported to Judah where, upon returning to Tekoa, he recorded his messages.

The actual length of Amos' prophetic ministry is uncertain, although it was probably very short. Perhaps the prophet's work lasted no more than three or four months. We know that Amos arrived in Israel during the reign of Jeroboam II (782-753 B.C.). In fact the prophet declared that the message was given two years before a great earthquake (1:1, see also Zech. 14:5). Since we cannot date the earthquake precisely, a date of about 760 B.C. would be appropriate. Jeroboam's reign was characterized by luxury, ease, and oppression. Trade with Phoenicia was significant while caravan traffic through Israel was booming. A rapid rise in the standard of living widened the gap between the rich and poor. Social evils abounded. Amos forcefully criticizes the moral and political corruption, abuse of luxury, and oppression of the poor. He called for a return to righteousness and justice. A refusal to repent would bring certain and swift judgment. Not all of Amos' message was negative. He also proclaimed a message of hope and salvation for those who repented and reaffirmed their faith in Yahweh. Like the other eighth century prophets, he looked for the coming of the Messiah and his kingdom (9:11-15).

God's Judgment on the Nations: 1:1-2:16

The book of Amos begins with a carefully orchestrated denouncement of Israel's neighbors. Amos' intention was to gain the attention and cooperation of his audience by pointing out the shortcomings of the nations surrounding the Northern Kingdom. One can almost hear the audience cheering Amos. Each of the nations surrounding Israel receives a clear declaration of judgment beginning with Damascus, the capital of Syria. The repeated indictment is "for three transgressions ... and for four ..." This formula is repeated eight times, and is an assertion that Israel's neighbors were deeply involved in sin, thus emphasizing their guilt. Damascus had cruelly threshed Gilead. Gaza (Philistia) and Tyre (Phoenicia) had captured and sold people into slavery. Both countries had sold their slaves to Edom who had no pity on the captured people. Apparently, the source of these slaves was Israel and Judah. Edom's pursuit of "his brother with a sword" probably refers to the fact that the Edomites, who were descendants of Esau, were selling their own relatives (Israelites) into slavery. Judgment is directed against Ammon because they committed terrible atrocities in Gilead. Moab showed no mercy when they attacked Edom. Each of these nations suffered for their evil, some at the hands of the Egyptians, others by the Assyrians.

Next, Amos declares that God's judgment will also fall upon Judah, Israel's sister nation. In contrast to the social and moral wrongs of the other nations, Judah is indicted on religious grounds. They had not kept the covenant nor the "law of the Lord." Judah had chosen a path of disobedience and rebellion. Thus Yahweh "will send a fire upon Judah." This pronouncement of judgment on the Southern Kingdom was undoubtedly well received by the Northerners. They were certainly aware of Judah's sins! Amos now turns his attention to Israel and declares that they too are worthy of judgment. From Israel's point of view, he had quit preaching and now had begun to meddle. It was perfectly acceptable to criticize Israel's neighbors, but not the Northern Kingdom itself. The indictments against Israel are significant. In many ways Israel (and Judah's) wrongs were worse than those of the surrounding nations. Israel had the covenant, the Mosaic Law, and the prophets, but they had abused and neglected them. The list of crimes are staggering (2:6-8). They sold innocent people into slavery. The well-to-do were so greedy that they foreclosed on a poor man's land without giving him an opportunity to pay his debt. Immorality and idolatry were rampant. In spite of all that God had done for them, they still preferred the courts of Baal to the temple of Yahweh. The rejection of God's mercy and grace meant that coming judgment was inevitable (2:12-16). Yahweh had sent Nazirites, and prophets, but the people would not listen to them.

Divine Judgment on Israel: 3:1-6:14

Yahweh had chosen Israel and delivered the nation from the bondage of Egypt. A covenant had been made with the nation. Therefore, they were responsible for their failure! Because the Northern Kingdom rejected God's direction, and preferred the worship of Baal, Amos delcares that Yahweh will bring a severe judgment on the nation. The indictments include not only religious perversions but social and moral corruption as well. The wealthy lived in luxury and their unsatiated demands produced even greater oppression of the poor. Excessive demands by the well-to-do women of Samaria (4:1) kept the majority of the people in poverty. God's judgment will come, then captivity and exile will result.

Religious life had reached such a low point that worship centers such as Bethel, Beersheba, and Gilgal had lost their vitality and had become Baal cult centers. Various judgments had been brought upon the nation. These were designed to create an awareness in Israel of her sin and disobedience. Drought, pestilence, and even famine had not succeeded in transforming the nation into a faithful servant of Yahweh. Amos' distress over Israel's failure to repent is reflected in chapter five where he presents a funeral lament over the sorry condition in Israel. Although the nation had not yet fallen, the inevitability of its collapse is all too real for Amos. The prophet calls upon the people to seek Yahweh's grace repudiating Baal and their idolatry. Only Yahweh can help them, but there must be a positive reordering of their private and public life. Crooked judges, oppression of the poor, and civil injustices must cease. The plea is that they "Seek good, and not evil that you may live..." (5:14). This repentance must be sincere. Israel anticipated the coming Day of Yahweh when the enemies of the nation were to be judged. They failed to discern that Israel would also be judged! Religious life in Israel had lapsed into formality and externalized religion. Amos warns of the pitfalls of false security. "Woe to those who are at ease in Zion" (6:1). Religious ritual had lost its meaning. The sacrifices and offerings were a sham. Only repentance could avert a national disaster.

The Coming Judgment Dramatized: 7:1-9:10

In a series of five visions Yahweh declares his impending judgment on Israel. In the first vision (7:1-3) a plague of locusts carry out a systematic destruction of the plants and grass of the land. This havoc brings out Amos' compassion for the people. He intervenes in their behalf, and the judgment is halted. The second vision (7:4-6) was related to the first for it portrayed a flaming fire in the land. Perhaps this was a dramatic depiction of a drought following the locust plague. Again, Amos intercedes and the judgment is stayed. With the third vision (7:7-17) a different situation prevails. Yahweh shows Amos a wall which he is about to inspect with a plumbline. The wall undoubtedly represents Israel. Amos knew the wall would not pass inspection for it was surely a crooked one. Israel had not kept the covenant. The nation had sought after Baal and, her sanctuaries had become centers of idolatry. In this vision Amos is forewarned that the judgment will not be rescinded. The Baal cult would be erradicated in the Northern Kingdom. This message was too strong for some of his listeners. In particular, Amaziah, the priest at Bethel, denounces him to King Jeroboam II. This action probably led to Amos' deportation. Amaziah even accused Amos of being a hired prophet sent by Judah to cause trouble in the North. However, Amos not only denies such a role, but emphatically declares that the only reason he is a prophet is because of Yahweh's command. In vision four, Amos is shown a basket of summer fruit (8:1-14). Israel failed to pass God's inspection with the plumbline, now the stress is upon the immediacy of judgment. The summer fruit came at the end of the harvest season and tended to be a bit overripe. So Israel is now approaching the end also. The judgment will not be delayed. The land was dominated by the wealthy who oppressed the poor and businessmen who detested the sabbath since they were not able to buy or sell on that day. Not only so, they used false scales and shoddy merchandise (8:4-6). A famine will fall upon the wealthy for their abuse of the poor. The final vision (9:1-10) is a graphic description of the destruction of the sanctuary, perhaps the one at Bethel or Samaria. Yahweh is described as standing at the altar ready to execute sentence on Israel. The judgment is certain and there is no escape from it. Captivity and exile (at the hands of the Assyrians) is a foregone conclusion. Yahweh had delivered them from the hands of the Egyptians, but he would not remove this judgment.

The book does not close with a negative note, however. A promise is set forth of a future restoration of the nation. The Kingdom will rise again. Israel will once more be the people of God (9:11-15).

The Book of Hosea:
Hosea, the Man:

Hosea's name literally means "salvation." Several other people in the Bible have the same name although the spelling varies somewhat. Included are Hoshea, the last king of Israel; Joshua, the successor to Moses; and Jesus, the Christ. Hosea's father Beeri is unknown beyond the reference to him in this book. Hosea himself was a contemporary of the eighth-century prophets Amos, Isaiah, and Micah. The prophet's ministry covered the reigns of Uzziah (790-739), Jotham (751-736), Ahaz (743-725) and Hezekiah (725-696), kings of Judah, as well as Jeroboam II

(793-753) king of Israel. Apparently, Hosea's ministry began about 750 B.C. and continued beyond the time of Jeroboam II to the fall of the Northern Kingdom in 722 B.C.

Historical Background:

The prophet Hosea was born and reared in a period of prosperity and peace. Toward the end of this era of Indian summer in the Northern Kingdom, Hosea was called by God to announce an impending judgment on the dynasty of Jehu. About the time Hosea began his prophetic ministry, Jeroboam II died (ca. 753-752 B.C.). In that same year his son Zechariah ascended to the throne for a short period of six months. His assassination by the hands of Shallum ended the dynasty of Jehu. After a one month reign Shallum was killed by Menahem, the next king. This rapid series of events obviously created a political crisis in Israel, although economically the nation still fared rather well.

Tiglath-pileser III's (Pul) ascension to the Assyrian throne in 745 B.C. signified the approaching end of the Northern Kingdom. Almost immediately the new Assyrian monarch began a western expansion. Nations feared him. His policy was not only to conquer but to relocate the conquered nation. Menahem was able to remain on the throne of Israel by pledging to pay tribute to Assyria. However, this proved to be only a temporary solution. Pekahiah came to the throne upon the death of his father, Menahem. The son ruled two years but was then assassinated for his pro-Assyrian policy. Pekah, the assassin, took over allying himself with Rezin, the king of Syria. This alliance proved to be futile since the Assyrians conquered Damascus in 732 B.C. and killed the king of Syria. Shortly thereafter the Assyrians took control of the Northern Kingdom. Pekah's murder in 732 B.C. led to Hoshea taking over the throne as an Assyrian vassal. Later, in 727 B.C., Shalmaneser V replaced Tiglath-pileser as the Assyrian monarch. Israel, under Hoshea, took advantage of the change and rebelled against Assyrian rule. After a couple of years' delay, Shalmaneser surrounds Samaria and sets up a three year siege of the city which finally capitulates in 722 B.C. Thus, within thirty years of the death of Jeroboam II, the Northern Kingdom lost its status as a vital independent nation. The territory that was once Israel's became an Assyrian province. Throughout this period of political turmoil Hosea served faithfully as God's spokesman.

Religious Background:

Amos spoke of Israel's impending spiritual collapse, but when Hosea was called to be a prophet, this prediction had been fulfilled. Hosea preached the love of God to a backsliding Israel. He pleaded, unsuccessfully, for the people to repent. Hosea was extremely sensitive to the sinful condition of his nation. Out of his own personal experience with Gomer he was to learn the unfailing love of God for his people.

Israel's primary religious problem was compromise. As a nation they had made a covenant with Yahweh to be his people. Yet they had invalidated the covenant by accepting the influence of Canaanite Baalism. According to the Baal cult, the deity was the owner of the land and through his beneficence fertility of the land was guaranteed. In order to gain Baal's good favor it was necessary to worship him as god. Essentially the demands of Baal were ritualistic, whereas Yahweh required an ethical response on the part of the faithful. There was only one Yahweh whereas there were many Baals. In addition, each Baal had a wife or consort known as Ashtaroth or Ashtoreth. Although the influence of Baalism had a long history in Israel, it was not until the time of Ahab and Jezebel that the cult became firmly entrenched in the religious life of the people. Jezebel introduced a pernicious form of Phoenician Baalism into Israel. Those who did not worship Baal were persecuted. Baal and Yahweh were integrated with Yahweh becoming, in practice, a super-Baal. Elijah and Elisha tried unsuccessfully to stem the tide of idolatry. Offerings to Baal included not only grains and animals, but human sacrifice as well. Baal was usually represented by a statue or a pillar. Worship of Baal included both self-mutilation and prostitution. The latter was supposed to induce magically the fertility of crops. Actually, Baal was a personification of nature and its reproductive power. Originally, Baal had been a sun-god who could be either beneficent or destructive. The sun could cause plants either to grow or die. Each local area had its Baal who, when properly approached, would grant good crops. This cult gradually infiltrated the religion of Israel, compromising the covenant between Yahweh and Israel. The book of Hosea is concerned with Israel's need to turn from Baal to the one true God - Yahweh.

Hosea's purpose was to reveal Yahweh's deep love for a sinful and disobedient people. The prophet's ministry was primarily to the Northern tribes. Israel is pictured under the symbolism of a faithless wife. Just as Gomer left Hosea for a life of prostitution so Israel turned her back on Yahweh committing adultery with Baal. Hosea pleaded for repentance on the part of both Gomer and the nation. He warns that judgment will come but promises the survival of a faithful remnant in Israel.

Hosea's Unfaithful Wife: 1:1-3:5

Gomer's unfaithfulness to Hosea is a problem. It is difficult to understand why the prophet's wife became a prostitute. It is even more difficult to understand why God would command a prophet to marry an immoral woman. Some scholars solve the problem by asserting that the account should not be taken literally but would be better understood as a symbolic description of Israel's defection. Others, insist that Yahweh commanded Hosea to marry a practicing harlot in order to teach Israel a lesson. Both of these views are doubtful. In the case of the first, there is very little reason for rejecting the literal interpretation since nothing in the story indicates that it is not factual. Three telling objections can be raised concerning the second view. First, if Hosea had known from the outset that Gomer was a harlot he would not have been surprised when she returned to her old profession. Secondly, Israel is pictured as a "virgin" (2:15, 9:10) when she came out of Egypt. On a symbolic level it is inappropriate to see Gomer as a prostitute at the time of marriage. Finally, the phrase "children of harlotry" looks to a future condition since, at the time of marriage, the children were not born. Similarly, a "wife of harlotry" looks to a future situation as well. It is better to hold that Gomer became a prostitute (probably dedicating herself to the Baal cult) after her marriage to Hosea. Thus 1:2 should be seen as a prophetic interpretation of God's command, the meaning of which Hosea learned through experience. In any case, Gomer represents an unfaithful Israel. Through Hosea's personal problems with his wife, the prophet learned the meaning and depth of Yahweh's love for Israel.

Each of the children born to Hosea and Gomer carried symbolic names. The first born was a son who was named Jezreel. "God sows." The name "Jezreel" is a declaration of Yahweh's judgment on the sin and disobedience of the Northern Kingdom. Israel needed religious reform but a half-hearted allegiance would not do. The impending downfall of the house of Jehu was a judgment on their failure to keep the covenant. Hosea sees the collapse of Jehu's dynasty as a signal of the eventual downfall of the Northern Kingdom. Lo-ruhamah, a daughter, was Hosea and Gomer's second child. The name Lo-ruhamah literally means "not-compassioned," due to Israel's failure to repent of her sins. Finally, a third child, a boy named Lo-ammi "not my people" was born. This third name represented the final stage of God's judgment. Since the people refused to repent and renew their covenant with Yahweh, they no longer could be classified as his people. There is, of course, still hope if Israel will return to Yahweh.

Gomer, like Israel, deserted her husband for the Baals. Presumably, Gomer left Hosea for religious reasons. The second chapter of Hosea indicates that Gomer became a prostitute in the service of the Baal cult. The close connection between the actions of Gomer and Israel makes it difficult to separate the two. Even as Hosea is willing to bring Gomer back from her erring ways and restore the once happy relationship, so Yahweh would bring Israel back and accept her once again. This new commitment will be based on a more personal and intimate relationship than the previous one. Yahweh declares:

> I will betroth you to me forever; I will betroth you to me in righteousness and in justice, in steadfast love, and in mercy, I will betroth you to me in faithfulness; and you shall know the Lord. (2:19-20)

In order to regain Gomer, Hosea had to buy her back from her paramour, a graphic picture of Hosea's unfailing love for his wife. Through this tragic experience Hosea learned the real meaning of Yahweh's great love for Israel.

Israel's Moral and Spiritual Corruption: 4:1-6:3

Israel's adultery is illustrated in the nation's failure to keep God's covenant. One commandment after another was broken. The list is appalling--swearing, lying, killing, stealing and adultery (4:2). Sadly, Israel chose to worship an idol instead of being a faithful servant of the One God. Foolishly they "inquire of a thing of wood" and are "joined to idols" (4:12a, 17a). Yahweh's judgment will come swift and sure. The only hope for Israel is repentance. Hosea pleads,

> Come, let us return to the Lord; for he has torn, that he may heal us; he has stricken. and he will bind us up. (6:1)

Restoration is possible, but it must be preceded by reformation.

Yahweh, the Righteous Judge: 6:4-10:15

Israel's love for God is as shallow as the morning dew is short lived. Yahweh's desire was for "steadfast love and not sacrifice" (6:6). Sacrifice and burnt offerings without right motive and relationship are meaningless. Ephraim, Hosea's favorite name for Israel, refuses to repent and permit Yahweh to heal them. The people had become a nation of bandits and adulterers. Ephraim is like an unappetizing half-baked cake. They foolishly seek help from Egypt and Assyria, but do not place their trust in Yahweh. When the people cry to God they are not sincere. The nation preferred Baal to Yahweh. At Samaria they fashioned an immobile and powerless golden calf. "They sow the wind, and they shall reap the whirlwind" (8:7). Idolatry had destroyed the nation's integrity. God's punishment will come as a means of refining. Israel's exile is not the end of the nation for a faithful nucleus will survive. Even at this late hour Yahweh would save them, if they would repent. But, the die is cast and the people will not change.

Yahweh, the Loving Father: 11:1-14:9

Israel's disobedience assured her judgment, but Yahweh cannot dispassionately correct his erring child. Yahweh still loves the nation, but they will not heed his pleas.

Tenderly Hosea describes Yahweh's concern:

> Yet it was I who taught Ephraim to walk. I took them up in my arms; but they did not know that I healed them. (11:3)

Again:

> How can I give you up, O Ephraim!... My heart recoils within me, my compassion grows warm and tender. (11:8)

The false faith of Israel left Yahweh with no other choice. In order to make them aware of their sin and guilt he had to bring judgment.

The book of Hosea closes with a call for Israel to return to Yahweh. There is still hope. However, restoration will only come after captivity and exile. Those who do turn to God will be saved. A remnant of faithful will survive the impending fall of Samaria and the Northern Kingdom. The faithful of the Ten Tribes were not lost!

Discussion - Questions to consider:

1. What is the significance and meaning of Amos' call to be a prophet?
2. What is the significance of Amos' judgment on the nations in chapters 1-2?
3. Outline and describe the "five visions" of Amos (7-9).
4. What are some of the central themes in Amos' preaching?
5. Why does God pronounce judgment on Israel?
6. How did Hosea's experience with Gomer give him an understanding of Yahweh's love for Israel?
7. What significance can be seen in the symbolic names of Hosea's children?
8. What could Israel have done to avert the tragic downfall of Samaria in 722 B.C.?
9. How does Hosea describe Yahweh's love for Israel in chapter 11?
10. Compare the messages of Amos and Hosea.

Resources for additional study:

Steve Barabas, "Baal," *ZPBD*

O. Bussey, "Amos," *NBC*

Robert O. Coleman, "Amos," *WBE*

A.E. Cundall, "Baal," *ZPEB*

H.L. Ellison, *The Old Testament Prophets - Amos, Hosea* (Zondervan)

Hobart Freeman, *An Introduction to the Old Testament Prophets - Amos, Hosea* (Moody)

J. Gray, "Baal," *IDB*

G.A. Hadjiantaniou, "Hosea," *NBC*

Homer Hailey, *The Minor Prophets - Amos, Hosea* (Baker)

R.K. Harrison, "Amos," "Hosea," *ZPBD, ZPEB*

E.S.P. Heavenor, "Hosea," *WBD*

A.K. Helmbold, "Gods, False," *WBE*

Abraham Heschel, *The Prophets* (Harper)

A.F. Kirkpatrick, *The Doctrine of the Prophets - Amos, Hosea* (Zondervan)

Jack Lewis, *Minor Prophets - Amos, Hosea* (Baker)

Neil R. Lightfoot, "Hosea", *WBE*

D.F. Payne, "Baal," *NBD*

Charles Pfeiffer, "Hosea," *WBC*

James Robertson, "Amos," "Hosea," *ISBE*

George L. Robinson, *Minor Prophets - Amos, Hosea* (Baker)

A.H. Sayce, "Baal," *ISBE*

Arnold Schultz, "Amos," *WBC*

R.B.Y. Scott, *The Relevance of the Prophets* (Macmillan)

J.D. Smart, "Amos," "Hosea," *IDB*

J.C.S.S. Thomson, "Amos," *NBD*

CHAPTER XVIII
The Hebrew Prophets of the Eighth Century B.C. - Isaiah, Micah
"Come now, let us-reason together, says the Lord: though your sins are like scarlet, they shall be as white as snow..."

Readings: Isaiah 1-66, Micah 1-7

The Book of Isaiah
The Prince of the Prophets:

According to rabbinic tradition, Isaiah was a member of the royal family of Judah. The prophet's father, Amoz, was probably a brother of King Amaziah. Significantly, the name Isaiah means "Yahweh is salvation" which reflects the theme of the entire book. From a literary point of view, Isaiah is generally considered to be the most capable writer among the prophets. Merrill Unger declares that he is unequaled in "splendor of diction, brilliance of imagery, versatility and beauty of style." In the Hebrew canon Isaiah is the first listed prophecy and the length of the book is greater than all the minor prophets combined. The quality and style of the Hebrew text of Isaiah is superb. B.A. Copass has appropriately described Isaiah as "the prince of the Old Testament prophets." Current evidence indicates that the prophet lived and prophesied in Jerusalem between 740 and 700 B.C. He conducted his prophetic ministry during the reigns of Jotham, Ahaz and Hezekiah, kings of Judah. Isaiah's call to the ministry came shortly after the death of King Uzziah in 740/739 B.C. According to 8:3, the prophet was married to a prophetess. The two sons of Isaiah had names which carried significant symbolic meaning. The oldest was called Shearjashub, "a remnant shall return" while the youngest was Mahershalalhashbaz, i.e. "the spoil speeds, the prey hastens." In the case of the first name there is an assurance that a faithful nucleus would survive the coming judgment and exile while the second name stresses the certainty of Yahweh's judgment. In addition to the prophetic book, Isaiah also wrote biographies of Uzziah (II Chron. 26:22) and Hezekiah (II Chron. 32:32) as well as the Vision of Isaiah the Prophet and the Book of the Kings of Judah and Israel (II Chron. 32:32). None of these books have survived.

Historical Background:

During the reigns of Jeroboam II of Israel and Uzziah of Judah Assyria was involved in a period of civil war. However, in 745 B.C. an Assyrian general by the name of Pul took over and unified the nation. He chose the throne name of Tiglath-pileser III. Immediately, he set out on a campaign of conquest. By the year 738 B.C. Rezin of Damascus, Hiram of Tyre, and Menahem of Israel had become Assyrian vassals. In 735 B.C. Pekah of Israel and Rezin of Syria attempted to revolt. They threatened an attack on Judah in order to force the Southern Kingdom into an anti-Assyrian alliance (see Isa. 7:1ff; II Kings 16:5ff; II Chron. 28:1-15). Ahaz, King of Judah, refused to join the Israelite-Syrian coalition. Instead, he appealed to Tiglath-pileser for help in opposition to the command of the prophet Isaiah (7:1ff). In 732 B.C., Damascus was conquered by Assyria and the leading inhabitants were taken captive. At the same time Israel, under Hoshea, lost the Transjordan area and Galilee (II Kings 15:29, 16:9; I Chron. 5:6-26). Later, Israel sought to break the Assyrian domination and revolted against Tiglath-pileser's successor, Shalmaneser V (II Kings 17:4). The inevitable result was the fall of Samaria and the Northern Kingdom in 722 B.C. Shalmaneser began the siege but, because of his death, the conquest was completed under his successor, Sargon (II Kings 17:5ff).

During this time Judah remained loyal to Assyria. However, in 715 B.C. Hezekiah, encouraged by Egypt, began to be uncooperative. Later, in 711 B.C., Judah sided with the Philistines against Assyria, yet escaped the wrath of the Assyrian army. Sennacherib followed Sargon on the throne of Assyria in 705 B.C. Shortly thereafter, most of the empire rose in revolt but Sennacherib firmly quelled these insurrections. By 701 B.C., he had defeated the Egyptians and surrounded Jerusalem demanding its surrender. Hezekiah refused to capitulate and asked for Yahweh's intervention. God delivered Judah by sending a "death" angel into the camp of the Assyrians. With his army decimated, Sennacherib gives up the siege and returns home where he is assassinated by his own sons (II Kings 19:35-37, Isa.

37:1-7). The Greek historian, Herodotus, refers to this event asserting that a plague of disease carrying rats destroyed the Assyrian army. Throughout this period the prophets Isaiah and Micah were faithful witnesses and spokesmen for Yahweh.

The Authorship of Isaiah:

Until the latter part of the eighteenth century no one seriously questioned that Isaiah of Jerusalem was the author of the book that bears his name. In 1775, J.C. Doederlein argued that Isaiah did not write chapters 40-66. These he attributed to a second Isaiah who wrote near the end of the Babylonian Exile (550-539 B.C.). Later, in 1892, Bérnhard Duhm divided Isaiah 40-66 and postulated a third Isaiah for chapters 55-66 who was supposed to have written in Jerusalem about the time of Nehemiah. Many modern scholars are convinced that the content, literary style, and theological sophistication of Isaiah 40-66 precludes any possibility of Isaiah of Jerusalem as being the author of the entire book, although chapters 1-39 are generally attributed to him.

On the other hand, the reasons for maintaining that there is only one Isaiah are very strong. In the first place, the New Testament recognizes only one author. Quotations from various sections of the book are referred to as being from Isaiah. No distinction is made as to different authors. Also, there is an unbroken tradition of Isaianic authorship in both Jewish and Christian history. This is true in Talmudic sources as well as in the writings of Josephus, the Jewish historian. Even the recently discovered Dead Sea Scrolls point to one author of Isaiah. Another factor to consider is that chapters 40-66 of Isaiah reflect a Palestinian background. There is no description of the land or religion of Babylon. Finally, if II and III Isaiah are much greater prophets than Isaiah of Jerusalem, as many scholars contend, why have they become anonymous with their material subsumed under a lesser light, Isaiah of Jerusalem? These points indicate that the entire book was written by Isaiah.

Purpose of the Book of Isaiah:

Isaiah's basic message was directed toward saving Judah from the twin problems of idolatry and degeneracy. Judah's fundamental fault was its refusal to keep the covenant. This failure to observe Yahweh's covenant not only brought about idolatry but wrong relationships with each other. As a result of their religious unfaithfulness, Judah's moral and social life degenerated. Without repentance the nation faced an inevitable collapse. Nevertheless, a faithful remnant will be saved! In time, through the faithful nucleus, the Messiah and Messianic Kingdom will be established bringing salvation to all (9:2ff, 53:1ff). This salvation will come because God's mercy and grace are sure.

Prophecies of Judgment and Blessing on Judah: 1-12

Isaiah's call to be a prophet is not recorded until chapter six. In contrast, most of the other prophets describe their call at the beginning of their prophecies. The first five chapters serve as an introduction to the whole book. All of the major ideas of the prophet are to be found in these first chapters. A careful reading of the introductory chapters will give the student a better understanding of the whole book. In these early chapters Isaiah describes the extremely sinful and immoral conditions of the nation. Judah had forsaken her God. The prophet describes the nation as less intelligent than an ox who has enough sense to return to its owner's crib for fodder. In some ways, Judah was worse off than Sodom and Gomorrah since the people had the covenant and a knowledge of Yahweh. Hypocrisy minimized the value of their sacrifices. Social injustices prevailed. Oppression of the poor, widows, and orphans was common (1:16-17). Sacrifice and prayer are meaningless unless accompanied by a spirit of contrition, humility, and obedience. Judgment will come on Judah for her sins (1:27-31). Yet, there is hope for the faithful and repentant (1:18-20).

Out of the impending judgment will come a faithful remnant that will become the basis for establishing the Messianic Kingdom. The coming judgment will be evenly applied. No matter one's rank or position, he will not be exempt from judgment. If one has sinned, he must face the consequences of his actions. The problem of Israel is vividly described in the parable of the Vineyard in chapter five. Israel is depicted as a lovely vineyard that produced "wild grapes" (5:1-2). Because the nation turned its back upon Yahweh, and his covenant, they will suffer the judgment of exile. The catalog of Judah's sins is revealing. Greed, indulgence in frivolous pleasures, and materialism permeated the society. In addition, immorality, pride, intemperance and injustice abounded (5:8-23). The situation was so bad that the people began calling "evil good and good evil" (5:20). Yahweh's sentence on their disobedience was destruction and defeat at the hands of their enemy (5:24-30). The purpose of this severe judgment was to encourage repentance and reaffirmation of the covenant.

Under these circumstances, God calls Isaiah, the son of Amoz, to be a prophet. Isaiah's prophetic commission comes in the same year as the death of King Uzziah (739-740 B.C.). Isaiah was in the temple when he had a vision of Yahweh and his glory. When Isaiah recognized the presence of God, he immediately realized that he was a sinner in the presence of the Holy One. At this moment of deep contrition, God cleanses the prophet of his sin. This act is symbolically depicted when one of the angelic creatures, known as seraphim, touches his lips with a hot coal. He was now prepared to be a spokesman for Yahweh. Illumination and challenge came when he heard Yahweh say, "Whom shall I send, and who will go for us?" Isaiah's response demonstrated his dedication and willingness to serve. He declares, "Here am I! Send me." (6:7). Isaiah's call was not without its frustrations. He was forewarned that most of the nation would refuse to heed God's call for repentance.

Interspersed with the declaration of judgment are the assurances of Yahweh that a faithful remnant would survive. Of particular interest are the Immanuel passages (7:1-17, 8:5-8, 9:2-7, 11:1-10). Characteristic of these sections is the declaration that Yahweh will send a Messiah to deliver Israel, and ultimately all the rest of mankind. For example, in chapter seven King Ahaz is worried about an impending invasion of Judah by the combined forces of Israel and Syria. Yahweh sends the prophet Isaiah to the king to assure him that he need not fear these armies. However, Ahaz refuses to ask for Yahweh's help. Apparently he was not all that interested in Yahweh's assistance. Nevertheless, a sign is given. A young woman (virgin) is to conceive and bear a son who will be called Immanuel (7:14). Before the boy reaches the age where he knows the difference between good and evil, the military threat of Israel and Syria will be eliminated (7:15-16). There is a twofold meaning here. In the first place a birth of a boy at the time of Ahaz would be a sign of Yahweh's deliverance of the nation then. Later, another child (Jesus the Christ) would be born who would bring eternal salvation to all people. Again, in chapter nine, there is a promise of a messianic king who would be called "Wonderful Counselor, Mighty God, Everlasting Father, Prince of Peace" (9:6b). Perhaps, as some think, the immediate reference here is to the reign of King Hezekiah. Even so, the ultimate reference is to the coming of Christ who brings permanent and eternal peace. In chapter eleven the Messianic King is described as the one who ushers in the Messianic Kingdom bringing love, justice, and mercy to all.

Prophecies Concerning the Nations: 13-23

In this section the prophet declares Yahweh's judgment on the various nations surrounding Judah. All of these nations had, to one degree or another, mistreated God's people. Therefore, they must stand judgment for their wrongs. For example, chapters 13-14 constitute a prophecy of judgment on Babylon. The normal word for expressing judgment in the prophets is **massā** which literally means "that which is lifted up" or "burden." For the prophet these national prophecies were a burden, i.e. a divine judgment which the offending nation had to bear. Isaiah 14:3-23 is a song of triumph over Babylon. This poem describes the fall of a Babylonian monarch, perhaps Belshazzar. The king of Babylon is described as being arrogant and pompous. He became so overconfident that he considered himself to be an equal of God. He even considered himself to be the Day Star (some translations read Lucifer). Although many commentaries interpret this verse as a specific description of Satan, it would be better to see the passage as an indirect reference. The king of Babylon was satanic in his ambitions and desires, but he was not actually Satan. Other judgments were pronounced on Philistia, Moab, Syria, Ethiopia, Egypt, Edom and Phoenicia.

The Coming Messianic Kingdom: 24-27

This section announces the impending downfall and captivity of Judah. Only a few will survive the coming judgment. However, from this nucleus there will be a faithful remnant which will become the basis of a restored community. Eventually, the Messiah will come and set up a permanent Kingdom.

The Coming Judgment on a Disbelieving Nation: 28-35

Chapters 28-34 contain a series of six "woes" which are pronounced against Judah and Israel as well as Assyria, the leading nation of the Middle East at that time. The probable setting for these judgments would be during the reign of Hezekiah, King of Judah (728-696 B.C.) and, before the fall of Samaria in 722 B.C. Each section begins with the word "woe" which aptly describes the coming consequences resulting from Yahweh's judgment. The first "woe" (28:1-29) is directed against Samaria and the Northern Kingdom for not keeping their covenant with Yahweh. Political and moral corruption was evident in every dimension of the nation's civil and moral life. Sermon two (29:1-14) is pronouncement of woe on the Southern Kingdom for its blatant hypocrisy. The third message (29:15-24) is a warning that Judah cannot hope to avert trouble by reliance upon Egypt. The fourth (30:1-33) and fifth (31:1-9) also warn of the folly of an Egyptian alliance. Yahweh's judgment will come at the hands of the Assyrians and there will be no way to avoid it. However, there is hope for Judah, if she will repent and return to her God. The nation's enemies will be defeated and, in time, Yahweh will establish the Messianic Age. The final woe is prophesied against Assyria. Although Assyria will be the means of judgment on both the Northern and Southern Kingdom, she too will face judgment for her own wrongs. While the Northern Kingdom of Israel completely collapses in 722 B.C., the Southern Kingdom of Judah will be saved when she faces near destruction at the hands of Sennacherib in 701 B.C. For the faithful, there is a promise of hope and an assurance of a new restored nation (35:1-10).

Judah's Deliverance from Assyria: 36-39
(see also II Kings 18-20; II Chronicles 28-33)

The setting for this section is the invasion of Judah by Sennacherib of Assyria in 701 B.C. After conquering Judah, the capital city of Jerusalem was surrounded. The king of Assyria sends the Rabshakeh to Hezekiah demanding that the city capitulate. Hezekiah, the king of Judah, refuses to surrender and appeals to God for help. Yahweh sends the prophet Isaiah to the king of Judah and assures him that the city will be spared. God then sends a plague destroying most of the Assyrian army. As mentioned before, the Greek historian, Herodotus, refers to this incident and describes the massive deaths as resulting from an invasion of plague-carrying rats. Perhaps God used such a means to accomplish his purpose. In any case, Sennacherib gave up the battle and returned to Nineveh. Later, Hezekiah became seriously ill, but, after praying to Yahweh, he was healed and restored to health.

Divine Salvation Promised: 40:1-56:8

Chapters 1-39 of Isaiah mostly reflect events and circumstances during the prophetic ministry of the prophet. Beginning with chapter forty the prophet turns from his own era to the distant future. He is especially concerned with the coming Babylonian Exile and its consequences. It may well be that Sennacherib's invasion, and near conquest of Jerusalem in 701 B.C., helped Isaiah to see the inevitable doom of the nation which took place over a hundred years later in 586 B.C. This portion of the book deals not only with Yahweh's judgment, but also with the promise and hope of restoration following the Babylonian captivity. Isaiah begins this section by speaking to the future exiles and assuring them that God will be with them. Israel is God's chosen servant (41:8-20). He will never totally forsake them.

The word "servant" is used twenty times in 41:8-53:12. In these verses the word "servant" is used in a dual sense. Collectively it refers to Israel, especially to the faithful nucleus that became the "true" Israel. The word "servant" also refers to the coming Messiah who would bring salvation both to Israel and the whole world (49:1-6). The "servant" is exalted through suffering. For Isaiah, the "ideal" servant is the one that suffers on behalf of others. The coming Messiah is righteous and innocent. He will bring pardon through vicarious sacrifice. Significantly, his death will bring redemption to all.

The Coming Kingdom of God: 56:9-66:24

At the time of Isaiah, Israel's religious practices were at variance with God's requirements. The nation's list of wrongs included idolatry, oppression of the poor, hypocrisy, social injustice, as well as violence and bloodshed (56:9-59:21). In contrast, Yahweh required a right relationship between himself and his people. This "right relationship" was to be based on a contrite and humble heart, genuine fastings, kindness to the oppressed, and dedication based on a meaningful inward faith. In this section, the coming of the Messiah and his kingdom is once again emphasized. God will be the final judge of all people. However, those who repent of their sins and turn to Yahweh will be redeemed. Israel was to be a "light" to the nations proclaiming to everyone the blessed hope of the coming Messianic Reign.

The Book of Micah:
The Man from Moresheth-Gath:

Micah's name is probably an abbreviated form of **Mikayahu** which translates "who is like Yahweh?" His home was at Moresheth in south-central Judah near the city of Gath. The prophet was a younger contemporary of Isaiah. Like Isaiah, he prophesied during the reigns of Jotham, Ahaz, and Hezekiah, all kings of Judah. Micah's prophetic work began about 740 B.C. and continued until approximately 700 B.C. In many ways Micah was like Amos. Both were from small villages in Judah. Characteristically both championed the cause of the poor and oppresssed. Micah, as well as Amos, predicted the downfall of Samaria (Mic. 1-5-7, Am. 2:6, 3:12) and Judah (Mic. 1:9-16; Am. 2:4). The prophet Micah says little about idolatry and politics. He is mainly concerned with the pursuit of wealth and its disastrous consequences. For example, he speaks out against unjust foreclosures and the general abusing of the rights of others by corrupt rulers and judges. While the leadership of the nation was content with right ritual, Micah stressed that Yahweh demanded right relationships as well. That which is good for Micah is "to do justice, and to love kindness, and to walk humbly with your God" (6:8b).

Religious and Historical Background:

Micah appeared on the scene at a time when Syria and Palestine were under the domination of Assyria. Micah's prophetic ministry began during the reign of Jotham as did Isaiah's. Uzziah, the father of Jotham, had been a rather powerful king with a good army and a strong economic policy. When Jotham became king he maintained the status-quo but, with the accession of his son, Ahaz, to the throne in 735 B.C., the Southern Kingdom became pro-Assyrian. Ahaz made an alliance with Tiglath-pileser of Assyria, and Judah thus became a vassal state of the eastern Monarch. In 732 B.C. Syria fell to Assyria. Later, in 722 B.C. Samaria was destroyed. Israel then lost its identity as an independent nation.

When Hezekiah ascended to the throne in ca. 725 B.C., he terminated the Assyrian appeasement. Sargon, the king of Assyria at the time, was busy with immediate problems at home, so he let Judah rebel for the moment. In order to prepare Jerusalem for an Assyrian retaliation, Hezekiah repaired the walls of Jerusalem and constructed the Siloam tunnel to bring water into the city. In addition, Hezekiah set in motion a number of religious reforms including the removal of altars and worship centers of Baal. Even the "bronze serpent," which Moses had made in the wilderness, was destroyed because it had become an object of worship. Hezekiah instituted a thorough religious reform, but after his death the people, under the leadership of Manasseh, returned to their old ways.

Throughout Micah's prophetic ministry repeated crises occurred in Judah and surrounding nations. During these turbulent times Micah faithfully proclaimed the message of Yahweh. Although he often spoke of impending judgment, he also stressed hope for the future of the nation. He assured them that the Messiah would come and set up a reign of Peace.

The Coming Judgment on Israel and Judah: 1:1-3:12

Micah begins his prophecy with a pronouncement of Yahweh's judgment on Samaria. The Northern Kingdom of Israel had turned from their covenant with Yahweh to the worship of idols, especially Baal. This deliberate violation of the first two commandments led to the breaking of others as well. For this, Micah announces an impending judgment on Samaria. The Southern Kingdom of Judah also turned from Yahweh and she too found herself facing a crisis. In chapters two and three, Micah clearly details the reasons for Yahweh's displeasure. In addition to idolatry, there were greedy landowners who unjustly acquired the lands of poor people through corrupt judges (2:1-5, 3:1-4). False prophets arose who spoke in favor of the rich and powerful when they were paid to do so (2:6-11, 3:5-8). For their wrongs the nation of Israel fell to the Assyrians in 722 B.C. Judah also would have collapsed two decades later in 701 B.C. except for her national repentance led by the great King Hezekiah. There was, of course, a nucleus of faithful worshippers in both countries. Eventually, this remnant became the basis of a restored community following the Babylonian Exile.

The Messiah and His Kingdom: 4:1-5:15

Micah 4:1-4 is a promise that a Messianic kingdom of love and peace will be firmly established in Zion. This assurance is clearly future. When the Messiah comes (see 5:2), then the eternal kingdom of God will be ushered in. The complete fulfillment of this prophecy will not occur until the End Time. These two chapters indicate that the faithful of Israel have a responsibility to share world-wide the good news of the Messiah and his kingdom. This messianic reign will be open to all people.

The Lawsuit of Yahweh: 6:1-7:20

In chapter six Yahweh brings a controversy ("lawsuit") against Israel for her failure to keep the covenant. Micah plays a dual role of prosecutor and defense attorney. The mountains and hills, symbols of unchanging justice, act as judges who hear the case impartially. The first indictment (6:1-5) by Yahweh is that he has been faithful to the nation, but they have chosen to be unfaithful by disobeying the covenant. Israel's immediate reply (6:6-7) is that she has been faithful in the observance of sacrificial obligations. Yahweh replies, through his messenger, that they have misunderstood. Sacrifice and ritual are insufficient. God requires a right relationship which includes doing justice, loving mercy, and a humble walk with Him (6:8).

Indictment number two (6:9-16) declares that wickedness is rampant among the chosen people. Dishonesty in business, oppression of the poor, lying and deceitfulness are all too common. To this charge Israel responds with an admission of guilt (7:1-10). This confession is followed by a sincere affirmation of repentance. The period reflected here is probably that of the revival of religious life under King Hezekiah.

The book ends (7:11-20) with a promise of blessing to follow the impending judgment. Micah closes by reaffirming his conviction that Yahweh is a God of forgiving love, redeeming power, and perpetual faithfulness (7:18-20).

Discussion - Questions to consider:

1. In what way was Isaiah distinctive? Is there any evidence that he was connected with the royal family of Judah?

2. Describe the occasion and implications of Isaiah's call to be a prophet. (6:1-9)

3. Discuss the problem of the Syria-Ephraimite alliance and King Ahaz. What role did Isaiah play?

4. What is the significance of Isaiah 7:14?
5. Discuss some of the key Immanuel (Messianic) passages in Isaiah. (7:1-17, 8:5-8, 9:2-7, 11:1-10)
6. What is the significance of the servant passages in Isaiah? (41:8-53:12)
7. What predictions did Micah make concerning the Messiah? Where are they found in his book?
8. What are some of the reasons for God's judgment on Israel and Judah?
9. What does Micah say about the establishment of the Kingdom of God?
10. What are some of the significant features of Yahweh's lawsuit against Israel?

Resources for additional study:

Oswald T. Allis, "Isaiah," *ZPBD; WBE*

Gleason L. Archer, Jr., "Isaiah," *WBC*

Paul T. Butler, *Isaiah* (College Press)

Charles L. Feinberg, "Micah," "Micah, Book of," *WBE*

W. Fitch, "Isaiah," *NBC*

A. Fraser, "Micah," *NBC*

Norman Geisler, *A Popular Survey of the Old Testament* (Baker) pp. 243-250

A.K. Helmbold, "Micah, The Prophet," *ZPEB*

E.A. Leslie, "Micah the Prophet," *IDB*

R. Laird Harris, "Isaiah," "Micah, Book of,"

R.K. Harrison, "Micah, Book of," *NBD*

C.R. North, "Isaiah," *IDB*

C. von Orelli, "Micah," *ISBE*

N.H. Ridderbos, "Isaiah, Book of," *NBD*

G.L. Robinson, "Isaiah," *ISBE*

_____. *The Book of Isaiah* (Baker)

S.J. Schultz, *The Old Testament Speaks* (Harper) pp. 299-324, 395-398

John T. Willis, *My Servants, the Prophets,* Vol. II (Biblical Research Press)

CHAPTER XIX

The Prophets of the Seventh Century B.C. - Zephaniah, Nahum, Habakkuk, Jeremiah

"The righteous shall live by his faith."

Readings: Zephaniah 1-3, Nahum 1-3, Habakkuk 1-3, Jeremiah 1-52

The Book of Zephaniah

When we turn to the seventh century B.C., we find that the Northern Kingdom of Israel no longer exists. Samaria, its capital, fell to the Assyrians in 722 B.C. While the eighth century prophets had warned of the imminent downfall of Israel, the seventh century spokesman stressed the impending collapse of the Southern Kingdom of Judah. Nearly two generations of silence mark the period between the ministries of Isaiah and Micah and that of Zephaniah. During this period there was a significant departure from Yahweh and his covenant, especially during the reign of Manasseh. With the ascension of Josiah to the throne in 639 B.C. a new day begins for Judah. We will now turn to Zephaniah who was probably the earliest of the seventh century prophets.

Zephaniah 1-3

Zephaniah appeared on the scene just prior to the famous reforms of Josiah. His message probably helped to trigger the religious revival of the young king. The name Zephaniah literally means "Yahweh hides or protects." The prophet was surely a great-grandson of king Hezekiah (1:1). Some object that the term king is not present in the text. However, it is unlikely that he would mention more than his father unless his greatgrandfather were a very important person. Zephaniah probably lived in Jerusalem and did most of his prophetic work there. He was a contemporary of Nahum, Habakkuk and Jeremiah.

Zephaniah clearly identifies his prophetic ministry as taking place during the reign of Josiah (639-609 B.C.). It appears likely that Zephaniah predated and probably influenced Josiah's reforms in 621 B.C. Several passages in the book (1:4-6, 8-9; 3:1-3) reflect conditions of low moral and religious vitality. In 1:4 the prophet speaks of the presence of foreign cults and idols. It is possible that Zephaniah had the ear of Josiah and was influential in helping to bring about the great Josian revival. The reforms of 621 B.C. (II Kings 22:1-23:30) included: repair of the temple, reaffirmation of the law of Moses, and, especially the reinstitution of the Passover. In addition, Josiah cleansed the land of idolatrous priests and pagan altars. This whole revival was spurred on by the discovery of the book of the law in the temple as it was being refurbished.

The main purpose of Zephaniah was to warn Judah of the coming day of Yahweh. He describes this day as one of judgment, but he also points out that there is a hope for a better day, if the people will repent. Eventually the nation will be delivered from destruction. A remnant of faithful souls will continue the nation's identity. Through these faithful few the Messiah will come and, by his action, the Kingdom of God will be established.

The Coming Day of Judgment: 1:1-3:15

Zephaniah begins his book with a phrase that is characteristic of the prophets - "The word of Yahweh came" (i.e. to me). In contrast to the priest who came by his office by right of birth, the prophetic call came by direct command of God. Yahweh's impending judgment on Israel could only be avoided by a genuine repentance on the part of the covenant people. It was necessary that they rid themselves of idolatry and disobedience. The major problem was that the people had become complacent and indifferent to the injustices about them.

A clear call to repentance is given in chapter two. The nation is invited to a convocation. Hope is possible, if they will repent! The call is "seek the Lord...seek righteousness, seek humility..." (2:3). Judgment had already been passed on the surrounding nations of Philistia, Moab, Ammon, Ethiopia and Assyria.

The final chapter closes with a two-sided emphasis; judgment and, yet, salvation is still possible for Judah. Although the leadership was corrupt and hypocritical, still God was present and available to aid the people, if they would turn to Him. While the majority of the people failed to heed this invitation, there is nevertheless, a faithful remnant who do hear. This nucleus of dedicated servants are cause for rejoicing. Through them Yahweh's future blessing will be manifested. Even though Josiah's reform in 621 B.C. averted immediate disaster, later, in 586 B.C., the nation falls to the Babylonians. Zephaniah concludes his message with a great promise to the faithful:

> And at that time I will bring you home,
> at the time when I gather you together.
> Yea, I will make you renowned and praised
> among all the peoples of the earth,
> When I restore your fortunes
> before your eyes, says the Lord. (3:20)

The Book of Nahum

Nahum's home was Elkosh (1:1). We do not know exactly where this town was located. In general, there are three views about the matter. Some say that Elkosh is the modern village of Elkush in Iraq, located near the ruins of the ancient city of Nineveh. However, this tradition is comparatively recent. This view was first advocated in the 16th century A.D. If this is the case, Nahum would have been a descendant of the captives deported from Samaria after its fall in 722 B.C. This site is probably incorrect since its tradition is too recent. A second possibility is a town in the territory of Simeon near the city of Lachish. While this location is possible, there is little evidence to support it. The most probable site is the city of Capernaum near the sea of Galilee. The word Capernaum means "village of Nahum." If this city is the correct one, then Nahum would have been a descendant of those Israelites who were left behind after the Assyrian conquest of Israel. Since the key point of this prophetic book is the imminent downfall of Nineveh, it is probable that Capernaum is the site of the ancient city of Elkosh.

Nahum's prophetic ministry occurred after the fall of NoAmon (Thebes) in 661 B.C. and before the fall of Nineveh (612 B.C.). The prophet whose name means "consoler" or "comforter" offers no criticism of Judah. This unusual omission probably indicates that the little book was written shortly after the reforms of Josiah. In agreement with this observation is the fact that the Assyrian empire began to crumble in 626 B.C. with the death of the great Assyrian monarch, Ashurbanipal. In addition, the Medo-Babylonian army attacked, but did not conquer, the city that same year. The handwriting was on the wall. Destruction finally came to Nineveh fourteen years later in 612 B.C. at the hands of the Neo-Babylonians. In light of the above discussion, the best date for the book would be about 620 B.C.

Yahweh's Majesty in Judgment and in Mercy: 1:1-15, 2:2

The prophet begins with a poetic description of Yahweh's judgment on his enemies. He cannot deal with the guilty as though they were innocent. God's judgments encompass the entirety of his creation. Any attempt to try to overcome or fight against God is ultimately futile. Assyria was used by God as a means of judgment on Israel, but now she must stand scrutiny for her own wrongs.

Nineveh's Fall is Imminent: 2:1-3:19

Chapter two is a song of impending doom on the capital city of Assyria. The poem begins with an ironical call for the city to prepare for an attack. Of course none of Nineveh's efforts would really prevail, but the great city was to be given an opportunity to defend herself. The actual siege of Nineveh is described in verses 3-7. The attacking armies wore red and scarlet, the respective colors of the Babylonians and Medes (v. 3). Nineveh's soldiers prepared to defend the city, but panic and dismay limited their effectiveness. Even the officers "stumbled" as they sought to organize a defense for Nineveh. In a mood of desperation, the citizens flooded the city to create difficulties for the invaders (vv. 6, 8). Nevertheless, the Medo-Babylonians plundered and destroyed the city. The destruction was so thorough that the city and its location were not rediscovered until 1845 A.D. when it was unearthed by the French archaeologist Henry Layard.

In 3:1 Nahum describes fallen Nineveh as "the bloody city," an apt designation since the city and its empire were built on conquest, violence, and murder. The moral failures of the city were well known (3:4-7). No one really bemoaned her demise. The city was not without warning. Nineveh should have learned a lesson from the downfall of NoAmon (Thebes) which was the capital and center of strength in Upper Egypt. In a way NoAmon had been better off than Nineveh for, at least, she had made alliances with neighbors. Assyria, on the other hand, had alienated and humiliated the nations surrounding her. Nineveh's condition was utterly hopeless (3:11-19). Her army had been reduced to a bunch of drunks who fought like untrained women. Because they had shown no mercy on others, the city's day of judgment was to be a severe one indeed. Preparation to fortify the city and to muster an army would be of no avail. The leadership of the city had lost its will to fight. The "shepherds" were asleep and the "people are scattered" (3:18). What was once a great military power was now reduced to a mere shadow of its former greatness. Internal problems as well as moral and religious degradation brought about the destruction. News of Nineveh's downfall was received with joy by her neighbors for she had shown no kindness or consideration for others. As Nahum predicts, the city collapses in 612 B.C. never to rise again.

This little book teaches that God is the judge of all people. No one can escape from the day of reckoning. Nineveh was to be an example to other nations. God simply will not tolerate sin indefinitely.

The Book of Habakkuk

Like other prophetic books, the name of this book comes from the author. The name Habakkuk means "to embrace," probably in two distinct senses. First, the word can be translated as "embracer" because of the prophet's love for God and, secondly, it can refer to his wrestlings or grapplings with God. Probably both ideas are true. Very little is known about the prophet. He may have been a member of the temple choir and thus a Levite (see 3:1, 19). The apocryphal work **Bel and the Dragon** describes him as "the son of Joshua of the tribe of Levi." Rabbinic tradition holds that he was the son of the Shunammite woman whom Elisha restored to life (II Kings 4:16), but this is highly improbable since his concern is with events toward the end of the seventh century B.C. If he had been born at the time of Elisha, he would have lived nearly three hundred years!

The book is difficult to date precisely, but the general historical context is clear enough. Habakkuk refers to the Babylonian (Chaldean) invasion of Judah (1:5-6). Accordingly, we should assign a date to the book sometime after the rise of the Neo-Babylonian empire (i.e. after 626 B.C.) but before the fall of Jerusalem in 586 B.C. The best date would probably be during the latter part of Josiah's reign (i.e. between 625-609 B.C.) or during the early reign of his son Jehoiakim (608-597). His message seems to indicate that Habakkuk prophesied after the discovery of the law in 621 B.C., perhaps even after the fall of Nineveh in 612 B.C.

Chapter one indicates that Babylon is a threat to Judah. The first significant invasion of Judah came in 605 B.C. After the Egyptians were defeated in the Battle of Carchemish, Babylon, under Nebuchadnezzar, then moved into Judah, laid siege to Jerusalem and made the territory a vassal state. At this time a number of leading Jews, including Daniel, were deported to Babylon. In light of the above discussion, a date between 610 and 605 B.C. would seem most appropriate. We will now turn to the text of the prophecy.

The Prophet's Questionings: 1:1-2:20

Habakkuk was a man of great sensitivity. He was especially concerned about wickedness that was all too evident in Judah (see 1:2). Violence, strife and corruption were rampant. The Mosaic law was being ignored and circumvented. Under these conditions, the prophet cries to Yahweh for guidance and help. Two significant questions are raised by Habakkuk. First, he complains about the unchecked sin in Judah and then asks God to do something about it. Yahweh answers by declaring that he will bring a judgment on the nation by means of the Babylonians (Chaldeans) (1:5-11). This answer disturbs the prophet and he then asks a second, more troubling, question. Habakkuk realized that Judah needed some kind of corrective discipline, but he could not understand why Yahweh would use a nation far worse than Judah (1:12-2:1). At this juncture, the prophet begins to fear that he had overstepped the bounds of faith by raising doubts about God's action. Yahweh responds with two assertions (2:2-20). In the first place, Habakkuk is told that the judgment will come, as promised, however "the righteous shall live by his faith" (2:4b). The point is clear. One who has an active living faith in God will trust Him completely! God will only do that which is good. The second point is that Babylon is simply an instrument of judgment. She too will be judged for her sins. Babylon is no more righteous than Judah! Chaldea's action in no way exonerates her guilt. Those who trust in God must have a faith that transcends doubt and self-reliance.

The Prophet's Prayer: 3:1-19

This closing psalm is a prayer demonstrating the prophet's complete trust in Yahweh for bringing salvation to his people. Habakkuk learned, through his questioning, a deeper meaning of faith than he had ever known before. He now understood that a really significant faith meant that one must trust God regardless of the circumstances of life. For Jacob, faith was based on a bargain with God (Gen. 28:20-21), while David understood faith as response to the goodness of God (Ps. 30:1-3), but now Habakkuk learns that faith is more than these (3:17-18). No matter what happens he will "rejoice in the Lord," for he knows that God's love and mercy will always be present.

The Book of Jeremiah
The Reluctant Prophet:

More biographical information is available on Jeremiah than any other Old Testament prophet. He was the son of Hilkiah, the priest. The prophet's hometown was the priestly city of Anathoth, just northeast of Jerusalem. Jeremiah ("whom Yahweh appoints") was about twenty years old when he was called to be a prophet (1:6). His prophetic call came in 626 B.C. during the thirteenth year of Josiah's rule (1:2, 25:3). He had a long ministry of over fifty years. After the fall of Jerusalem in 586, he chose to remain behind with the remnant of the nation. Later, when Gedaliah, the Babylonian appointed governor, was assassinated, he was taken to Egypt, against his will, by some of his countrymen. Apparently he died there.

When Jeremiah began his ministry, he prophesied that Jerusalem would be destroyed by an enemy from the North (i.e. Babylon). This was to be God's judgment on a disobedient and faithless nation. However, five years after Jeremiah's call (i.e. 18th year of Josiah) there was a temporary stay of judgment. The "book of the law" was discovered in 621 B.C. and Josiah instituted a series of religious reforms that led the nation back to Yahweh for a short period of time. Josiah set out to cleanse the nation of idolatry and, at the same time, reinstitute the Mosaic law. Undoubtedly, Jeremiah was influential, along with other prophets, in bringing about this revival. Important as this reform was, it did not last.

With the death of Josiah in the Battle of Megiddo (609 B.C.), the people again drifted from God. The death of the king also left Jeremiah without royal backing. The priests, and even Jeremiah's own family, turned against him (11:18-23, 12:6). Jehoahaz (Shallum), Josiah's son, had a short reign of three months. He was deposed by Pharaoh Necho, the Egyptian king, who had defeated

Josiah in the Battle of Megiddo. Jeremiah announced ahead of time the downfall of Jehoahaz (22:11-17). Jehoiakim, another son of Josiah, was placed on the throne of Judah by Pharaoh Necho. He proved to be an unfaithful servant of Yahweh. In fact, this opposition to Jeremiah was so intense that he destroyed the first copy of Jeremiah's prophecy (36). (Here it should be noted that Jeremiah dictated his prophecy to the scribe Baruch. With the second edition, additions were made. The result was that the material in the book is not in strict chronological order.) During Jehoiakim's reign, the Egyptians were conquered at the Battle of Carchemish (605 B.C.). Thereafter, Judah came under the orbit of Babylon's control.

In 605 B.C. Nebuchadnezzar besieged Jerusalem and took captives back to Babylon making Judah a subservient state. During this period, Jeremiah proclaimed a seventy year captivity of the nation (25:11). Later (in 597 B.C.), Jehoiachin (Coniah), the son of Jehoiakim, ruled Judah for three months, but he was uncooperative with the Babylonians, so they deposed him. A third son of Josiah, Zedekiah, now becomes king (597-586 B.C.). He proves to be the last monarch in Judah. Although Zedekiah was appointed by the Babylonians, he soon rebelled and refused to cooperate by paying the required taxes. He even sought a futile alliance with Egypt. Jeremiah insisted that the king remain faithful to Babylon. For this, he was accused of being a traitor and was thrown into prison. However, Jeremiah's real reason was due to the fact that the Babylonian conquest was a judgment of God which the nation had to accept. Later, when Jeremiah was moved from the dungeon to a cistern, he was rescued by an Ethiopian by the name of Ebed-melech (38:7-13).

Throughout the latter years of the kingdom of Judah, Jeremiah was Yahweh's faithful witness. At times the opposition grew so strong that he came close to quitting, but he could not forsake his commission. At one point he reached such a low ebb that he declared, "I will not mention him, or speak any more in his name." However, he goes on to say, "There is in my heart as it were a burning fire ... and I cannot" (20:9). The prophet simply could not hold back his message of Yahweh. The word of God had to be proclaimed, no matter what the opposition. Jeremiah genuinely sought to help the nation avert disaster but they would have no part in the message of repentance and reconciliation. The people of Judah assumed they were Yahweh's children, regardless of what they did. The verdict of history was on Jeremiah's side. Nevertheless, a faithful remnant survived the downfall of Judah. These people later became the basis for a restored Israel after the Babylonian exile.

The Call of Jeremiah: 1:1-19

The book contains an account of both the prophet's life and message. Jeremiah was a priest by birth, but a prophet by calling. Anathoth, his hometown, was the residence of priests. The prophetic word came to Jeremiah by inspiration. Even before Jeremiah was born, he had been chosen by God to be a prophet. When the actual call came, he objected on the grounds that he was too young. In that day a young man would normally not have been accepted as a leader. In Jeremiah's case, his message was an unpopular one. Contrary to Jeremiah's disclaimer, he was the man for the job. God's foreknowledge enabled him to choose the right person ahead of time. Of course the prophet could have refused the call, but God knew he would accept the challenge of his own free will. Yahweh assures Jeremiah that he will have the Lord's guidance. This assurance did not guarantee that he would have an easy life, rather the promise was that Yahweh would be with him at all times.

Reproofs and Admonitions: 2:1-20:18

This section of the prophecy constitutes a series of six (perhaps seven) sermons that Jeremiah delivered during the reigns of Josiah and Jehoiakim. The first message centers on the theme of Israel's unfaithfulness to Yahweh. In her early days, following the Exodus, she had been faithful to the covenant, but now the nation had forsaken Yahweh. Israel's defection led to alienation from her God. The people's appetite for foreign deities was evident in their love of the Baals (2:23-28). The various idols of wood and stone were utterly worthless. Even when Yahweh withheld rain as a corrective judgment, they ignored him.

Jeremiah's second sermon speaks of the downfall of the Northern Kingdom warning that Judah should learn a lesson from this tragedy (3:6-6:30). In a way, Judah was even more guilty in her disobedience than was Israel for she had an example to follow. The nation could yet be saved, if she would repent and return to Yahweh, but the Lord's plan was frustrated by their continued unfaithfulness (3:14-23). The situation was so deplorable that Yahweh sent Jeremiah through the streets of Jerusalem looking for one righteous person (5:1-3). One honest person would have saved Jerusalem when it would have taken ten to save Sodom! Rather than reform, the people chose a path of stubbornness and rebellion (5:23-29).

The third message of reproof was Jeremiah's famous Temple Sermon (7-10). The prophet's audience was skeptical about the coming judgment. After all, they were Yahweh's people and they had the temple in Jerusalem. God would surely not destroy his own temple! Jeremiah points to the ruins in the North and stresses the fact that the Tabernacle at Shiloh did not save that city nor the Northern Kingdom. Thus, the Temple in Jerusalem would not insure their protection. The people falsely assumed that right ritual was sufficient. However, the key to a right relationship with God was faithfulness and obedience, not mere formalities and ritual. Nevertheless, Jeremiah is grieved over the impending judgment. He seeks to intercede for Judah, but Yahweh will not permit it (7:16). Idolatry is everywhere. Jeremiah wants to help the nation, but they will not heed (8:18-21). There is "balm in Gilead" and the great physician is willing to heal them, if they will turn back to Yahweh (8:22).

Judah's rejection for breaking Yahweh's covenant is the theme of the fourth message (11:1-13:27). Through dramatic illustrations (the marred waist cloth and the wine jars) the prophet seeks to encourage a national reaffirmation of the covenant, but to no avail. Judah still remains disobedient and indifferent. In the fifth message (14:1-17:27) Jeremiah asserts that the judgment is certain. The prophet intercedes again for the nation claiming that she has been misled by false prophets. Yahweh responds that they had adequate guidance and it was rejected. As symbolic of the imminent judgment, Yahweh tells Jeremiah not to marry for it would be an inappropriate time to do so. After the judgment, restoration will come. Later, as a sign of Jeremiah's confidence in the future of the nation, he buys property at a time when real estate had become almost worthless. The sixth and final sermon has two symbolic lessons (18:1-20:18). The first message was drawn from the potter's house showing how God could turn a worthless vessel, like Judah, into a useful one. Jeremiah reaffirms the coming destruction of Jerusalem with a broken bottle. As punishment for this affrontry, Pashur, the priest, beats Jeremiah and puts him in stocks overnight. Nevertheless, God's judgment does come.

Prophecies and Incidents Prior to the fall of Jerusalem: 21:1-39:18

This part of the book is evidently topical rather than chronological in its arrangement. Chapters 21-29 deal with God's punishment of King Zedekiah and the people of Judah. The setting for this dialogue between Zedekiah and Jeremiah is the siege of Jerusalem which began in January, 588 B.C. Under the circumstances, the king is concerned about prospects for deliverance. In the past, he knew, Yahweh had miraculously intervened in behalf of Israel. In response to Zedekiah's inquiry, Jeremiah declares that this time Yahweh will not save the nation. The only possible salvation is through surrender and capitulation. Judah must accept her punishment in order to be cleansed of her guilt. Israel's real hope lay in the future. Earlier, in the reign of Jehoiachin (597 B.C.), the king and some leading citizens were deported to Babylon. The ones who were left behind assumed they were better people (see chapter 24) and favored by God. However, in Jeremiah's vision of the two baskets of figs, it is obvious that the good figs are those who are in exile while those who remained are bad figs to be discarded. The faithful remnant will come from the exiles.

During Jehoiakim's reign, which followed, Jeremiah had told the people that, by ignoring the warnings of Yahweh, they would face a seventy year exile (25:11). In another temple sermon he again predicts that Jerusalem will be destroyed (26). In chapters 27-29 Jeremiah uses an unusual method to put across this message. Zedekiah had assembled emissaries from surrounding countries to conspire against Babylon. The prophet appears before the assembly wearing an ox yoke about his neck. He then insisted that the nations must submit to Nebuchadnezzar's rule as a judgment of Yahweh. Refusal to do so would bring destruction and exile. Later, Jeremiah sends a letter to the Jews in Babylon telling them to expect a long exile.

Chapters 30-33 deal with the coming Messianic Kingdom. At that time the remnant will be restored and a new covenant will be made. Features of this new covenant include: a religion that is personal, universal and spiritual, as well as a kingdom of priests who will have total forgiveness of their sins. All of this was to be fulfilled with the coming of the Messiah (Christ). The new law will not be written on tablets of stone, but on the very heart of the person who accepts the new covenant. In chapters 34-35 Jeremiah illustrates faithfulness to God by the example of the Rechabites. These nomadic people, named after Rechab the son of Jonadab, were staunch worshippers of Yahweh who refused to compromise their convictions. Even when the prophet Jeremiah tried to get them to break their regulation of not drinking wine, they would not do so. In contrast to the people of Judah, the Rechabites would rather have died than violate their consciences.

The Work of Jeremiah After the Fall of Jerusalem: 40:1-51:64; 52:1-34

After Jerusalem was captured, the Babylonian commander, Nebuzaradan, released Jeremiah from prison and gave him the option of going to Babylon, as a free man, or remaining behind to help the demoralized nation. The prophet opted for the latter choice. He became an advisor to Gedaliah, the territorial governor, who was later murdered by Ishmael. These anti-Babylonian leaders then feared for their life choosing to retreat to Egypt. Jeremiah denounced both the assassination and the Egyptian emigration. However, the people refused to listen and forced Jeremiah to go to Egypt against his will. In Egypt, the survivors once again turned to idolatry refusing to heed Jeremiah's warnings. Chapters 46-51 comprise a series of nine oracles against nations surrounding Judah. Like the covenant people, they too would face judgment for their evil deeds. Among the nations receiving Yahweh's judgment were Egypt, Moab, Edom and Babylon. The book closes with an historical appendix (52:1-34). This account of the siege and fall of Jerusalem is identical to II Kings 24:18-25:30. Perhaps Jeremiah was the author of both passages.

Jeremiah was a prophet who fought valiantly to save his people from destruction. However, the nation did not heed his warning. He dearly loved the people, but they refused to listen to his advice. Judah's refusal to heed the covenant and the admonition of the prophets sealed their doom. Yet there is still hope, for a faithful minority will survive even the exile.

Discussion - Questions to consider:

1. What does Zephaniah say about the coming Day of the Lord (Yahweh)?

2. What is the central message of the book of Nahum?
3. Discuss the implications of Habakkuk's questionings.
4. Who were the kings reigning in Judah during Jeremiah's ministry? What interaction did the prophet have with them?
5. Why was Jeremiah arrested and put in prison during the siege of Jerusalem? Who rescued him from the cistern?
6. Why did Jeremiah advocate capitulation to Babylon? How did the people react to this?
7. Discuss the implication of Jeremiah's temple sermon (chapter 7).
8. How can we reconcile God's promise of a "sure kingdom" to David with the downfall of Judah?
9. Why did Jeremiah use unusual methods to put across his message?
10. What does Jeremiah say about the coming Messianic Kingdom?

Resources for additional study:

A. Cohen, *The Twelve Prophets* (Soncino)

D.W. Deere, "Jeremiah," "Jeremiah, Book of," *WBE*

F.C. Eiselen, "Habakkuk," "Nahum, Book of," "Zephaniah, Book of," *ISBE*

C.F. Feinberg, "Zephaniah," "Zephaniah, Book of," *WBE*

Arthur B. Fowler, "Zephaniah," *ZPBD*

Hobart Freeman, *An Introduction to the Old Testament Prophets* (Moody) pp. 225-260

John B. Grayhill, "Jeremiah, Book of," "Habakkuk," *ZPBD*,

R. Laird Harris, "Nahum, Book of," *ZPBD*

R.K. Harrison, *Jeremiah and Lamentations* (Intervarsity, TOTC)

Theo Laetsch, *Jeremiah* (Concordia)

E.A. Leslie, "Habakkuk," "Nahum," "Zephaniah, Book of," *IDB*

A.F. Kirkpatrick, *The Doctrine of the Prophets* (Zondervan)

J. Muilenberg, "Jeremiah the Prophet," *IDB*
C. von Orelli, "Jeremiah," *ISBE*

CHAPTER XX

The Prophets Of The Exilic Age The Sixth Century B.C. - Obadiah, Ezekiel, and Daniel

"Such was the appearance of the likeness of the glory of the Lord."

Readings: *Obadiah, Ezekiel 1-48, Daniel 1-12, Lamentations 1-5*

The Book of Obadiah

This little book of one chapter does not identify the prophet. All we know about him is his name. At least twelve men in the Old Testament have this name, but we cannot prove that any of them is the author of the book. The name Obadiah means "servant" or "worshipper" of Yahweh. The prophet's parentage, social status and occupation are unknown. Obadiah 1-9 closely parallels Jeremiah 49:7-16, although the order is different.

Evidence for the date of the book of Obadiah is not clear. The prophecy refers to a time when Edom was allied with the enemies of Israel and, at the same time, participated in the sack of Israel (10-14). There are two possible dates that would fit these circumstances. During the reign of Jehoram (ca. 843 B.C.) the city of Jerusalem was plundered by the combined forces of the Philistines and Arabians (II Chron. 21:16-17). Several objections can be raised to this view. To begin with, there is no mention of Edom in the Chronicles account. Also, the Chronicles account indicates that the event was a raid whereas Obadiah describes a full scale invasion. In addition, the book of Kings makes no mention of the invasion which would seem unlikely, if it were as significant as Obadiah and Jeremiah declare it to be. The only other instance that will fit Obadiah's description is that of the fall of Jerusalem in 586 B.C. At that time, Edom was allied with Babylon and participated in the plunder of Jerusalem. In consideration of the above discussion, it appears probable that we should date Obadiah shortly after 586 B.C.

The basic message of the prophecy is that Edom's unjust action toward Judah will be punished. At the same time, there is an assurance that a faithful remnant from Judah will be saved.

The Book of Ezekiel
The Prophet-Priest of the Exile

Ezekiel whose name means "God is strong" or perhaps "God strengthens" was the son of a priest named Buzi. Ezekiel, who was also a priest, was deported to Babylon in 597 B.C. along with King Jehoiachin and other leading people. Apparently, the prophet was born in 621 B.C., the same year of Josiah's reforms. Ezekiel's call to be a prophet came, in 593 B.C., the fifth year of King Jehoiachin's exile (1:2). It would appear that he was thirty years of age at the time (1:1). When the prophetic call came, he was probably living at Tel-abib by the river Chebar (1:3). This river was actually a canal southeast of the city of Babylon. Some have suggested that Tel-abib was a worker's camp for the Babylonian irrigation system. Tragically, Ezekiel's wife died on the very day that the siege of Jerusalem began (i.e. January 15, 588 B.C. - see 24:1-15,18). The prophet's ministry lasted at least until 571 B.C. (29:17) and probably longer. Ezekiel is the first prophet to date his visions chronologically. This he does by referring to the years of King Jehoiachin's exile. Ezekiel was Yahweh's dynamic and sympathetic spokesman during the early trying years of the exile. In clear contrast to the prophets who preceded him, Ezekiel did not stress social nor moral reform. Rather, he sought to encourage and comfort the discouraged captives. He also prophesied that God, in time, would bring about a restored and renewed nation built on a truly spiritual foundation.

Ezekiel's Call and Commission: 1:1-3:27

Along with the prophetic call (1:1-3), Ezekiel received a strange vision of a chariot with four living creatures (1:4-28). Numerous attempts have been made to interpret this unusual vision. The key is found in the last verse of chapter one where the prophet says, speaking of the strange chariot, "such was the appearance of the likeness of the glory of the Lord." The vision was designed to bring comfort and hope to the discouraged and despondent exiles. In the first place, they learned, through the vision, that Yahweh was not limited in jurisdiction and power to Palestine. The heavenly chariot was a clear indication that their God was present with them in Babylon. He was not, like most ancient deities, territorial. The "living creatures" appear to be the cherubim who directly represent Yahweh himself. After all, Israel's God was the creator of heaven and earth. Secondly, the chariot's ability to move in all directions instantaneously symbolized the omnipresence of God, i.e., he could be anywhere and everywhere. The whole universe is open to him. No spot, including Babylon, is inaccessible. The third lesson to be learned from the vision is that God is all powerful and absolute sovereign of his creation (1: 22-25). Finally, the general human form, along with the several faces of the living creatures, expresses the dignity and majesty assigned by God to his creation. Upon casual examination the vision of chapter one seems puzzling indeed, but the context clearly shows that the vision was an illumination of God's majesty, power, and concern.

Chapters two and three of the prophecy detail Ezekiel's commission to be a "watchman" over the house of Israel. Ezekiel was to be Yahweh's spokesman at a time when the people had lost their moorings. They needed encouragement and guidance in a most difficult time. Ezekiel is designated as the "son of man," a title indicating his calling as a true man among men. Yahweh's message symbolically came to the prophet by means of a scroll which he had to eat and digest. God's word was to permeate thoroughly his heart and soul. He, in turn, was to share the message with the exiles.

Prophecies Against Judah and Jerusalem: 4:1-24:27

Ezekiel was a pastoral prophet. Some suggest that chapters 4-24 are directed to the people in Jerusalem. However it is much more likely that he is talking to the "Israel" that was in Babylon. On occasions, when the people would not listen to the prophet, he had periods of "dumbness" when he would refrain from speaking as a sign of Yahweh's displeasure (3:26, 24:27, 29:21, 33:22). These periods of silence were times of prophetic inactivity.

Ezekiel's prophecies of Jerusalem's fall begin four and one-half years before the actual siege. As a symbolic demonstration of Israel and Judah's impending exile, Ezekiel lays on his side for 390 days (4:4-7). The coming siege of Jerusalem is acted out with clay bricks and a plate of iron (4:1-3). On another occasion, the prophet is told to cut his hair and beard and then divide it into three parts. In order, the three parts were to be burned, cut with a sword, and scattered to the wind with the exception of a few hairs which he was to save (5:1-4). This strange act was designed to portray vividly the siege and destruction of Jerusalem. The few hairs that were retained represented a faithful remnant that would be redeemed. As with the other prophets, Ezekiel points to idolatry as the basic reason for the demise of Israel. Chapter eight details this point. In a trance state Ezekiel has a vision of the temple where he sees idolatry being practiced in that holy place. Images were worshipped, Baal and Tammuz, gods of vegetation, were adored. The priests were even leading the people in the worship of the sun (8: 15-18). For this, divine judgment must and will come (9-11), but Yahweh will show mercy on those who are in exile in Babylon. In chapter sixteen the prophet depicts the sad history of Israel by means of a powerful allegory of a foundling child who becomes a faithless wife to her benefactor.

The eighteenth chapter of Ezekiel is a most important section of the book. A significant change of perspective is evident here. Prior to the exile, the Israelites had held to a community or group view of responsibility. Thus the proverb, "The fathers have eaten sour grapes and the children's teeth are set on edge." Now, however, Yahweh says that responsibility for wrong will rest with the individual alone. No longer were children to be condemned for the action of their parents, rather "the soul that sins shall die" (18:4). Individual responsibility for good or bad now takes priority over a family or community one. Each wicked person will be tried for his own sins while each righteous individual will be exonerated for his own deeds. Even in the case of the wicked person forgiveness will be given, if that individual repents. This chapter reflects the nature of restored Israel where religion will be an individual and personal matter.

Chapters 25-32 are a series of judgments on Judah's neighbors. The list is similar to that of other prophets such as Jeremiah, Isaiah, and Amos. The general purpose of these prophecies is the same.

Prophecies of Hope: 33:1-39:29

The material in these chapters should probably be dated shortly after the fall of Jerusalem. As the watchman over the house of Israel, it was Ezekiel's job to give warning and aid to the people. The problem is that many would not hear his message, especially the leaders of the people. Judah's judgment is not totally irrevocable. Through the faithful, Yahweh will restore the nation once again. This promise is vividly portrayed in the vision of the Valley of Dry Bones (37). Here Ezekiel sees a valley of bones to whom he is told to prophesy. As he speaks, the bones and the flesh return to life. Similarly, Yahweh will bring the remnant back to the Holy Land and Israel will live once again. There will be a national resurrection.

Messianic Prophecies of the New Israel: 40-48

These final visions in the book deal primarily with the spiritual quality of the New Israel. When the Messiah comes, there will be a new Temple, a new worship, and a new land. The new Temple will not be physical like the old Solomonic one. The new Temple symbolizes the presence of God. Yahweh's glory will return, and he will once again dwell with his people. This new Temple is an eternal one where the Glory of God is permanently present. The restored temple is not a physical building, but the Kingdom of God. Establishment of the new worship will come through a faithful people who will constitute a universal priesthood. Worship of God will be personal and intimate. Finally, a new land will be given to the people of God. Unlike the Old Israel, it will be a place of peace, happiness, joy and abundance. God will provide every need. This new land will have a new Jerusalem (see Revelation 21-22). The most important feature of this new city is the fact that "the Lord is there."

The Book of Daniel
The Prophet-Wise Man of the Exile

The name Daniel can be translated as "God is my Judge." He was born in Judah during the reign of Josiah. During the third year of Jehoiakim's reign (605 B.C.) he was taken, along with the first group of captives, to Babylon (1:1-3). At the time of exile, he was probably in his early teens. He was chosen, with three other youths, to be educated by the Babylonians in their learning and language. While yet a young man, Daniel became famous for his godliness and wisdom (Ezek. 14:14, 20, 28:3). Daniel was given the name Belteshazzar by the Babylonians. Significantly, the book was written in both Hebrew (1:1-2:4a, 8:1-12:13) and Aramaic (2:4b-7:28). Aramaic was the universal language of the ancient Middle East. The reason for the change to Aramaic in 2:4b is probably due to the fact that the Babylonians begin to speak at that point. Chapter eight returns to the Hebrew language since at 8:1ff Babylon comes under Medo-Persian control. In the Jewish canon, Daniel appears in the "writings" section because of its historical-prophetic character. The last known event in Daniel's life takes place in the third year of Cyrus (ca. 536 B.C.). Daniel probably died around 520 B.C.

The Problem of Authorship and Date

For the most part, conservative Biblical scholars hold that the book of Daniel was written by a man by that name during the Babylonian Exile. Liberal scholars generally deny that the author is Daniel while placing the date of the book during the Maccabean era (ca. 167 B.C.). The major arguments in favor of Daniel are significant. To begin with, Jesus quotes from the Book Daniel (Mt. 24:15; cf. Dan. 9:27, 12:11) declaring that his reference is to the words of the prophet Daniel. On several occasions the writer speaks in the first person (7:2-6, 8:1, 15, 9:2, 10:2) and, in 12:4, the prophet is commanded to preserve his words in a book. Both Jewish and Christian traditions ascribe the book to Daniel. In addition, I Maccabees 2:59-60 refers to incidents in the book of Daniel. This reference seems odd if the book of Daniel were written at about the same time. Those who reject the Daniel of the exile as the author usually do so on the grounds that the book contains historical errors. For example, Daniel 1:1 refers to the third year of Jehoiakim whereas Jeremiah says it was the fourth year of the king's reign. This apparent discrepancy may well be due to Daniel's use of the Babylonian method of dating which does not count the year of accession to the throne. Another problem is that Daniel describes Belshazzar as king of Babylon whereas his father Nabonidus was. Babylonian inscriptions show that Nabonidus, who was a scholar and archaeologist, did not want the kingship. He delegated the royal authority to Belshazzar and then went off into the desert to study. In Daniel five, Nebuchadnezzar is called the father of Belshazzar whereas he was actually his grandfather. This particular use of father-son relationship was common in the Biblical world. The head of a royal house was considered to be the father of all the members of the dynasty. Some scholars contend that there is no historical evidence for Darius, but this does not disprove his existence. Another small problem is the use of "satrap" which is a Persian, not a Babylonian, term. However, if Daniel wrote at least part of his book during the time of Cyrus, then the use of "satrap" is understandable. The position of the book in the writings section of the Hebrew Bible seems to imply that it was written as the last of the prophets. This point is inconclusive. Some manuscripts of the Septuagint place Daniel among the prophets. A significant number of Scholars hold that the theological ideas of the Messiah, angels, and the resurrection are too advanced for the sixth century B.C. However, such ideas are found in a less developed form in earlier parts of the Old Testament. In addition, the above mentioned ideas were current in the thought of the Medo-Persians at that time. Finally, some scholars hold that Apocalyptic literature did not arise until the Hellenistic period, but this is not certain since such ideas are found in Zoroastrianism, which is much earlier. In addition to Daniel, both Ezekiel and Zechariah have Apocalyptic sections. The key emphasis of Daniel is that Yahweh is superior to all of the "gods" of the other nations. These nations, and their deities will pass, but the God of Israel will erect a kingdom that will never be destroyed.

Events During the Reign of Nebuchadnezzar: 1:1-4:37

The book begins with an account of the choosing of Daniel, and his three friends for special training in Babylonian language and culture. At the same time, they are tested when Daniel and his friends refuse to compromise their convictions, particularly in regard to the food laws. Nebuchadnezzar's famous dream of the image and uncut stone is found in chapter two. Nebuchadnezzar had a troubling dream, but he could not remember it. His advisors could not tell him either the content or meaning of the dream. Daniel, however, through the direction of God, was able to do both. The "image" in the king's dream symbolized four kingdoms. The head, made of gold, represented Babylon while the breast and arms, which were made of silver, was the Medo-Persian empire which succeeded Babylon. Greece, the next empire, was depicted by a bronze waist and thighs. A mixture of iron and clay in the legs and feet of the image symbolized Rome as the last of the four great kingdoms. Finally, God's eternal kingdom is portrayed as a rock cut without human hands that breaks up these four empires. The point of the dream was to inform Nebuchadnezzar that only the Kingdom of God was permanent. All other kingdoms deteriorate and eventually collapse. Nebuchadnezzar had a forty-three year rule which lasted until 561 B.C. He was then followed by

Awel-Marduk (2 years), Neriglissar (4 years) and Nabonidus (566-539). During the latter part of Nabonidus' reign, he turned the throne over to his son Belshazzar. With Cyrus, the Medo-Persian empire became supreme. Later, under Alexander the Great, Greece took control of the area. In turn the Romans ousted the Greeks. The story of the "fiery furnace" is the theme of chapter three. Shadrach, Meshach, and Abednego were tossed into a hot furnace for refusing to worship an image of Nebuchadnezzar. Their deliverance by God was a vindication of the faith they had in Yahweh. Nebuchadnezzar has another dream (chapter four) and becomes temporarily insane as a judgment of God on his pride.

Visions and Events During the Reign of Belshazzar: 5:1-30, 7:1-8:27

Since Nabonidus preferred the pursuit of knowledge over the prestige and power of the throne, he turned over the rule of Babylon to his son Belshazzar. However, the son proved to be both incompetent and unpopular. An example of his lack of discernment is found in chapter five where an account is given of his misuse of the sacred vessels that were taken from the Jerusalem temple. During the debauchery that accompanied the use of the temple vessels a mysterious hand wrote in Aramaic on the wall of the palace. This message, when later interpreted by Daniel, proved to be a judgment of God on Belshazzar and his kingdom. The Babylonian king learns that his rule will collapse and the nation will be conquered by the Medo-Persians. On another occasion Belshazzar has a dream (7:1-28) concerning four beasts which Daniel explains as referring to four great kingdoms (apparently Babylonia, Persia, Greece and Rome). The meaning of this dream is similar to the one of Nebuchadnezzar concerning the "image." Daniel's vision of the "ram" and "he-goat" (8:1-27) depicts the coming of the Medo-Persians in the first instance and the conquest of the Greeks under Alexander in the latter. The point here is that God's judgment reaches to the wickedness of nations as well as that of individuals.

Visions and Incidents During the Early Rule of the Medo-Persians: 5:31-6:28, 9:1-12:13

Daniel's famous vision of the "seventy weeks" refers to the time decreed by God for the accomplishment of the restoration of his people. The exile will become a means of redemption. Following the restoration of Israel after the Babylonian exile, God will, in due time, send the Messiah. This interval is symbolized by the "seventy weeks." When the Messiah comes, he will "put an end to sin," "atone for iniquities," and "bring in everlasting righteousness" (9:24). With the coming of the Messiah, the eternal kingdom of God will be ushered in for all peoples. Daniel's deliverance from the lion's den is a well known incident (6:1-28). Significantly, Daniel was saved from the lions not only to prove the superiority of Daniel's God, but to demonstrate, as well, the value of a committed faith. Apparently, the Persian king who threw Daniel to the lions was Gubaru the Mede who was appointed governor of Babylon by Cyrus. Later, Cyrus himself takes over the rule of Babylon.

In the last three chapters of the book (10-12) there are a series of visions and prophecies that relate to the future historical development of the Persian and Greek empires. Much of chapter eleven is devoted to the persecution of the Jews during the rule of the Seleucid, Antiochus Epiphanes (175-163 B.C.). Antiochus unsuccessfully attempted to Hellenize the Jews. Under the leadership of Judas Maccabeus, Antiochus and the Seleucids were overthrown. For a time Israel became an independent state, only later to fall under Roman domination. The final chapter of Daniel deals with the End Time. Here the righteous are assured everlasting life through the resurrection of the dead. This prophecy is both a warning of coming tribulations and a promise of eternal life for the faithful.

The Book of Lamentations

This little book of five chapters is difficult to date. The theme of the prophecy is a succession of laments concerning the fall of Jerusalem. Traditionally, the book has been ascribed to the prophet Jeremiah, although this is uncertain. The tone and content of the book certainly reflects the writing of an eyewitness. Accordingly, the book could be dated somewhere from 586 B.C. to about 536 B.C. The arrangement of the book is interesting. Each of the first four chapters is set up as an acrostic following the letters of the Hebrew alphabet. Obviously, this feature is only discernible in the original language.

As the author sees Jerusalem in ruins, he reflects back over the great history of the city's past. The city's predicament arose because the people preferred disobedience to faithfulness. Now the city and even the Temple have been razed. False prophets and priests led to Jerusalem's downfall. The final chapter is a prayer of hope for the future. The prophet is confident that God's mercy will assure a restoration of the nation following her exile.

Discussion - Questions to consider:

1. Who was Obadiah and what was the central theme of his prophecy?
2. Describe the significance and meaning of Ezekiel's vision of the "four living creatures" (chapter 1).
3. How did Ezekiel's prophetic function differ from that of the prophets who preceded him?
4. How and why does Ezekiel distinguish individual from community responsibility (chapter 18)?
5. Discuss Ezekiel's prophecies concerning the "restoration" of Israel.
6. What is the main theme of the book of Daniel?
7. What is the significance of Nebuchadnezzar's dream of the "great image" (2:1-49)?
8. Why does Daniel refer to Belshazzar as the last king of Babylon when history shows that Nabonidus was?
9. What is the significance of the "seventy weeks" in chapter nine of Daniel?
10. What does the book of Daniel say about "last things"?

Resources for additional study:

J.G. Aalders, "Ezekiel," *EC*

Paul T. Butler, *Daniel* (College Press), *Obadiah* (College Press)

H.L. Ellison, "Ezekiel, Book of," *NBD, Ezekiel, the Man and His Message* (Paternoster Press)

Charles L. Feinberg, "Ezekiel," *WBE; Ezekiel* (Moody Press)

Arthur B. Fowler, "Obadiah," *ZPBD*

S.B. Frost, "Daniel," *IDB*

Hobart Freeman, *An Introduction to the Old Testament Prophets* (Moody)

John B. Grayhill, "Ezekiel," *ZPBD*

R.K. Harrison, "Daniel," "Daniel, Book of," *WBE*

R. Laird Harris, "Daniel," *EC*

C.C. Howie, "Ezekiel," *IDB*

Clyde J. Hurst, "Daniel," "Daniel, Book of," *WBE*

Wilhelm Moller, "Ezekiel," *ISBE*

W.J. Martin, "Daniel," *NBD*

James Muilenburg, "Obadiah, Book of," *IDB*

J. Barton Payne, "Daniel," "Daniel, Book of," *ZPBD*

John Rea, "Ezekiel, Book of," *WBE*

John Richard Sampey, "Obadiah, Book of," *ISBE*

A.C. Schultz, "Ezekiel, Book of," *ZPEB*

S.J. Schultz, "Obadiah, Book of," *WBE*

John B. Taylor, *Ezekiel* (TOTC- Intervarsity)

J.A. Thompson, "Obadiah," "Obadiah, Book of," *NBD*

John D.W. Watts, *Obadiah* (Eerdmans)

R. Dick Wilson, "Daniel," "Daniel, Book of," *ISBE*

E.J. Young, *The Prophecy of Daniel* (Eerdmans)

CHAPTER XXI
The Prophets Of The Restoration - Haggai, Zechariah, Malachi
"I am with you, says the Lord."

Readings: *Haggai 1-2, Zechariah 1-14, Malachi 1-4*

Return from Exile

Pre-exilic prophets had predicted both the fall of Jerusalem and the return of a faithful remnant. For example, Jeremiah declared that Judah's collapse would bring about a seventy year exile followed by a restoration of the nation (Jer. 25:11-12, cf. Dan. 9:2). Babylon fell to the Medo-Persians under the leadership of Cyrus in October, 539 B.C. Cyrus then permitted the Jews to return to their homeland in order to rebuild the Temple and the city of Jerusalem. In 536 B.C. about 50,000 exiles returned to Palestine and began to restore the Temple. From the outset hostility from the Arabs and Samaritans hindered the rebuilding process. Opposition, coupled with indifference, soon led to the total abandonment of the project with little more than the foundation completed. Sixteen years later in 520 B.C., God stirred up the prophets Haggai and Zechariah to urge on the restoration of the Temple. The people responded enthusiastically, and the Temple was completed in a short four years (516 B.C.). Later, under Nehemiah, the wall around Jerusalem was reconstructed.

The Book of Haggai

The name Haggai means "festive" or "festal." He may have been so named because he was born on a feast day. The prophet is the only person in the Old Testament with the name Haggai. He was a contemporary of the prophet Zechariah. Details of Haggai's personal life are unknown. He, along with Zechariah, encouraged the people to return to rebuilding the Temple which had begun sixteen years earlier only to be abandoned shortly thereafter. Haggai delivered four prophetic messages stressing the need to rebuild the Temple. All four sermons came within a period of three months during the year 520 B.C. Haggai was the first postexilic prophet to minister to the returned remnant. Apparently he was born during the exile and was among the first group of returnees to Palestine. The date of the book is clear enough. It was written during the second year of Darius the Mede's reign (520 B.C.). Not only did Haggai urge the rebuilding of the Temple, he also emphasized the glory of the coming Messianic Kingdom.

A Call to Rebuild the Temple 1:1-15

Although the returned exiles began the restoration of the Temple in 536 B.C., they abandoned the project. A lack of faith in Yahweh combined with a general indifference to the task created an atmosphere of self-interest that led to a sixteen year delay in the Temple's construction. The people assumed that they could not afford the completion of the Temple, yet they were able to line their houses with expensive wood. Stone for their houses was cheap, but wood was costly. Their neglect of the Temple had led to God's withdrawal of his blessings from them (1:7-11). A return to the rebuilding of the Temple would restore Yahweh's blessings (2:15-19). Three weeks after Haggai began preaching, the people heeded his message and the work on the temple was finally completed in 516 B.C.

A Message of Comfort and Hope 2:1-23

Chapter two of Haggai is essentially a statement of encouragement for the exiles. Yahweh assures the people that the glory of the second Temple will be greater than the first. The Second Temple's greatness lay in its spiritual quality in contrast to the opulence of the Solomonic one. Coupled with the need for urgency in rebuilding was a great concern, on the part of the prophet, that the people maintain both personal and national holiness. Finally, 2:20-23 is a promise to the Jewish governor Zerubbabel that Yahweh will be with him firmly establishing his, and Judah's, authority and jurisdiction in Palestine.

The Book of Zechariah

A contemporary and fellow worker with Haggai was the prophet Zechariah. The name Zechariah ("Yahweh remembers") is a common one in the Old Testament. At least twenty-nine persons had the name. Zechariah's prophetic ministry began about two months after that of Haggai. It is probable that the prophet was a member of the priesthood. Zechariah, the son of Berechiah, was a young man when he began to prophesy. The book is divided into two clear divisions. Chapters one through eight are primarily concerned with the rebuilding of the Temple and should be dated about 520 B.C. The second section (chapters nine through fourteen) centers around the future needs of the community. Here the special concern of the prophet is with the coming Messiah and his Kingdom.

When Zechariah began his ministry, Darius I was king of Medo-Persia. Israel, at that time, was under the guardianship of Persia. Zerubbabel had been appointed governor while Joshua was the high priest. The historical background of the first eight chapters is the same as that of the book of Haggai. The last six chapters were probably written much later for they reflect a change in writing style and subject matter. These differences are due to changed conditions following the reestablishment of the Temple and its worship services.

Zechariah abounds in allusions to the coming of the Messiah and the Messianic Kingdom. Well known events such as the Triumphal Entry (9:9-10), the Messiah's betrayal (11:12-13) and crucifixion (12:10) are predicted. Even as the prophet sought to inspire the returned exiles to complete the task of rebuilding the Temple, he also encouraged them by assurances that the Messiah would come bringing salvation to all people.

The Visions of Zechariah: 1-6

The prophet begins with a call for the people to return to God by rededicating themselves to the task of rebuilding the Temple. In a series of eight night visions he visualized the spiritual truths that undergirded the community's faith and trust in God. Visions one through three are primarily concerned with the task of reconstructing the Temple. These include "the angel among the myrtles" which stresses Yahweh's guidance and care for his people. The "four horns and four craftsmen" symbolize God's assurance that the task of building will be achieved. In the case of the third vision Zechariah sees an unnecessary "measuring line." There is no need to measure the city of Jerusalem. Yahweh is to be both their "wall" and center of security. The next two visions concern Joshua and Zerubbabel, the spiritual and civil leaders of the returned remnant. In vision four, Joshua the priest symbolizes the people as a nation of priests while at the same time prefiguring the coming of the Messiah. Vision five pictures a "lampstand and two olive trees." Here Joshua and Zerubbabel, as the "two olive trees," represent the dual dimensions of the Messiah's ministry which will include both royal and priestly functions. Finally, the last three visions present the spiritual transformation that the coming Messiah will bring. The "flying scroll" symbolized the "law" which was to be the basis for right actions in the Kingdom of God. The seventh vision of the "ephah" depicted the removal of wickedness from Israel. Finally, the "four chariots" of divine judgment stress the sovereignty of God's rule and power over the entire earth. In the sequel (6:9-15) to the first eight visions, Joshua the priest is crowned, not as a sign of royalty but of honor. Joshua then becomes a type of the Messiah.

The Problem of Piety: 7-8

This section begins with Zechariah questioning God about the value of fasting. Yahweh responds by emphasizing the inward quality of fasting (7:4-14). Piety must be honest and sincere, or it is of little significance. The first part of chapter eight pictures a future glorified Jerusalem because it will be ruled by God "in truth and righteousness" (8:8). This future Jerusalem will be characterized by spiritual prosperity (8:9-17). Jerusalem, itself, will be the religious center of the world (8:18-23).

Establishment of the Messianic Kingdon: 9-14

Chapter nine details a coming judgment on three of Judah's enemies (9:1-10). The last half of the chapter is Messianic (9:11-17). Deliverance from the captivity is assured. Judah will be restored and will once again be a nation of considerable significance. This theme is continued in chapter ten where the complete redemption of the nation is promised. If the people will serve God and remain faithful to him, great blessings will be theirs. Physical prosperity as well as spiritual vitality will be indicative of the restored community. The eleventh chapter appears to be in contradiction to the previous two, but this is not the case. This chapter is intended as a warning that the restoration of Israel will not eliminate the need for faithful obedience to Yahweh. Unfaithfulness and the rejection of the "good shepherd" (i.e. the Messiah) will bring their own judgment. Apparently 11:1-6 refers to the future destruction of Jerusalem by the Romans (70 A.D.). Ultimately, a repentant Israel will turn to God and follow his Messiah. However, they will be guilty of killing the king. Later, they will realize their mistake and repent of the wrong. Through the Messiah, true Israel will be cleansed and saved after a chastisement for rejecting the Messiah (13). The last chapter of Zechariah describes the final triumph of the Messiah and his Kingdom. While some stress the physical features of the coming kingdom, it would be better to understand these final chapters as an affirmation of the spiritual quality of the Messianic Kingdom. Zechariah's particular concern is with the coming of the Messiah and the glorious salvation that he will bring.

The Book of Malachi

Malachi meaning "my messenger" is probably a shortened form of **Malakiyah** "the messenger of Yahweh." Some Bible scholars hold that Malachi is a title applied to the prophet rather than his actual name. In that case, the author would be anonymous. Very little is known of the prophet's life. Tradition says that Malachi was a member of the "Great Synagogue" and was a Levite born in Supha in Zebulun. However, there is no certain information other than the fact that the author of the book is the last of the Old Testament prophets.

The date of the book can only be approximated. Malachi was definitely written later than the prophecies of Haggai and Zechariah. The Temple was now complete and sacrifices were being offered (1:7-10, 3:8). Enough time had elapsed for various abuses to develop in the religious life of the nation. Piety of both the people and the priests had degenerated (1:6-8). Payment of the tithe was being neglected and mixed marriages had become a serious problem (3:8-10, 2:10-12). The immediate historical context was the period of Nehemiah's governorship of Judah. Around 433 B.C. Nehemiah was recalled to Babylon for consultations with the Persian ruler. It may have been during the governor's absence that lax religious conditions developed. On this basis, the book was probably written during the latter part of the fifth century B.C. A date of about 425 B.C. is likely.

The central theme of Malachi's prophecy is an emphatic declaration of the sovereignty of God. God is declared to be a father (1:6), master (1:6), king (1:14), and heavenly governor (1:7-8). Judgment is decreed for those who sin and disobey, but grace and mercy will be bestowed on those who repent (3:7-12). Malachi's purpose is twofold. In the first two chapters he outlines and describes the sin and apostasy of Israel. Then, in the final two chapters he stresses judgment on sin, but mercy and blessing to those who repent.

Malachi's Message 1-4

Significantly Malachi begins his prophecy with a strong affirmation of Yahweh's love for Israel (1:1-5). Sadly, the nation failed to respond in kind. Instead of showing love and respect, they became spiteful and hypocritical. This attitude was reflected in the use of blind and lame animals in their temple sacrifices. Even the priests became irreverent and disobedient (2:1-17). However, the nation's unfaithfulness would not prevent the fulfillment of Yahweh's promise to send the Messiah (3:1-5, 4:5-6). Hope is available, if the people will repent of their ways. Should the people quit robbing God and reinstitute the full tithe, then an "overflowing blessing" will be theirs (3:6-12). The book closes with a final call to repentance and reaffirmation of the law of Moses which will prepare the nation for the Messianic Kingdom. Before the Messiah arrives, Elijah the prophet will come preparing the way for the Lord's anointed. In the Gospel accounts Jesus clearly indicates that this prophecy is a reference to John the Baptist who was the forerunner of the Christ (Mt. 11:14, Mk. 9:11, Lk. 1:17). Thus, Old Testament prophecy closes with a promise of redemption and salvation.

Discussion - Questions to consider:

1. When and under what circumstances did the exiles begin to return from Babylon?

2. Why did the returning exiles fail to complete the rebuilding of the Temple?

3. When was the Temple finally completed?

4. What role did Haggai and Zechariah play in rebuilding the Temple?

5. Discuss the meaning and significance of Zechariah's visions.

6. What do the post-exilic prophets say about the coming Messiah and his Kingdom?

7. What reasons do we have for believing that Malachi was the last of the Old Testament prophets?
8. What is the central theme of Malachi's message?
9. What was the general religious attitude of Israel at the time of Malachi?
10. What is the significance of Malachi's prophecy of the coming of Elijah (4:5-6)?

Resources for additional study:

Steven Barabas, "Zechariah, Book of," *ZPBD*

A. Cohen, ed., *The Twelve Prophets* (Soncino)

G.N.M. Collins, "Zechariah," *NBC*

H.L. Ellison, *The Old Testament Prophets* (Zondervan)

Charles L. Feinberg, "Zechariah, Book of," *WBE; WBC*

A.B. Fowler, "Haggai," *ZPBD*

Hobart Freeman, "Malachi," *WBE;*, *An Introduction to the Old Testament Prophets* (Moody)

John B. Grayhill, "Malachi," *ZPBD*

R.K. Harrison, "Haggai," "Malachi," "Zechariah, Book of," *ZPEB*

Carl. F. Keil, *The Twelve Minor Prophets* Vol. II, (Eerdmans)

Jack Lewis, *The Minor Prophets* (Baker)

W. Neil, "Haggai," "Malachi," "Zechariah, Book of," *IDB*

George L. Robinson, "Haggai," "Malachi," "Zechariah," *ISBE;*, *The Twelve Minor Prophets* (Baker)

S.J. Schultz, "Haggai, Book of," *WBE*

J.S. Wright, "Haggai, Book of," "Zechariah, Book of," *NBD*

E.J. Young, "Malachi, Book of," *NBD*

CHAPTER XXII
The Books of Ezra, Nehemiah, and Esther
"So we built the wall...for the people had a mind to work."

Readings: *Ezra 1-10, Nehemiah 1-13, Esther 1-10*

The Book of Ezra
Historical Background

In 539 B.C., after having conquered Babylon, Cyrus permitted the exiled Jews to return to their homeland. They were given permission to restore the Temple and the city of Jerusalem. This action contrasted with the Babylonian policy of deportation and relocation of conquered peoples. The Persians even restored the sacred vessels of the Temple (Ez. 1:8-10). Zerubbabel (Sheshbazzar) led 42,360 people in the initial return to the Holy Land. If the above number represented only the heads of the households, then the actual number of returnees would have been much higher. Soon after returning, the Jews built a burnt-offering altar and laid the foundations for the Second Temple. The Samaritans offered to help rebuild the Temple, but their assistance was rejected on religious grounds. The Samaritans were only half-Jews. Thereafter, the Samaritans applied their energies toward thwarting the rebuilding of the Temple. Because of this opposition and general laxity of the people, the project was abandoned for nearly sixteen years. In 520 B.C. under the urging of the prophets Haggai and Zechariah, the work on the Temple began again. Four years later in 516 B.C. the Second Temple was dedicated.

The Book of Ezra includes two distinct historical periods with the first six chapters covering from the return under Zerubbabel to the completion of the Temple (539-526; 520-516 B.C.), while 7-10 detail events after the completion of the Temple. Ezra, the priest, appeared in Jerusalem during the seventh year of Artaxerxes of Persia (ca. 458 B.C., see Ez. 7:7). Ezra's mission was to rekindle the dwindling religious fervor of the people. In particular, he was concerned that mixed marriages with non-Jews be repudiated. By far the most important reform was the reaffirmation and reinstitution of the Torah in the religious life of the community. Ezra's contribution to the development of Judaism was most significant (see also Neh. 7-10).

In the Hebrew Bible the book of Nehemiah is the second part of the book of Ezra. Nehemiah arrived in Jerusalem about twelve years after Ezra. Nehemiah was appointed governor of Jerusalem in ca. 445 B.C. While an exact date is uncertain, the events recorded in the book of Esther are probably a little bit earlier than those described in Ezra-Nehemiah (ca. 486-465 B.C.). Part of the book of Ezra (4:8-6:18; 7:12-26) is written in Aramaic. The book itself is a continuation of the narrative of Judah's history begun in the books of Chronicles with special emphasis on the restoration of the religious and civil life of the nation after the Exile. Ezra was either written by the priest himself or edited by him about 450 B.C. The book covers about eighty years of history although there is a sixty year period of silence between chapters six and seven. Perhaps the key verse of the book is the very first one which stresses the fulfillment of Jeremiah's prophecy that the exiles would return and re-establish the nation of Israel (see Jer. 29:10).

Return to the Holy Land: 1-2

Cyrus, after conquering Babylon, issued an edict permitting the Jews to return to Palestine in order to rebuild the Temple. Under the leadership of Zerubbabel a large number of people returned home. Chapter two contains a list of the various families who availed themselves of the opportunity to re-establish Israel as a nation.

Building of the Second Temple: 3-6

The first official act of the Jews upon returning to their homeland was the building and dedication of the altar of sacrifice. Then the rebuilding of the Temple began but, after restoring the foundation, work was halted because of local opposition and a lack of enthusiasm on the part of the people (4). After a sixteen year hiatus work on the Temple began again due to the encouragement of the prophets Haggai and Zechariah (5). Four years later in 516 B.C. the Temple was completed and dedicated with the celebration of the Passover (6).

Ezra's Return and Israel's Reform: 7-10

An interval of about sixty years passes before the writer resumes his narrative with the return of Ezra the scribe and priest. The material here parallels that of Nehemiah 7-10. Ezra was a direct descendant of Aaron, the high priest and brother of Moses. The Scribe's return was directly commissioned by the Persian king Artaxerxes. With a large caravan, Ezra reaches Jerusalem with high hopes only to discover that the religious life of the people had deteriorated due to mixed marriages. The problem with marrying non-Jews was that the religious life of the people was compromised by the idolatry of the offender's spouse. In order to maintain the purity of the Jewish faith, Ezra insisted that the violators give up their foreign wives, which they did. Nehemiah 7-10 also tells us that the people reaffirmed the Law of Moses and their covenant with Yahweh.

The Book of Nehemiah
Nehemiah the Governor

The historical setting of this book is the same as that of the first six chapters of Ezra. In the Hebrew Bible Ezra and Nehemiah constitute one book in the Writings (Ketuvim) section which also includes the books of Poetry and Wisdom. Nehemiah's name means "whom Yahweh has comforted" while Ezra probably means "Yahweh helps." According to the Talmud, Ezra was author of both his book and Nehemiah's, although this is unlikely since the latter book is an autobiography. Nehemiah probably arrived as the appointed governor of Jerusalem a dozen or so years after Ezra, though some would hold that he preceded the Scribe. A date of about 440 B.C. seems probable for Nehemiah's first visit (2:1). Even though some scholars dispute the matter, available evidence points to the fact that Ezra and Nehemiah were contemporaries. Nehemiah's trip to Jerusalem was occasioned by the distressing news he had received from his kinsman Hanani. The major contribution of Nehemiah was the rebuilding of the walls of Jerusalem in order to re-establish the city as the capital and assure the future development of the nation. Chapters 1-6 of the book are autobiographical while 7-10 describe the renewing of the Law and Covenant. The final three chapters are also autobiographical and detail the stabilization of the religious and civil life of Jerusalem following the Exile. II Maccabees 2:13 adds that Nehemiah "founded a library and collected the books about the kings and prophets and the writings of David..."

Rebuilding the Walls Around Jerusalem: 1-6

Nehemiah's immediate reaction to the news that the returned exiles had not re-established Jerusalem nor rebuilt the walls around the city was one of sorrow and distress. After being appointed governor of the territory and receiving permission from the Persian king Artaxerxes to restore the city and its walls, Nehemiah goes to Jerusalem and inspects its ruins. Immediately, he sets out to rebuild the walls of the city even though the project was opposed by the local inhabitants, especially Sanballat and Tobiah. In addition, the Jews themselves were unenthusiastic about the matter. Finally, after numerous difficulties, the wall was begun and completed in a record fifty-two days. Nehemiah's enthusiasm and dedication not only encouraged the exiles but inspired them to extra effort as well.

Reaffirmation of the Law and the Covenant: 7-10

During Nehemiah's stay in Jerusalem, both he and Ezra, the Scribe led the people in a public reading and interpretation of the Law of Moses. The community joyfully responded to God's word by celebrating the Feast of Tabernacles followed by a fast and a renewal of the covenant with Yahweh (8-9). Later, the problem of mixed marriages was dealt with again. Then, the nation made a solemn promise to keep all of their covenant obligations (10:32-39).

Nehemiah's Second Reform: 11-13

After a twelve year stay as governor of Jerusalem Nehemiah returned, for a time, to the Persian court. During his absence, conditions deteriorated and it became necessary for Nehemiah to visit Jerusalem a second time. His return led to the formal dedication of the city walls and a series of religious reforms. Included in the latter was the cleansing of the Temple, financial undergirding of the priesthood, reaffirmation of the Sabbath, and additional marriage reforms. Nehemiah concludes his book by saying,

Thus I cleansed them from everything foreign, and I established the duties of the priests and the Levites, each in his work. (13:30)

I and II Chronicles

These two books were originally one. They were divided into two books in the Greek Old Testament. The books were written about 450 B.C., probably by Ezra the Scribe. For the most part, the contents parallel the material of I and II Kings. The main difference is that Chronicles is almost exclusively concerned with the history and life of the Southern Kingdom of Judah. These books were placed in the Writings section of the Hebrew Bible.

The Book of Esther
Setting and Context

Even though the book of Esther follows Nehemiah in the Old Testament, the events recorded in the book precede those in Nehemiah. The incidents described in Esther took place at Susa, the Persian capital, during the reign of Ahasuerus (ca. 486-465) who is better known by his Greek name Xerxes. Esther is the heroine of the account. Her name is a Persian word meaning "star." The book itself is part of the "Five Scrolls" in the Ketuvim or Writings section of the Hebrew Bible. The actual author of the book is uncertain. Both Mordecai and Ezra have been suggested, but it appears that the author is anonymous. However, it is clear that the author was very familiar with Persian customs and history.

The central theme of the book is its concern with the deliverance of the Jews at a time when their national existence was threatened by persecution. The book is unusual among Old Testament writings since it is much more patriotic than religious. In fact, the name of God is not mentioned once although it does occur in acrostic form in the Hebrew text. Nevertheless, the deliverance of the Jews by the intervention of Esther is very important in Jewish history for she saved the nation at a time when total destruction was imminent. This particular event became so significant to the Jews that it continued to be remembered by a celebration known as the Feast of Purim. By the time of Jesus, this Feast had become one of the most important days in the religious calendar. Although the book of Esther is not particularly religious, it does reflect the background of deep faith in God. Matthew Henry's comment is most appropriate: "If the name of God is not there, His finger is."

The Persian Court and its Intrigues: 1-2

During a boisterous meal in preparation for a battle against the Greeks, Vashti, the wife of Ahasuerus, refused to appear at the drunken feast. As a result, she was deposed as queen on the recommendation of the king's counselor, Memucan. The king then began an extensive search for a beautiful young woman as her replacement. Esther, whose Hebrew name was Hadassah ("myrtle"), was chosen as Vashti's replacement. Mordecai, Esther's uncle who had raised her as his own daughter, remained with her as an advisor.

Conflict Between Haman and Mordecai: 3-7

The promotion of Haman the Agagite to the position of second in command of the kingdom created problems for Mordecai. Since Mordecai refused to bow down and worship Haman, the latter, in a fit of fury, used his influence and position to set in motion a pogrom to destroy the Jews. Once Mordecai learned of the seriousness of the threat, he appealed to Esther for help. Esther, now the king's favorite, was able to convince Ahasuerus to stop the slaughter. A gallows that was built to execute Mordecai was now used to hang Haman. Mordecai was then promoted to chief minister. Through the intervention of Esther, the Jewish nation was saved at a most difficult moment in its history.

Institution of the Feast of Purim: 8-10

In commemoration of Esther's deliverance of the Jews, a special feast was declared. This feast continued to be celebrated yearly as a day of happiness and joy. The holiday became known as Purim from the Persian word "Pur" meaning "lot." The word is in reference to the "lots" that were cast in favor of the destruction of the Jews. Now, however, the word came to signify deliverance. The feast was celebrated on the fourteenth day of the twelfth month of the Jewish calendar. According to Esther 9:27-28 the Jews vowed to keep the feast of Purim perpetually. The book of Esther gives us a significant insight into an important moment in Jewish history.

Discussion - Questions to consider:

1. Describe the general historical setting of the books of Ezra, Nehemiah, and Esther.
2. What problem did the Jews have with the building of the Second Temple?
3. Under what circumstances did the Jews return to the Holy Land after the Exile?
4. What contributions did Ezra make to the re-establishment of Israel after the exile?
5. Why was Nehemiah so concerned to rebuild the walls around Jerusalem?
6. What reforms did Nehemiah set in motion?
7. Why is the book of Esther important?
8. How would you explain the absence of any reference to God in Esther?
9. Who were Mordecai and Haman?
10. Why are the three books in this chapter significant in understanding Jewish history?

Resources for additional study:

J.G. Aalders, "Esther," "Ezra," *EC*

W.F. Adeney, *Ezra, Nehemiah and Esther,* Expositor's Bible (Armstrong)

Steve Barabas, "Ezra," "Ezra, Book of," *ZPBD*

L.H. Brockington, *Ezra, Nehemiah and Esther,* Century Bible (Nelson)

A. Cohen, ed., *Soncino Books of the Bible,* (Ezra, Nehemiah, and Esther)

Robert B. Dempsey, "Esther," "Esther, Book of," *WBE*

Clyde E. Harrington, "Esther, Book of," *ZPBD*

R. Laird Harris, "Ezra," "Ezra, Book of," *ZPBD;* "Ezra," *ZPEB*

D. Harvey, "Esther, Book of," *IDB*

W.J. Martin, "Nehemiah," *ZPEB*

R.H. Pfeiffer, "Ezra and Nehemiah, Books of," *IDB*

John Urquharat, "Esther," "Esther, Book of," *ISBE*

John C. Whitcomb, "Ezra," "Nehemiah," "Esther," *WBC*

R. Dick Wilson, "Ezra," "Ezra-Nehemiah," "Nehemiah," *ISBE*

J.S. Wright, "Esther," "Esther, Book of," "Ezra," "Ezra, Book of," "Nehemiah," "Nehemiah, Book of," *NBD;* "Esther," "Esther, Book of," "Ezra, Book of," "Nehemiah, Book of," *ZPEB; NBC*

Kyle M. Yates, "Ezra, Book of," "Nehemiah," "Nehemiah, Book of," *WBE*

CHAPTER XXIII
The Book of Job
"Though he slay me, yet will I trust him..."

Readings: Job 1-42

Nature of Hebrew Poetry:

Poetry is a characteristic feature of the Old Testament. At least one-third of the Old Testament is poetic in form. Some books such as Psalms, Proverbs, Micah, and Nahum are written entirely in poetry. There are significant poetic sections in most of the other Old Testament books. Only six books contain no poetry at all. These include: Ruth, Ezra, Nehemiah, Esther, Haggai, and Malachi.

The structure of the Hebrew language is uniquely appropriate for poetry. Hebrew words express things and actions more than ideas. The musical quality of the language readily lends itself to poetic structure.

Parallelism is the most significant feature of Hebrew poetry. This poetical technique was first clearly identified by Robert Lowth in 1753. Lowth made three basic observations. First, Hebrew poetry is mainly a matter of sense to which sound and form are loosely linked. The emphasis is on balancing ideas and phrases rather than on strict meter. Secondly, he held that the original meter was lost and that it was not possible to reconstruct Hebrew Poetry on the basis of classical poetic forms. Finally, he insisted that the most significant poetic device used by the Hebrew poet was "parallel members" which consisted of a balance or distribution of thought sense rhythm. Thus, the Hebrews used thought rather than word arrangement for versification. This counter balancing of verse members was the general form of poetic structure in the ancient Near East.

Three principal types of parallelism, synonymous, antithetic, and synthetic, have been distinguished. Of these, the most obvious, as well as the most frequent, is the synonymous parallel. Essentially, this form is a repetition of the same thought with equivalent expressions. Thus, the first line of a stanza is reinforced by the second. Parallels may be either complete or incomplete. Psalm 103:3 is an example of the former, and Jeremiah 17:9 of the latter. These examples may be schematically represented as follows:

Psalm 103:3
"who forgives all your iniquity   a.b.
   who heals all your diseases"   a'b'

Jeremiah 17:9
"The heart is deceitful above all things,   a.b.c.
   and desperately corrupt; who can understand it?"   b'c'

The incomplete form is a deliberate variation and makes the poem more fluid and poetically attractive.

Antithetic parallelism is the repetition of a contrasting thought in the second line for the purpose of emphasizing or confirming the first thought. The second line may recapitulate the thought of the first negatively, or, as is usually the case, the thought of the second is in total opposition to the first. Further, this thought may be either complete or incomplete. Thus:

Psalm 1:6
"for the Lord knows the way of the righteous,   a.b.
   but the way of the wicked will perish."   b- c

Proverbs 14:28
"In a multitude of people is the glory of a king,   a.b.
   but without people a prince is ruined."   a- b-

The third kind of parallelism cited by Lowth is known as synthetic. Central to this form is the progressive flow of thought in which the second or following lines either add something to the first or explain it. Technically, the two lines are not parallel except in the sense that any straight line is parallel with its beginning. Parallelism of form exists although parallelism of thought is not actually present. An example of synthetic parallelism is Psalm 1:3.

He is like a tree
   planted by streams of water
that yields its fruit in its season,
   and its leaf does not wither.
In all that he does, he prospers.

Since the time of Lowth, several other types of parallelism have been identified including emblematic, stairlike and introverted.

A second significant feature of Hebrew poetry is rhythm. This is the effect produced by the recurrence of stressed or accented syllables at more or less regular intervals. In Hebrew poetry, the rhythm of the line is determined by a balance of thought or meaning. The basic unit of Hebrew poetry is the line which comprises the essential element of a parallelism. The line then is formed into a larger poetical unit, namely the verse. Normally two lines combine to form a verse although three or four are not uncommon. Individual verses display a uniformity of accent as its norm of rhythm. This is generally known as beat or meter. The actual number of beats to a line varies. Rigid uniformity is not characteristic of Hebrew verse. A common meter in Hebrew poetry is the lament which has a 3:2 beat. Many examples of this type of beat can be found in the book of Lamentations. However, for the most part, meter in Hebrew poetry is fluid. Various other types of literary forms are found in Old Testament poetry, but they are not peculiar to Hebrew.

The Book of Job
Job and His World:

The title of the book of Job comes from the main character of the book. Job lived southeast of Palestine in the land of Uz (1:1). Some have identified his home with Teman. In any case he was a pious worshipper of God, and he was probably a Hebrew although this is not certain. In addition to this book, Job is mentioned in two places in the Bible, Ezekiel 14:14,20 and James 5:11. The context and content of the book points to a historical person, although some have expressed doubts on the matter. We do not know who wrote the book. Suggestions as to the author include Job, Elihu, Moses, Solomon, Isaiah, Hezekiah, and Baruch. Probably the best suggestion would be Job himself, but we cannot be sure.

There is no way to be precise about the date of the book since firm historical references are lacking. However, it does appear that the book is pre-exilic and probably even predates Solomon. The atmosphere depicted in the book, especially the Prologue, is patriarchal. Job appears as his own priest. His wealth is determined by his ownership of cattle. There is no reference to the law of Moses nor to the prophets. In light of these points some have dated the events in the book as occurring during the time of Abraham, but it probably is better to date the book at about 1,000 B.C. Any date, however, is conjecture.

The central theme of the book is a recurring one in history and life. It is, why do the righteous suffer and the wicked prosper? The corollary question is, how can this be reconciled with the belief in a good God? For Job the answer had to come through faith and trust in an all wise and loving God. The proof of God's presence in one's life is not to be found in either prosperity or success, but rather in the relationship between God and the individual. Ultimately, God's justice will correct any apparent inequities. Job's friends, however, saw his suffering as a proof of guilt and sin. As far as they were concerned, a righteous man simply does not experience reverses and serious illness in this life. Thus, they held that suffering, sickness and trouble, in general, are evidences that God is punishing the guilty for his sins. Job's friends were quite wrong since suffering is not necessarily a judgment of God on wickedness. Sometimes affliction is a means of strengthening the righteous person. In other cases it may arise simply because of the general consequences of sin in the world as a whole.

Job has long been cited as an example of great faith and patience, and rightly so. His trials were not directly caused by his sin. Under the most trying circumstances, he maintained a vigorous and affirmative trust in God. It has sometimes been said that Job never waivered in his faith, but this is not exactly true. Under the extreme criticism of his friends, he found it necessary to defend himself and his own righteousness. In doing so he overstated his defense and found himself becoming a bit arrogant and overconfident. It finally became necessary for God to intervene and reprimand Job (see chapter 38). However, Job's suffering not only demonstrates that he was truly a man of God, but his experience becomes a challenge and an inspiration to all. The book falls into the "wisdom" class of literature which will be discussed in more detail in the next chapter. Job is a unique composition. The best way really to understand it is to read it.

Prologue: 1-2

Almost all of the book of Job is written in poetry, except the first two chapters, 32:1-5 and 42:7-17. This epic poem with its prose prologue and epilogue has been acknowledged as one of the greatest literary works of all time. Its structure, style, and argument are skillfully and cogently developed.

The prologue itself is set up as a one act drama with five scenes. This preliminary drama sets the stage for the main attraction which is a confrontation between Job and his friends concerning the questions of justice and righteousness. The first scene (1:1-5) is set in the land of Uz. Job is described as a pious well-to-do worshipper of God. In the second scene, which is set in heaven, Satan, the adversary, appears before Yahweh accusing Job of being a coddled self-seeking saint. Yahweh then permits Satan to remove some of Job's benefits to test his faith. Scene three (1:13-22) revolves around a series of tragedies that befall Job and his family. In quick succession he lost both his wealth and his children. In the face of these disasters, Job's trust in God remained firm. The fourth scene (2:1-6) takes place in heaven again. Satan presents himself declaring that Job's piousness would be broken if he should have to suffer physical pain. Yahweh then permits this second examination of Job's religious integrity. The final scene (2:7-13) takes place in the land of Uz. Job is covered with boils from head to toe. Now his wife enters the drama and suggests that he "curse God and die," but he refuses to do so. Thus, Satan fails to tempt Job into rebellion against God. This scene closes with the appearance of Job's three friends, Eliphaz, Bildad, and Zophar who came, supposedly, to comfort him. As it turned out, they spent seven days with him not saying a single word. Obviously their attitude was more detrimental than helpful. The next twenty-nine chapters detail a discussion between Job and his three friends over the issue of his righteousness.

Poetical Dialogue: Job and his Friends 3-31

The poetic section of the book begins at 3:1 and continues to 42:6. In chapter three Job breaks the silence of his friends with a speech in which he reflects upon the deep emotion and tragedy of his life. He expresses clearly his feelings and holds back no punches. Job makes three apparently negative points. First, he says that he would have been better off if he had not been born (3:1-12). Then he states that non-existence is desirable (3:13-19). Finally, he declares that he would be better off dead. All of these statements reflect an element of despair, but not total desperation. Job does not really want to die, he is only seeking to communicate the depth and feeling of his inner turmoil. These comments open the door for a series of criticisms by his three friends.

Eliphaz the oldest, and perhaps the wisest, begins the discussion (4-5). At first Eliphaz appears to be kind and diplomatic, but he quickly turns to censure. Sadly, what Job really needed was neither theology nor philosophy, but compassion and understanding, neither of which his friends were willing to provide. According to Eliphaz, all suffering arises from wickedness. Job's suffering was in rebellion against God. Suffering, according to the eldest of Job's comforters, is a direct punishment of God (5:17). Eliphaz begs Job to seek God and repent of his sins. Like many after him, Eliphaz wanted a simple solution for a complex problem. While some suffering does arise from sin, it is certainly not true that all troubles arise directly from rebellion against God. Sickness and tragedy touch the righteous and wicked alike. Eliphaz' big mistake was that he presumed to know fully the will and providence of God.

Job's answer (6-7) is that those who are afflicted should have pity and compassion, especially from one's friends. Eliphaz assumed that he had all the answers. He was trying to play God. Job was distressed by the fact that his friend's view was not based on hard evidence. Job pleads for more than a mere theory (6:24-30). He wants solid evidence of his guilt. In chapter seven Job describes the power and nature of human suffering. This chapter is both a prayer to God and a plea for understanding by his friends.

Bildad's speech in chapter eight presents basically the same argument as that of Eliphaz, except he is much less sympathetic. Each friend, in turn, is more assertive, less tolerant. Bildad is quite unkind. He endorses the doctrine that righteousness pays in prosperity here and now. This view was an established truth for Bildad. He simply makes the facts fit his theory. It is a common contention that righteousness will bring prosperity. This was the view of Calvin and the Puritans, but certainly not of Jesus! There are two main objections to this position. First, no one is really righteous enough to deserve blessings on the basis of merit. Secondly, the opinion makes a vile sinner of every person who is poor or ill. Bildad's defense of his assertions was based on past experience of the failures of some wicked men. While this situation holds in many cases, it is not universally so. In fact, some unrighteous people do prosper, at least in this world.

Job's reply to Bildad is that true righteousness is often rewarded, but not always. Sometimes even the righteous suffer. Even though Job knew himself to be innocent, he nevertheless was aware of the fact that, like everyone else, he was a sinner. Further, the full nature of God and his purposes are too complex for a mere human to fathom. Chapter ten is Job's attempt to understand this problem, but he finds the answer too difficult to ascertain. Like

Habakkuk, who later was to learn the same lesson, he must simply trust God and accept him on faith.

The third speech (11) came from Zophar who, probably being the youngest of the comforters, was last to speak. Basically, Zophar parrots the ideas of the other two speakers. He was not particularly original in his comments. Without sufficient evidence, he becomes quite critical of Job's insistence upon his innocence (11:6). Zophar actually contradicts himself in verse seven. He had argued previously that he knew why God makes a person suffer, now he declares that one cannot really understand God. Zophar knows that he cannot limit God, yet he tries to do so anyway by assuming that all who suffer are being punished by God for their sin. This fairweather friend closes his tirade by asserting that Job is vain because he assumes that he is wise and innocent. He suggests that Job will be restored, if he will only admit his guilt and put away his iniquity.

Again, Job's response (12) is to deny the accusations. For Job, God is totally aware of all things. He is all powerful and wise yet inexplicable. God's providence is greater than any human evaluation of his actions. In chapter thirteen Job declares that his friends were being dishonest with their false and baseless accusations. Job continues to defend his own integrity and confidently asserts that he will be vindicated. In many ways, chapter fourteen is the most important part of the book. Here Job speaks to God seeking some understanding of his predicament. He honestly yearns for relief from his suffering. He also declares that he is unable to cope with his troubles without God's help.

Chapters fifteen through twenty-one contain a second cycle of speeches. Most of the discussion is the same as the first series, except the criticism of Job is more severe. Job's third and final series of discourses with his three friends are recorded in chapters 22-31. In this last cycle of speeches only Eliphaz and Bildad speak. Job is again accused of being a severe sinner and is encouraged to repent, then God will restore what he has lost. Job refuses to acknowledge guilt and insists that he be tried impartially by God himself. In a long discourse, Job admits the majesty and power of God and the deity's distaste for wickedness. The patriarch then rehearses his past life and present suffering while still refusing to admit guilt on his part. Job acknowledges the dilemma of his life, but he is unwilling to admit that his troubles have arisen from sin. He continues to maintain his innocence even though he is hard pressed to explain his predicament. In some sense Job realizes that he is experiencing a test, but he does not really understand it.

The Arguments of Elihu: 32-37

Beginning with chapter thirty-two, the three friends cease their arguments. Elihu then enters the discussion as an outside observer. He was younger and perhaps more reflective than the other three speakers. He proves to be more objective than they were. Elihu's speeches are longer and more incisive than his predecessors. He was disturbed that the "three friends" did not really answer Job's questions. In his argument he tries to correct what he sees as their errors. The main point of Elihu is that God is just and Job's affliction is disciplinary and corrective. At least some suffering does have meaning. This view is essentially stressed in chapter thirty-three. In chapters 34-37, Elihu emphasizes the point that God is not unjust and that all of his actions have meaning and purpose. However, from a human point of view, God's ways are often inscrutable. Elihu makes a significant contribution to the basic problem of the book of Job. He points out that even suffering can be a learning experience. For Elihu, Job's suffering is no mystery, it is a revelation of God's involvement in human affairs. Job does not respond to Elihu. There was no need to do so since no biased criticism was made.

God's Rebuke of Job: 38:1-42:6

The dramatic poem now turns from Job and his friends to God's reprimand of the patriarch. Because Job's friends insisted that his plight arose from his sin, Job was forced to defend himself. In doing so he overstated his case and became overconfident. Job so strongly affirmed his own innocence that he lost his perspective and humility. God speaks out of the whirlwind and reproves Job for his arrogance. Chapter thirty-eight suggests that there is some distance between man and God. God is the creator and humans are the creation. There is no way a person can fully understand the complexity of creation (38:16-38). Even the mysteries of biological life itself are unfathomable (38:39-39:30). God's speech is really a series of rhetorical questions with the obvious answer that no human being can completely probe the meaning of existence. This whole section clearly shows the limitations of human knowledge. Both Job and his friends are wrong. Job's predicament was neither a result of sin nor a total mystery. God's purpose was to test Job's faith and trust. While Job's faith did weaken a bit, he never abandoned his trust in God. The discourse closes with Job reaffirming his dedication to God. Job had to learn the lesson that, even when events are unexplainable, the saint always remains true to his God.

Epilogue: 42:7-17

This long dramatic poem began with Job as a happy and prosperous man. Satan, however, enters this idyllic scene and accuses Job of serving God out of self-interest. The experiences that follow demonstrate that Job, contrary to Satan's assertion, did not serve God purely out of self-seeking. On the other hand, the series of events do reveal that human righteousness is never sufficient in itself, a problem that is not solved in the book of Job. It is only later, through the Messiah, that a final solution will be found. Some scholars are a little disturbed that Job's prosperity is restored in the final scene. However, we must remember that Job's blessings were removed as a test. It is fitting that they should be restored. Those who serve God ultimately find a happy ending to their lives.

Discussion - Questions to consider:

1. What do we know about Job and the world in which he lived?
2. What is the central theme in the book of Job?
3. What was the general viewpoint of the three friends concerning Job's suffering?
4. What is the relationship of the Prologue and Epilogue to the total story of Job?
5. Who was Elihu? What contribution did he make to the arguments in the book of Job?
6. How did Job's wife react to his suffering?
7. Why was Satan so concerned to break Job?
8. Were Job's three friends really friends?
9. What is the significance of God's "whirlwind" speech?

10. How does the book of Job, and its message, relate to the present day world?

Resources for additional study:

Francis I. Anderson, *Job* (Intervarsity, TOTC))
Wesley C. Baker, *More Than A Man Can Take* (Westminster)
Albert Barnes, *Job* (Baker)
E.M. Blaiklock, "Poetry," *NBD*
T. Winton Davies, "Poetry, Hebrew," *ISBE*
H.L. Ellison, "Job, Book of," *NBD; A Study of Job* (Zondervan)
John F. Genung, "Job, Book of," *ISBE*
N.K. Gottwald, "Poetry, Hebrew," *IDB*
Norman C. Habel, *The Book of Job* (Cambridge)
Anthony and Mary Hanson, *Job* (Torch)
R.K. Harrison, "Hebrew Poetry," *ZPEB*
Dale Hesser, *Job* (Sweet)
Philip C. Johnson, "Poetry," *WBE*
Meredith B. Kline, "Job," *ZPBD;* "Job," "Job, Book of," *WBE*
Andrew MacBeath, *The Book of Job* (Shield-Baker)
Marvin H. Pope, "Job, Book of," *IDB*
H.H. Rowley, *Job* (New Century Bible)
Emmet Russell, "Poetry," *ZPBD*
E. Smick, "Job," *ZPEB*
Ralph L. Smith, *Job-A Study in Providence and Faith* (Convention Press)
Sanford C. Yoder, *Poetry of the Old Testament* (Herald Press)

CHAPTER XXIV
The Book of Proverbs
*"The fear of the Lord is the
beginning of knowledge..."*

Readings: Proverbs 1-31

The "Wise" and Their Function

Old Testament Wisdom Literature is a product of a class of religious leaders known as the "wise." Normally, Wisdom Literature includes Job, Proverbs, Ecclesiastes, and certain Psalms (for example, 19, 37, 104, 107, 147, 148) as well as a few short passages elsewhere. In addition, the Apocryphal books of Ecclesiasticus and the Wisdom of Solomon are also part of the same type of literature. Although Hebrew Wisdom Literature does not deal exclusively with religious subjects, the context and setting of the writings are always religious. Proverbs, for example, is mostly concerned with morality in everyday life, yet the basis for conduct is "fear of the Lord." While Wisdom Literature often centers in the practical dimensions of life, books such as Job and Ecclesiastes seek to probe the deep mysteries of life.

The central contribution of the wise, which included both men and women, was in the area of counsel and guidance, especially in practical affairs. Wise men had the capacity to be clever, prudent, and even shrewd. These counselors sought a realistic approach to the problems of life. In particular, they sought to harmonize everyday life with the law of God. The primary concern of the wise was with the practical exposition of mores and ethics. This moral concern developed under the influence of the prophets and priests as well as within the context of their own experience. The wise were involved in the deep questions of life, death, suffering, innocence, and, especially, prosperity and wickedness. This quest was directed much more toward the individual than institutions. Ultimately the search for wisdom was to lead directly to God.

The Book of Proverbs
Introduction: 1:1-7

The book of Proverbs is largely composed of maxims to guide one in this life. Wisdom in Proverbs begins with a reverence and respect for God. Proverbs has an optimistic view of the world. God's word and creation are trustworthy. The book is actually an anthology of at least five collections of proverbs. Not all of Proverbs were written by one author. In addition to Solomon, we can identify the "men of Hezekiah," Agur, Lemuel and an author known as "the wise." The final date for the collection and editing of Proverbs could be as late as 400 B.C. It is best to see the book of Proverbs as the work of a number of authors ranging over a period of several hundred years. However, most of chapters 1-29 are associated with Solomon.

Proverbs contain many short pithy sayings, but there are also long discourses such as the one on wisdom (1:8-9:18). In general, the proverbs stress prudence (managing one's affairs sensibly), sobriety (earnestness), and diligence. Those who follow such practices find peace, security, happiness, and a long life. On the other hand, Proverbs warns against the dangers of drunkenness, idleness, adultery, lying, and stupidity. Underlying these admonitions is the need for a strong religious faith. Wisdom is seen not as human achievement, but as a divine gift.

The word proverb comes from a Hebrew word **(mashal)** meaning "to represent" or "to be like." Proverbs are really analogies between the natural and spiritual world. In many ways the proverb is very much like Jesus' parable. However, there are also non-analogies and general observations about life. In the book of Proverbs, the aim is to apply the law of God to the whole of life. Almost all of Proverbs is poetic in form. Generally, the proverbial thought is expressed in a short couplet.

Verses 2-7 of the first chapter stress that wisdom begins and ends with a deep faith in God. The admonition is to seek wisdom by seeking God.

Lessons on Wisdom: 1:8-9:18

This rather large section is devoted to a lengthy discussion of the acquisition and utilization of wisdom. In particular, a child should heed the teaching and instruction of his parents. Wisdom, here in Proverbs, is set in a religious context. It is more than shrewdness, skill or intelligence. In Proverbs, wisdom is reflected in a life of integrity and uprightness, both morally and religiously. Proverbs 1-9 personifies wisdom as a righteous woman who can be trusted under all circumstances. Wisdom is contrasted with foolishness. This section on wisdom warns against its neglect and stresses the benefits and rewards of seeking its insight. Wisdom is considered to be more precious than money and more valuable than wealth. Those who are wise receive honor. In contrast, the unwise are wicked and devious. The wise individual opts for fidelity in marriage and willingly accepts the responsibilities of the marital state. The discussion includes a strong warning against idleness and perversion. The infamous seven deadly sins are listed in 6:16-19. A special admonition is given about the dangers of sexual immorality in 6:20-7:27. This long discourse closes with a description of the beauty and power of wisdom (8-9).

Miscellaneous Proverbs: 10:1-22:16

Proverbs in this section are generally held to be Solomon's. Chapters 1-9 serve as an introduction to this portion which constitutes the main body of the book. Previously the discussion had centered on the virtues and values of wisdom. Now we have a collection of proverbs in the true sense. In this part of the book there are many pithy sayings which express practical wisdom about conduct, attitudes, and general moral living. The sayings are not organized or structured according to a logical sequence. Rather, these proverbs deal with various aspects of human life. The proverbs in this group tend to be non-religious, but the context in which these admonitions are given is clearly religious. Right action is recommended because it pays. Evil deeds are to be avoided because they are detrimental to one's life. For the most part, these sayings were directed to the ordinary person who needed to learn that "honesty is the best policy."

Examples of the moral admonitions in this section include the value of hard work (10:4-5), the value of money (10:15-16), the insecurity of the wicked (10:24-25), the problem of pride (11:2), the rewards of generosity (11:24-26) and the virtues of having a good wife (12:4). Kindness is to be displayed to all, even animals (12:10). Many of the proverbs deal with the right and wrong use of words (12:6, 13-14, 17-19). The extremes of laziness and anxiety both have their price (12:21-25). While children need discipline (13:24), they also need love and understanding (15:1). Throughout this entire section three emphases are evident. First, the wise man trusts in God. Secondly, those who are wise weigh carefully their actions. Finally, a wise person is an individual of great integrity. Certainly a wise individual avoids alcoholic beverages (20:1) and seeks to be honest in all his dealings (20:17, 21:6, 21:29, 22:1).

The Words of the Wise: 22:17-24:34

Apparently these proverbs were written by a number of different people. The proverbs in 22:17-24:22 are similar to a group of Egyptian sayings known as the **Wisdom of Amen-em-opet**. Clearly there is some borrowing of ideas here. If the **Wisdom of Amen-em-opet** were written about 600 B.C., as many have held, then the Egyptian writer could have utilized the Hebrew proverbs. In this section there are thirty sayings which admonish the hearer to choose true knowledge and righteousness. An interesting description of the folly of drunkenness is found in 23:29-35.

Solomonic Proverbs: 25:1-29:17

According to 25:1 these proverbs were originally spoken by Solomon, but finally edited by King Hezekiah's scribes. Within this group of sayings there are two collections 25:1-27:27 and 28:1-29:27. In the case of the first, the proverbs deal with the matter of kingship, problems of gossip, counsel for a good life, hazards of laziness, and general lessons on life. The second collection includes observations on the value of teaching and learning as well as with issues that deal with right conduct and a good life.

The Sayings of Agur: 30:1-33

The final two chapters of Proverbs contain a sort of appendix to the Solomonic materials. Probably both Agur and Lemuel were Arabs. They both belonged to the land of Massa which is associated with Abraham's son Ishmael (Gen. 25:14). Agur begins by asserting his human limitations in contrast to the all encompassing knowledge of God. In verse seven Agur begins with a series of numerical proverbs. He wants no part of falsehood and lying. He prefers neither the extremes of poverty nor riches. His desire is to know the Lord. Agur, recognizes the problems of life, but he also affirms its beauty as well. For Agur the wise person is one who finds a balance between the excesses of life.

The Words of Lemuel: 31:1-31

By far the most important portion of this final chapter is the famous poem on the "ideal wife." This portrait of a virtuous woman is an alphabetical acrostic in the original Hebrew. The author of this beautiful poem is unknown. The key thought of the closing message of Proverbs is clear. A good wife (or husband) is a valuable treasure indeed (31:10-11). An excellent wife makes an exceptional home. She is a woman who utilizes well the resources at her disposal. She is not self-centered, but loving, kind, and generous. Whatever she seeks to do, she does well. What is significant about the ideal wife, and mother, is not her external beauty, exceptional skills, and abilities, but rather it is her love for God, family, and neighbor that makes her distinctive. In a real sense she becomes a model for everyone.

Discussion - Questions to consider:

1. Was the entire book of Proverbs written by Solomon?
2. What was distinctive about the "wise men" of the Old Testament.
3. Compare the function of the wise man with that of the prophet and priest.
4. What does the word "proverb" mean?
5. How would you define "wisdom" as it appears in the Book of Proverbs?
6. Why do most of the proverbs deal primarily with practical matters?
7. Is the book of Proverbs a religious book?
8. Why does a "wise" person seek to be honest at all times?
9. What is the main theme of the "sayings" of Agur?
10. What is your evaluation of the "ideal woman" in chapter thirty-one?

Resources for additional study:

Sheldon H. Blank, "Proverbs, Book of," *IDB*

Donald K. Campbell, "Proverbs, Book of, *WBE*

A. Cohen, *Proverbs* (Soncino)

John Franklin Genung, "Proverbs, Book of," *ISBE*

Edgar Jones, *Proverbs and Ecclesiastes* (Torch)
R. Laird Harris, "Proverbs, Book of," *ZPDB*
A.K. Helmbold, "Proverbs, Book of," *ZPEB*
R.F. Horton, *The Book of Proverbs* (Expositor's Bible)
Donald Hunt, *Pondering the Proverbs* (College Press)
Derek Kidner, *Proverbs* (Intervarsity - TOTC)
J.W. Nutt, *Proverbs* (Ellicott's Bible Commentary)
J.I. Packer, "Proverbs, Book of," *NBD*
J.C. Rylaarsdam, *Proverbs to Song of Solomon* (Layman's Bible Commentary)
R.B.Y. Scott, *Proverbs and Ecclesiastes* (Anchor Bible)
Marvin E. Tate, *Commentary on Proverbs* (Broadman Bible)
Andrew F. Walls (and W. A. Rees Jones), "Proverbs," *NBC*
Earl C. Wolf, *Proverbs* (Beacon Bible Commentary)
R.N. Whybray, *The Book of Proverbs* (Cambridge Bible Commentary)

CHAPTER XXV
The Books of Ecclesiastes and The Song of Solomon
"Remember now your Creator in the days of your youth..."

Readings: *Ecclesiastes 1-12, Song of Solomon 1-8*

The Preacher and his Message

For many people the book of Ecclesiastes is a puzzle. At times the book appears to be baffling and inexplicable. There are a number of words which are not found in the rest of the Old Testament that appear only in Ecclesiastes. The book seems to be negative, but it really is not. Rather, the writer presents a penetrating and critical view of human life. From personal experience the author shares insights into the deep questions of life.

The title Ecclesiastes is a Greek translation of the original Hebrew word Qoheleth. Qoheleth is derived from the word **qahal** which means a public assembly. It is possible that the message of the book was delivered as a sermon at a public gathering. For this reason the writer is often referred to as a preacher. In 12:9 the writer calls himself "the Preacher." The message of the book stresses the vanity of living only for this life. Ecclesiastes is critical of those who leave God out of their affairs. For the preacher, God is involved in the life and history of the world. One should not forget either God's immanence nor his transcendence. He is both in this world and beyond it. The book opposes all attempts to reduce religion to secularism. Utopia will not be found in this world. Only God can solve the twin problems of death and evil. Human institutions and ideas, without God, are ultimately futile or, as the Preacher says, they are "vanity." Ecclesiastes sees vanity as a description of sin's corruption of creation. When the author asserts that all is vanity, he is not speaking of life in general, but misdirected human life. Although the tone of the book is negative, its message is not really one of despair. The preacher wanted to remove false and illusionary hopes. Real happiness is to be found only in one's trust of God. The world is not evil in itself. It is only when a person treats the world as an end in itself that it becomes vanity. Ecclesiastes' skepticism revolves around the preacher's rejection of human wisdom when it becomes a substitute for the knowledge of God. Whoever seeks God will find new meaning and purpose in his life.

The question of the authorship of Ecclesiastes is still debated. Traditionally, the book has been assigned to Solomon on the basis of 1:1, 12, 16. These verses indicate that the writer was the son of David and a king in Jerusalem. If Solomon is held to be the author, then a date of about 930 B.C. would be appropriate. Those who assume that the author is someone else do so primarily on literary and philosophical grounds. For example, it is contended that the book reflects Greek and Babylonian thought which postdate Solomon. However, these arguments are quite subjective and inconclusive.

The Book of Ecclesiastes
A Series of Futile Quests: 1-11

As stated above, the key point of the preacher is that no matter how successful, popular, or powerful one may be, a life without God is worthless. The writer enumerates no less than seven such futile quests that are common in human endeavor. In the first place, some people are workaholics. They work hard to accumulate money and even prestige, but these prove to be vain since they cannot satisfy the inner need of the soul (1:3, 3:9-10, 4:4-8). Other people, including the author of Ecclesiastes, choose a second route. They attempt to find happiness and satisfaction in life by accumulating great knowledge. This also proves to be futile since knowledge and wisdom, by themselves, are unsatisfactory (1:13-16, 2:12-17, 7:23-25). Ultimately, wisdom and knowledge come from God (2:26). Many seek a third approach. They try to find the meaning of life in sensual pleasure. Often the philosophy is "eat, drink, and be merry." Pleasure is not bad in itself (2:24-25, 3:11-13), however the sensual does become detrimental when it is sought as an end in itself (2:1-3).

Some people find the accumulation of possessions a consuming passion. This fourth quest is reflected in 2:4-11. The author had amassed houses, vineyards, gardens, servants, livestock, silver, and gold, but none of these things had brought happiness. Status symbols, while attractive, are never really satisfying. Wealth rapidly looses its glamour and appeal. When the "preacher" considered the toil, tears, and turmoil of acquiring great possessions, he found the effort to be "vanity and a striving after the wind" (2:11).

Next, the author tried to divert his wealth into setting up an estate for his family (2:18-23). On the surface this effort appears to be a noble one. However, the problem arises as to whether or not the heirs would be hindered more than helped. The wise use of an inheritance is important, but no one can guarantee that the heirs will be better off. So the preacher concludes that this sixth road is also "vanity." Oddly enough the old preacher even tried the "unchaser quest" (12:1-3). He had permitted himself to grow old without real purpose and meaning in his life. To drift aimlessly without a real concern for yourself or others is pointless. One who fails to use his time in service to God and others is cheating himself out of the best things in life. Of course, the seventh and inevitable quest is death itself. When life loses its meaning and purpose, then death takes over (12:4-7). For those who leave God out, life becomes a big fat zero. However, this final road need not be futile. This leads to the quest that the "preacher" wishes he had taken.

The best way of life is the religious one. Those who trust in God find life both good and challenging. This is especially so in the case of those who commit themselves to the Creator God while they are still young (12:1). Having surveyed the various futile attempts that are commonly used in seeking the "good life," the writer of Ecclesiastes appropriately concludes: "The end of the matter; all has been heard. Fear God, and keep his commandments, for this is the whole duty of man" (12:13). When one considers the entire book of Ecclesiastes, it becomes obvious that the author's message is not a negative one, but a positive declaration that the only life really worth living is the one that puts God first.

The Song of Solomon
Introduction

The Song of Songs is the only Old Testament book that has love as its sole theme. Actually, the book comprises a series of dramatic poems. From the title (1:1) of the book we learn either that the author of the book was Solomon or that the Song was composed about him. If the traditional authorship of Solomon be accepted, then a date of about 950 B.C. should be assigned to this book.

According to the Midrash, the Song of Solomon was composed in Solomon's youth while Proverbs was written during his mature years and Ecclesiastes in his waning ones.

For the most part, the Song of Songs has been an embarrassment for both Jews and Christians. The explicit descriptions of love seem too human and gross to many. In order to circumvent this problem, Jewish and Christian scholars have resorted to allegorical and symbolic interpretation of the story. In general, there have been three basic methods of interpreting the book. The most common one is the allegorical. Jewish rabbis saw the account as a description of the spiritual marriage between God and Israel (Hos. 2, Isa. 42, Jer. 21, Ezek. 16). Accordingly, the first half of the book pictures Israel before the captivity and the second half after the return. Christians who use this method argue that the book describes the relationship of love between Christ and his Church. While one could draw an analogy between the story and God's love for his people, it is doubtful that such was the intended meaning.

Another approach is to abandon the allegorical view and opt for the drama theory. Thus, the story is a play with acts, scenes, and actors. This view was first set forth by Franz Delitzsch in his commentary. While there may be some truth in this opinion, there is no evidence that the Jews ever acted out the story, or even considered it to be a drama. A third view that has become popular recently is the one that considers the long poem a wedding Song. Thus, the song was used as a part of the wedding ceremony. Sections of the song were supposedly sung on each of the seven days of the wedding feast. While this suggestion is appealing, there is no evidence that it was written for the wedding ceremony. When all factors are considered, it is better to see the Song of Solomon as a simple, but beautiful love story. Theologically, the poem communicates the abiding value of human love and, by analogy, the meaning of divine love.

A Love Story: 1:1-8:14

The story begins with a young woman in the palace of a king fondly recalling her beloved while being enticed by the promise of expensive jewels (1:1-2:7). In the next scene, the maiden recalls a delightful visit by her loved one. This is followed by a dream in which she reaffirms her love for him (2:8-3:5). Following this, Solomon visits and tries to win her favor with praise and flattery

(3:6-4:7). However, the young woman is not impressed. She still remembers her shepherd lover and wants to marry him, not the king (4:8-5:1). In the next scene, the girl relates a dream describing her beloved (5:2-6:3). Solomon once again visits the maiden and attempts to win her affection (6:4-7:9). However, the young woman continues to remain loyal to her absent lover. She longs to be with him rather than with the king (7:10-8:3). Finally, the girl is permitted to return home to her first love. She had remained faithful to him in the face of great temptation (8:4-14).

This whole account is a fabulous story of love and faithfulness. None of the enticements of the royal court were sufficient for the young woman to abandon her beloved. Undoubtedly this poem was included in the Old Testament canon to demonstrate the quality of true love.

Discussion - Questions to consider:

1. Why do some people consider the book of Ecclesiastes to be an enigma?
2. What does the word Ecclesiastes mean?
3. What would you consider the main theme of Ecclesiastes to be?
4. Why did the writer of Ecclesiastes consider all of his quests to be futile?
5. Why does the book of Ecclesiastes appear to be negative? Is it?
6. What quest does the "preacher" wish he had followed?
7. Why do some people find the Song of Solomon embarrassing?
8. What are the weaknesses and strengths of the allegorical approach to the Song of Solomon?
9. Is there any problem in considering the Song of Solomon a simple, but beautiful, love story?
10. Why is the Song of Solomon such an unusual Old Testament book?

Resources for additional study:

Walter F. Adeney, *The Song of Solomon* (Expositor's Bible)
G.L. Archer, "Ecclesiastes," *ZPEB*
Willis J. Beecher, "Ecclesiastes," *ISBE*
S.H. Blank, "Ecclesiastes," *IDB*
Wick Broomall, "Ecclesiastes," *ZPBD*
W. Gordon Brown, "Ecclesiastes, Book of," *WBE*
W.J. Cameron, "Song of Solomon," *NBC*
Samuel Cox, *The Book of Ecclesiastes* (Expositor's Bible)
A. Cohen, *The Five Megilloth* (Soncino)
Don DeWelt, *Song of Solomon* (College Press)
R.K. Harrison, "Song of Solomon," *ZPEB*
F. Delitzsch, *Commentary on the Song of Songs* (Eerdmans)
N.K. Gottwald, "Song of Songs," *IDB*
Andrew Harper, *The Song of Solomon* (Cambridge Bible)
R. Laird Harris, "Ecclesiastes," *EC*
G.S. Hendry, "Ecclesiastes," *NBC*
D.A. Hubbard, "Song of Solomon," *NBD*
Edgar Jones, *Proverbs and Ecclesiastes* (Torch)
G.A.F. Knight, *Esther, Song of Songs, Lamentations* (Torch)
R.J. Kidwell, *Ecclesiastes* (College Press)
J.P. Lange, *Proverbs-Song of Solomon* (Zondervan)
Robert Laurin, "Ecclesiastes," *WBC*
Marvin H. Pope, *Song of Songs* (Anchor Bible)
J.C. Rylaarsdam, *Proverbs to Song of Solomon* (Layman)
J.R. Sampey, "Song of Songs," *ISBE*
John Watt, *Two Neglected Books - Ruth and the Song of Solomon* (Loizeau)
Sierd Woudstra, "Song of Solomon," *WBC*
J.S. Wright, "Ecclesiastes," *NBD*
Edwin M. Yamauchi, "Solomon, Song of," *WBE*

CHAPTER XXVI
The Book of Psalms
"The earth is the Lord's and the fulness thereof, the world and those that dwell therein."

Readings: Psalms 1-150

Introduction

In a very real sense the book of Psalms was both a hymn and prayer book for the Jews. The freshness and enduring quality of the Psalms is due to their spiritual intensity. Psalmists sought to worship and praise God in their writings. They also wished to portray vividly the dynamic quality of life that comes from dedicated service to God. Three main themes constantly recur in the book of Psalms. First, the writers stress their personal encounter with God. For the psalmists, God is real! There are no doubts on this point at all. In the second place, the natural order is important because God is both its creator and sustainer. Thirdly, history is central in their thoughts since it is the stage upon which God works. The choice of Israel as a nation was not only historical but a demonstration of God's grace as well.

The Hebrew name for the book of Psalms is "Songs of Praise." Psalms is not a Hebrew word at all but is derived from the Greek word **psalmos** which means "to play instrumental music, and then to sing to musical accompaniment" (A. Cohen). In the temple services the psalms were sung by a choir of Levites accompanied by string and wind instruments (II Chron. 29:25).

Although David wrote many Psalms, he is not the author of all of them. The basic collection in the Psalter is a large group of Davidic hymns (2-41 except 33, 51-72, 108-110, 137-145). Of these psalms, some were probably not written by David, but rather were dedicated to him as an outstanding psalmist. Psalm 72:20 indicates that not all the psalms were by David. The notation there says "the prayers of David, the son of Jesse are ended." The title of the next Psalm is "A Psalm of Asaph." There are two collections of Levitical Psalms, Korahite 42-49 and Asaphite 73-83. These Psalms tend to be more didactic than the other Psalms. Two

Psalms, 72 and 127, are by Solomon. Some Psalms are clearly anonymous, for example 1, 33, 84-89. Psalms 90-91 have traditionally been assigned to Moses.

Dating of the Psalms varies from the time of David ca. 1000 B.C. to the post-exilic period ca. 400 B.C. There are even psalms outside of the Book of Psalms. For example, Exodus 15, Deuteronomy 15, II Samuel 22-23, Jonah 2, Habakkuk 3 and Numbers 23-24 are psalms. The Psalter can be broken down into five books based, apparently, on the structure of the Pentateuch. The first book comprises Psalms 1-41. Most of these Psalms are Davidic. The most common word for God in book one is Yahweh. Both David and the sons of Korah are the basic authors of Psalms 42-72. El or Elohim is the most frequent word for God in this section. Book three consists of Psalms 73-89. Most of these Psalms are by Asaph who usually uses the word Elohim for God. The fourth book (90-106) is mostly anonymous psalms. Finally, book five contains the remaining Psalms (107-150). Some of this final group are attributed to David, one is by Solomon and the rest are anonymous. Yahweh is the predominant word for God in this concluding book.

The Psalms have been classified in many ways. Some of the more common ones are: acrostic poems, Messianic psalms, historical psalms, thanksgiving hymns, lamentations, songs of trust, hymns of penitence, pilgrim psalms and festival hymns. The themes commonly found in the Psalms are both personal and communal. The Psalms are concerned with instruction (1, 19, 39) trust (3, 27, 31, 46, 56, 103, 107, 116), penitence (6, 32, 38, 51, 143), aspiration (42, 63, 80, 137) as well as many other topics.

Probably the most troubling Psalms are those classified as "imprecatory." An imprecation is the act of invoking a judgment or calamity on another person or nation. Psalms such as 69, 83, and 109 appear to be vindictive and stern. However, the psalmist is not being vengeful, he is simply declaring that one reaps what he sows. It is not necessary to see in the psalmist's words a spirit of personal spite and cruelty, rather we should understand his assertions as clear declarations that wrongs should be punished.

Since the book of Psalms is a book of Hebrew poetry, it is important to be aware of its special characteristics. Here it would be useful to review the discussion on the nature of Hebrew poetry in Chapter XXIII. It is especially important to realize that, in the case of a synonymous parallel, the writer is not stating something new in the second line of the parallelism, but rather is repeating the same thought with different words. For example, in Psalm 103:3 the author is not speaking directly of physical health. It is spiritual healing that concerns him. This device is a common one in Hebrew poetry. (See also Psalms 25:1, 46:7.)

Book I - Psalms 1-41

Most of these Psalms are attributed to David, although not all of them were actually written by him. The first Psalm is not Davidic but was probably written as an introduction to the book of Psalms. Psalm one introduces a basic theme of the entire collection, i.e. that people fall into two classes, the Godly and the ungodly. The life of righteousness is a happy one, but the way of the wicked leads to ruin. Psalm two is Messianic stressing the final triumph and victory of the coming Messiah. Psalms 3-7 are personal prayers of David regarding his distresses and problems, while Psalms 8-10 stress praise and thanksgiving to God. A strong affirmation of courageous faith is detailed in Psalm 11. Psalms 12-14 center in the problems of evil and wickedness. Psalm 15 describes the kind of person who dwells in the house of God while Psalm 16 is Messianic, predicting the death, burial and resurrection of the Christ. In Psalm 17, David prays for deliverance from his enemies. Psalm 18 is an expression of thanks to God for his deliverance. The 19th Psalm is famous for its affirmation of faith in God's revelation through his creation and word. Psalms 20-21 are royal psalms, dedicated to David, asking for God's direction in battle. The 22nd Psalm is Messianic. It predicts the coming Messiah's suffering and glorification. The 23rd Psalm is probably the best known and most beloved of all the psalms. This psalm of David is a personal confession of faith and trust in God as the loving Shepherd.

Psalm 24 is a processional hymn that was probably sung by pilgrims on their way to worship in Jerusalem at the Temple. The use of **selah** which appears in this psalm, and elsewhere in the book of Psalms, is significant. The word comes from a Hebrew root meaning "to lift up." The word is a liturgical and musical notation indicating an interlude in which singing would cease and the orchestra would play. The 25th Psalm is an acrostic. Each verse begins with a different letter of the Hebrew alphabet. The hymn is a prayer for guidance, protection and forgiveness. Psalms 26-28 are prayers asking for divine help in times of difficulty and distress. The 29th Psalm is a hymn of praise to God as the Lord of creation. The remaining psalms in this section (30-41) are hymns of praise and thanksgiving to God for his deliverance and aid in the time of trouble.

Book II - Psalms 42-72

Several of the Psalms in this section are by the "sons of Korah." One is by Asaph, and another is attributed to Solomon. Most of the Psalms in Book II are Davidic. Psalms 42-49 are songs of the "sons of Korah." The 42nd and 43rd Psalms constitute one poem. These two psalms reflect the author's thirst for God's presence and direction in his life. Psalm 44 is a bit unusual since it is a cry for help by the whole nation rather than just an individual. Various suggestions have been made as to the date of this psalm, but it seems best to date it during the reign of Hezekiah when Jerusalem was being threatened by the Assyrians under Sennacherib. The 45th Psalm is a royal marriage song. Verses six and seven are used by the writer of Hebrews (1:8-9) to describe the kingship of Christ. Psalms 46 through 48 should be dated about 700 B.C. since they reflect joy over God's redemption of the "city of God." Here God intervenes and saves Jerusalem from the Assyrian invasion because of Hezekiah's intercession. Psalm 49 is a sermon on the folly of trusting in wealth. The 50th Psalm declares that God's judgment is an impartial one. Neither hypocrisy nor wickedness will be accepted by God. Psalm 51 is usually held to be a prayer of David confessing his sins and asking forgiveness from God. This psalm is the greatest penitential prayer in the Bible. It strikes a responsive chord in the heart of every servant of God. Psalms 52-53 describe the fate and folly of the wicked. Generally, it has been held that Psalms 54-59 are poems of faith. The emphasis is not only on the psalmist's need of God but equally upon the conviction that aid will come. For the most part, Psalms 64-71 are prayers for deliverance, both personal and national, in times of great distress. The poems reflect a deep confidence in God's intervention in behalf of his people. Psalm 72 is generally attributed to Solomon and is a description of an ideal king and his reign. Many have seen Messianic implications in this hymn.

Book III - Psalms 73-89

Most of the Psalms in this section are ascribed or dedicated to Asaph, a Levite and contemporary of David, who was well-known for his musical ability (I Chron. 15:17ff, 16:4ff). All of Asaph's psalms are characterized by an emphasis on teaching and instruction. Psalms 73 through 83 are of this type. The psalmist is troubled by the prosperity of the wicked (Psalm 73) but he realizes that ultimately only the righteous will prosper. Psalm 74 is a plea for God's help against a powerful enemy. This psalm reflects the circumstances at the time of Jerusalem's destruction by the Babylonians in 586 B.C. Both Psalm 75 and 76 express praise and thanksgiving to God for his aid. Psalms 77-83 describe God's faithfulness and goodness in the face of Israel's hypocrisy and unfaithfulness. The psalmist is aware of God's providence even at times of great national stress. He reflects this faith in his positive understanding of the nation's trials. Psalms 84-85 are hymns by the "sons of Korah." The former describes the joy and happiness of a pilgrim who visits the Temple while the latter is an affirmation of God's love and faithfulness. Psalm 86 is a prayer of David for assistance in the time of trouble, but it is also a declaration of assurance of God's mercy. The next Psalm (87) describes the privileges of being in God's kingdom whereas the 88th Psalm is a petition for help in a troubled time. Book III closes with the 89th Psalm which details the Davidic covenant and its significance for Israel.

Book IV - Psalms 90-106

With the exception of Psalm 90, which is attributed to Moses, most of the psalms in this section are anonymous. The ninetieth psalm is entitled "A Prayer of Moses." The content and language of this psalm resembles Deuteronomy 33. The theme of this hymn is the transitory nature of man as contrasted with God who is eternal. This psalm inspired Isaac Watt's famous hymn "O God, Our Help In Ages Past." Psalm 91 is a declaration of faith in the promises of God while 92 is an expression of praise for God's goodness. The 93rd is a short psalm describing God as the King of the universe. Psalm 94 is an appeal for divine judgment on the wicked. With Psalm 95, and continuing through 100, the psalmist returns to the theme set forth in the 93rd Psalm. This group of psalms emphasize the enthronement of God as the king of his whole creation. These psalms carry a Messianic message. In addition, they reflect the reaffirmation of Israel's faith in God, as the king of the universe, following the return from the Babylonian Exile. The spirit of these psalms is one of joy and happiness.

Psalms 101-103 are probably Davidic. They describe an ideal king as one who worships and serves God with dedication and fervor. The final three psalms in this section (104-106) are hymns of praise to God. The 104th praises God as creator and sustainer of the universe while 105 and 106 praise God for keeping his covenant and showing mercy to the disobedient nation of Israel.

Book V - Psalms 107-150

This final section has a collection of thirteen Davidic Psalms. One psalm is attributed to Solomon and the rest are anonymous. The 107th psalm is closely linked to the preceding one, even though it begins the fifth and final book of Psalms. The emphasis here is upon divine providence. The psalmist expresses his thanks to God for his deliverance. Psalms 108-110 are Davidic. The first two of these psalms reflect great confidence and trust in God while the third (110) is Messianic. In particular, Psalm 110 describes the Messiah as being a priest after the order of Melchizedek (Hebrews 5-7). Psalms 111-118 are a series of hymns that praise God for his goodness and kindness towards his people. In each of these psalms there is a particular stress on the writer's thankfulness to God. The 117th is the shortest of all the 150 psalms. Its theme is "praise the Lord." In contrast, the 119th psalm is the longest poem in the entire Bible. This psalm has 176 verses set up in 22 stanzas of eight lines each. Each stanza represents a different letter in the Hebrew alphabet from beginning to end. The theme of this long acrostic poem is that the only good life is the one that follows the law of God. The key verse is "Thy word is a lamp to my feet and a light to my path" (119:105).

A series of fifteen psalms (120-135) bear the title "Songs of Ascent." The exact meaning of this phrase is uncertain but apparently it refers to the hymns that were sung by pilgrims going up to Jerusalem for one of the three great yearly Festivals. Psalm 120 is a prayer for deliverance from one's enemies whereas 121 is a great poem affirming deep trust in God's mercy. Psalms 124-126 are thanksgiving hymns that praise God for his deliverance and protection. The 127th psalm is ascribed to Solomon. Its theme is the uselessness of work without God's guidance. Psalm 128 is a prayer of blessing on those who seek to do God's will. The 129th psalm is a cry for judgment of Israel's enemies. In Psalms 130 and 131 there is an expression of hope and assurance in God's care. Psalm 132 describes David's intent and desire to build the Temple.

both the 133rd and 134th psalms are brief hymns of three verses. The former stresses brotherly unity while the latter is a call to trust God. The final psalm in this series (135) praises God for his greatness and goodness to his people. The 136th psalm is a similar hymn of praise. Psalm 137 is unusual for it depicts the plight of the Israelites while they were exiles in Babylon. Psalms 138-145 are Davidic hymns describing the faithfulness, power, protection and goodness of God. The remaining five psalms are by various authors. The general theme of these final psalms is a plea for the entire creation to praise God as the Lord of all. The last verse of Psalm 150 declares, "Let everything that breathes praise the Lord."

Although the book of Psalms is a lengthy book, it is one that stirs deeply the heart and soul of every reader. The spiritual intensity of these hymns and prayers arise from the psalmist's personal experience of God. They therefore carry a message that is timeless.

Discussion - Questions to consider:

1. Did David write all of the Psalms?
2. How appropriate is the Hebrew title, "Songs of Praise"?
3. How important is the study of Hebrew poetry for an understanding of the Psalms?
4. What is the significance of the fivefold division of the Book of Psalms?
5. Why have the Psalms proven to be so popular?
6. Which Psalm do you consider to be the most unusual? Why?
7. What is the significance of the Messianic psalms?
8. What does "selah" mean?
9. Are psalms found outside of the book of Psalms in the Old Testament?
10. Which is your favorite Psalm? Why?

Resources for additional study:

A.A. Anderson, *Psalms* (2 volumes - New Century Bible)

A. Cohen, *The Psalms* (Soncino)

M.J. Dahood, *Psalms* (3 volumes - Anchor)

F. Delitzsch, *Biblical Commentary on the Psalms* (Eerdmans)

J.H. Eaton, *Psalms* (Torch)

J. Hempel, "Psalms, Book of," *IDB*

Derek Kidner, *Psalms* (2 volumes - Intervarsity, TOTC)

A.F. Kirkpatrick, *Psalms* (Cambridge Bible)

Leslie S. McCaw, "Psalms," *NBC*

J. Barton Payne, "Psalms, The Book of," *ZPBD, ZPEB*

A.B. Rhodes, *Psalms* (Layman)

J.R. Sampey, "Psalms, Book of," *ISBE*

R.L. Smith, "Psalms, Book of," *WBE*

J.G.S. Thomson, "Psalms, Book of," *NBD*

Kyle M. Yates, "Psalms," *WBC*

C. Yoder, *Poetry of the Old Testament* (Herald Press)

Bibliography

Adeney, Walter F. *The Song of Solomon* (Expositor's Bible), New York: A.C. Armstrong and Son, 1903.

――――――. *Ezra, Nehemiah and Esther* (Expositor's Bible). New York: A.C. Armstrong and son, 1903.

Albright, William F. *The Archaeology of Palestine*. Baltimore: Penguin Books, 1960.

Allen, Leslie C. *The Books of Joel, Obadiah, Jonah and Micah* (NICOT). Grand Rapids: Wm. B. Eerdmans Publishing Co., 1976.

Anderson, A.A. *The Book of Psalms* (2 Volumes - New Century Bible). London: Oliphants, 1972.

Anderson, Francis I. *Job* (Tyndale Old Testament). London: Inter-Varsity Press, 1976.

Archer, Gleason. *A Survey of Old Testament Introduction*. Chicago: Moody Press, 1964.

Baker, Wesley C. *More Than a Man Can Take*. Philadelphia: The Westminster Press, 1966.

Barnes, Albert. *The Book of Job*. New York: George A. Leavitt, 1852.

Benedict, Robert P. *Journey Away From God*. Old Tappan: Fleming H. Revell Co., 1972

Bright, John. *A History of Israel*. Philadelphia: The Westminster Press, 1952.

Butler, Paul T. *Daniel*. Joplin: College Press, 1970.

――――――. *Isaiah*, Volumes I - III. Joplin: College Press, 1975-1978

――――――. *Minor Prophets* - Hosea, Joel, Amos, Obadiah, Jonah. Joplin: College Press, 1968.

Buttrick, George A., ed. *The Intepreter's Dictionary of the Bible*. Nashville, Tennessee: Abingdon Press, 1962.

Clarke, Adam. *Commentary of the Bible*, abridged by Ralph Earle. Grand Rapids: Baker Book House, 1961.

Cohen, A. *The Five Megilloth*. London: The Soncino Press Ltd., 1952.

――――――. *Proverbs*. London: The Soncino Press, Ltd., 1952.

――――――. *The Psalms*. London: The Soncino Press, Ltd., 1950.

――――――. *Ezra, Nehemiah and Esther*. London: The Soncino Press, Ltd., 1962.

――――――. *The Twelve Prophets*. London: The Soncino Press, 1961

Cohen, Joseph H. *I Have Loved Jacob*. New York: ABMJ, 1948

Cox, Samuel. *The Book of Ecclesiastes.* (Expositor's Bible) New York: A.C. Armstrong and Son, 1903.

Crawford, C.C. *Genesis,* Volumes I - IV. Joplin: College Press, 1966, 1970, 1971

Cundall, A.E. and Morris, Leon. *Judges and Ruth* (TOTC). London: InterVarsity Press, 1968.

Dahood, Mitchell J. *Psalms* (3 volumes - Anchor Bible). Garden City: Doubleday & Company, Inc., 1970.

Davidson, Francis, ed. *The New Bible Commentary.* Grand Rapids, Michigan: Wm. B. Eerdmans Publishing Co., 1963.

Dean, B.S. *An Outline of Bible History.* Cincinnati: Standard Publishing, 1912.

Delitzsch, F. *Biblical Commentary on the Psalms.* Grand Rapids: Wm. B. Eerdmans Publishing Co., 1971.

_____. *Commentary on the Song of Songs.* Grand Rapids: Wm. B. Eerdmans Publishing Co. 1971.

Dewelt, Don. *Sacred History and Geography.* Grand Rapids: Baker Book House, 1955.

Douglas, J.D., ed. *The New Bible Dictionary.* Grand Rapids: Wm. B. Eerdmans Publishing Co., 1962.

Eaton, J.H. *Psalms* (Torch) London: SCM, Press, 1967.

Edersheim, Alfred. *The History of Israel and Judah.* New York: Fleming H. Revell Co., n.d.

Erdman, Charles. *Book of Exodus.* New York: Revell, 1959.

_____. *Genesis.* New York: Revell, 1950.

_____. *Book of Leviticus.* New York: Revell, 1951.

_____. *Book of Numbers.* New York: Revell, 1952.

Ellison, H.L. *Ezekiel, the Man and His Message.* Exeter: The Paternoster Press, 1967.

_____. *The Old Testament Prophets.* Grand Rapids: Zondervan Publishing House, 1973.

_____. *A Study of Job: From Tragedy to Triumph.* Grand Rapids: Zondervan Publishing House, 1973.

Francisco, Clyde T. *Introducing the Old Testament.* Nashville: Broadman Press, 1950.

Free, Joseph P. *Archaeology and Bible History.* Wheaton: VanKampen Press, 1950.

Freeman, Hobart. *An Introduction to the Old Testament Prophets.* Chicago: Moody Press, 1968.

Geisler, Norman. *A Popular Survey of the Old Testament.* Grand Rapids: Baker Book House, 1977.

Habel, Norman C. *The Book of Job* (Cambridge Bible). New York: Cambridge University Press, 1975.

Hailey, Homer. *A Commentary on the Minor Prophets.* Grand Rapids: Baker Book House, 1972.

Haldeman, I.M. *The Tabernacle, Priesthood and Offerings.* New York: Revell, 1925.

Harper, Andrew, ed. *The Song of Solomon* (Cambridge Bible). Cambridge: The University Press, 1907.

Harrison, Roland K. *Introduction to the Old Testament.* Grand Rapids: Wm. B. Eerdmans Publishing Co., 1969.

_____. *Jeremiah and Lamentations.* (TOTC) London: The Tyndale Press, 1973.

Heidel, Alexander. *The Babylonian Genesis.* Chicago: The University of Chicago Press, 1963.

_____. *The Gilgamesh Epic and Old Testament Parallels.* Chicago: University of Chicago Press, 1946.

Heschel, Abraham J. *The Prophets.* New York: Harper and Row, 1962.

Hesser, Dale. *Job.* Austin: R.B. Sweet Co., Inc., 1965.

Horton, R.F. *The Book of Proverbs* (Expositor's Bible). New York: A.C. Armstrong and Son, 1891.

Hunt, Donald. *Pondering the Proverbs.* Joplin: College Press, 1974.

Hunt, I. *The World of the Patriarchs.* Englewood Cliffs: Prentice-Hall, Inc. 1968.

Jauncey, James. *Science Returns to God.* Grand Rapids: Zondervan Publishing House, 1968.

Jones, Edgar. *Proverbs and Ecclesiastes* (Torch). London: SCM Press, 1961.

Keil, Carl F. and Delitzsch, F. *The Twelve Minor Prophets,* Vol. I & Vol. 2. Grand Rapids: Wm. B. Eerdmans Publishing Co., 1961.

Keller, Werner. *The Bible as History.* New York: William Morrow & Co., 1961.

Kenyon, Kathleen M. *Archaeology in the Holy Land.* New York: Frederick A. Praeger, 1965.

Kidner, Derek. *Genesis.* (TOTC) London: Tyndale Press, 1971.

_____. *Proverbs.* (TOTC) London: Tyndale Press, 1968.

Kidwell, R.J. and DeWelt, Don. *Ecclesiastes and Song of Solomon.* Joplin, Missouri: College Press, 1977.

Kirkpatrick, A.F. *The Doctrine of the Prophets.* London: MacMillan and Co., Limited, 1927.

_____. *Psalms* (Cambridge Bible). Cambridge: University Press, 1921.

Knight, G.A.F. *Esther, Song of Songs, Lamentations.* London: SCM Press, 1955.

Kuntz, J. Kenneth. *The People of Ancient Israel: An Introduction to Old Testament Literature, History and Thought.* New York: Harper & Row, 1974.

Laetsch, Theo. *Jeremiah* (Bible Commentary). St. Louis: Concordia, 1965.

Lange, J.P. and Peter, John. *Proverbs-Song of Solomon* (Commentary on the Holy Scriptures). Grand Rapids: Zondervan Publishing House, n.d.

Lewis, Jack, *Minor Prophets.* Austin: R.B. Sweet., 1966. (also Baker)

Lockyer, Herbert. *All the Doctrines of the Bible.* Grand Rapids: Zondervan Publishing House, 1964.

MacBeath, Andrew. *The Book of Job* (Shield). Grand Rapids: Baker Book House, 1966.

Maclear, G.F. *A Classbook of Old Testament History.* Grand Rapids: Wm. B. Eerdmans Publishing Co., 1964.

Merrill, Eugene H. *An Historical Survey of the Old Testament.* Nutley: The Craig Press, 1966.

Meyer, F.B. *Joseph, Beloved - Hated - Exalted.* Grand Rapids: Zondervan Publishing House, 1955.

Montgomery, John W. *The Quest for Noah's Ark.* Minneapolis: Bethany Fellowship, Inc., 1972.

Morris, Henry M. *The Bible and Modern Science.* Chicago: Moody, 1968.

Mould, Elmer W.K. *Essentials of Bible History.* New York: The Ronald Press Co., 1951.

Nutt, J.W. *Proverbs* (Ellicott's Commentary on the Whole Bible, Vol. IV). Grand Rapids: Zondervan Publishing House, n.d.

Orr, James, ed. *The International Standard Bible Encyclopedia.* Grand Rapids: Wm. B. Eerdmans Publishing Co., 1939.

Palmer, Edwin H., ed. *The Encyclopedia of Christianity.* Wilmington, Delaware: The National Foundation for Christian Education, 1964.

Parrot, Andre'. *Abraham and His Times.* Trans. by James H. Farley. Philadelphia: Fortress Press, 1962.

Payne. D.F. *Genesis and Exodus.* Scripture Union Bible Study Books. Grand Rapids: Wm. B. Eerdmans, 1965.

Payne, J. Barton. *Theology of the Older Testament.* Grand Rapids: Zondervan Publishing House, 1962.

Pfeiffer, Charles F.,ed. *The Biblical World.* Grand Rapids: Baker Book House, 1966.

_____. *Old Testament History.* Grand Rapids: Baker Book House, 1973.

_____. Charles F. and Harrison, Everett F., ed. *The Wycliffe Bible Commentary.* Chicago Moody Press, 1975.

_____. Charles F., Vos, Howard F. and Rea, John ed. *Wycliffe Bible Encyclopedia.* Chicago: Moody Press, 1975.

Pope, Marvin H. *Song of Songs* (Anchor Bible). Garden City: Doubleday & Co., Inc., 1977.

Pritchard, James B., ed. *Ancient Near Eastern Texts.* Princeton: Princeton University Press, 1969.

Purkiser, W.T., ed. *Exploring the Old Testament.* Kansas City: Beacon Hill Press, 1955.

Rhewinkel, A.M. *The Flood.* St. Louis: Concordia Publishing House, 1951.

Rhodes, Arnold B. *Psalms* (Layman's Bible Commentary) Vol. 9. Atlanta: John Knox Press, 1974.

Rimmer, Harry. *Harmony of Science and Scripture*. Grand Rapids: Baker Book House, 1950.

Ringinberg, Loyal R. *The Word of God in History*. Butler: The Higley Press, 1953.

Robinson, G.L. *The Book of Isaiah*. Grand Rapids: Baker Book House, 1954.

_____. *The Twelve Minor Prophets*. Grand Rapids: Baker Book House, 1953.

Robinson, T.H. *Prophecy and the Prophets in Ancient Israel*. London: Gerald Duckworth & Co., Ltd., 1923.

Rowley, H.H. *Job* (New Century Bible). London: Oliphants, 1970.

Rylaarsdam, J.C. *Proverbs to Song of Solomon* (Layman's Bible Commentary). London: SCM Press, Ltd., 1964.

Schaeffer, Francis A. *Genesis in Space and Time*. Downers Grove: Inter-Varsity Press, 1972.

Sellin, Ernst and Fohrer, George. *Introduction to the Old Testament*, Trans. David E. Green. New York: Abingdon Press, 1968.

Schultz, S.J. *The Old Testament Speaks*. New York: Harper and Row, 1960.

Scott, R.B.Y. *Proverbs and Ecclesiastes* (Anchor Bible). Garden City: Doubleday and Co. 1965.

_____. *The Relevance of the Prophets*. New York: The Macmillan Company, 1945.

Sears, Jack Wood. *Conflict and Harmony in Science and the Bible*. Grand Rapids: Baker Book House, 1969.

Smith, Ralph L. *Job - Study in Providence and Faith*. Nashville: Convention Press, 1971.

Smith, Wm. *Bible Dictionary*. Philadelphia: John C. Winston Co., 1884.

Suetonius, Gaius. *The Twelve Caesars*, Trans. Robert Graves. Harmondsworth: Penguin Books, 1957.

Tate, Marvin E., Jr. *Commentary on Proverbs* The Broadman Bible Commentary, Vol. 5. Nashville: Broadman Press, 1971.

Taylor, John B. *Ezekiel - An Introduction and Commentary* (TOTC). London: Tyndale Press, 1969.

Taylor, William. *David, King of Israel*. Grand Rapids: Baker Book House, 1961.

_____. *Moses the Law Giver*. Grand Rapids: Baker Book House, 1961.

Tenney, Merrill C., ed. *Zondervan Pictorial Bible Dictionary*. Grand Rapids: Zondervan Publishing House, 1963.

_____. *The Zondervan Pictorial Encyclopedia of the Bible*. Grand Rapids: Zondervan Publishing House, 1975.

Thiele, Edwin R. *The Mysterious Numbers of the Hebrew Kings*. Grand Rapids: Wm. B. Eerdmans Co., 1965.

Thompson, J.A. *Archaeology and the Old Testament*. Grand Rapids: Wm. B. Eerdmans Co., 1959.

Tribble, H.W. *Old Testament Biographies*. Nashville: Broadman Press, 1939.

Unger, Merrill. F. *Archaeology and the Old Testament.* Grand Rapids: Zondervan Publishing House, 1954.

_____. *Introductory Guide to the Old Testament.* Grand Rapids: Zondervan Publishing House, 1956.

Vos, Geerhardus. *Biblical Theology, Old and New Testaments.* Grand Rapids: Wm. B. Eerdmans Publishing Co., 1948.

Watt, John. *Two Neglected Books - Ruth and the Song of Solomon.* New York: Loizeaux Brothers, n.d.

Watts, John D.W. *Obadiah.* Grand Rapids: W. B. Erdmans, 1969.

Whitcomb, John C. and Morris, Henry M. *The Genesis Flood.* Philadelphia: The Presbyterian and Reformed Publishing Co., 1961.

Whybray, R.N. *The Book of Proverbs.* (The Cambridge Bible Commentary). Cambridge: University Press, 1972.

Willis, John T. *My Servants, The Prophets.* Vol. I - III The Way of Life Series, No. 116. Abilene, Texas: Biblical Research Press, 1971.

Winter, W.W. *Studies in Joshua, Judges, and Ruth.* Joplin: College Press, 1969.

Wolf, Earl C. *Proverbs* (Beacon Bible Commentary). Vol. III Kansas City: Beacon Hill Press, 1967.

Wood, Leon. *A Survey of Israel's History.* Grand Rapids, Michigan: Zondervan Publishing House, 1970.

Wright, G. Ernest. *Biblical Archaeology.* Philadelphia: The Westminster Press, 1966.

Yoder, Sanford C. *Poetry of the Old Testament.* Scottsdale: Herald Press, 1948.

Young, E.J. *Genesis 3.* London: The Banner of Truth Trust, 1966.

_____. *The Prophecy of Daniel.* Grand Rapids: Wm. B. Eerdmans, 1949.

_____. *Introduction to the Old Testament.* Grand Rapids, Wm. B. Eerdmans, 1949.

The Divided Kingdom
An Analytical Outline

The Two Kingdoms 931-722 B.C.

JUDAH *(Southern Kingdom)*	**ISRAEL** *(Northern Kingdom)*
Tenth Century B.C.	**Tenth Century B.C.**

Rehoboam 931-913 B.C.
I Kings 14:21-31; II Chronicles 10-12

   a. son of Solomon
   b. reigned 17 years (began at age 41)
   c. "did evil in the sight of the lord"
   d. Shishak, king of Egypt, looted Temple
   e. at war with Jeroboam

Jeroboam 931-910 B.C.
I Kings 12:2-14:20

   a. soldier under Solomon
   b. unified the Northern ten tribes
   c. set up calf worship at Dan, Bethel
   d. established first of nine dynasties
   e. became a symbol of evil in Israel

Abijah 913-910 B.C.
I Kings 15:1-8; II Chronicles 13

   a. son of Rehoboam
   b. reigned three years
   c. won a few cities for Judah from Israel

Nadab 910-909 B.C.
I Kings 15:25-32

   a. son of Jeroboam
   b. reigned two years
   c. evil, assassinated by Baasha

Asa 910-869 B.C.
I Kings 15:9-15; II Chronicles 14-16

   a. son of Abijah
   b. reigned 41 years
   c. basically a good king
   d. however hired Behhadad of Syria to attack Israel, reproved by the prophet Hanani
   e. rid the country of sodomy, but left the "high places" (cult centers)

Baasha 909-886 B.C.
I Kings 15:33-16:1

   a. reigned 24 years
   b. killed all the house of Jeroboam and set up the second dynasty in the North
   c. evil, Jehu the prophet announced the end of his family because of his sin

Ninth Century B.C.   Ninth Century B.C.

Jehoshaphat 872-848 B.C.
I Kings 22:41-51; II Chronicles 17-20

   a. son of Asa
   b. reigned 25 years

Elah 886-885 B.C.
I Kings 16:8-10

   a. son of Baasha
   b. reigned two years

JUDAH - (Cont.)

c. reversed policy of Asa, made an alliance with Israel (King Ahab)
d. Jehu spoke against this pact
e. on the whole he was a good king

ISRAEL - (Cont.)

c. a drunkard, slain while drunk by Zimri
d. last king of the second dynasty

Zimri 885 B.C.
I Kings 16:11-22

a. reigned 7 days, shortest reign, dynasty
b. rejected by the people, he set fire to the king's house and died in the fire
c. only member of the third dynasty

Omri 885-874 B.C.
I Kings 16:23-28

a. reigned twelve years
b. he was the people's choice, began the fourth dynasty
c. moved the capital from Tirzah to Samaria
d. worse than his predecessors

Ahab 874-853 B.C.
I Kings 16:29-22:40

a. son of Omri
b. reigned 22 years
c. married Jezebel, daughter of Ethbaal, king of Sidon
d. encouraged Baal worship with the help of his wife
e. Elijah, the prophet, defeated the prophets of Baal in a contest on Mt. Carmel
f. Ahab stole the vineyard of Naboth
g. the king died in a battle with the Syrians according to Micaiah's prophecy

Jehoram (Joram) 848-841 B.C.
II Kings 8:16-24; II Chronicles 21

a. son of Jehoshaphat
b. reigned 8 years
c. married Athaliah, daughter of Ahab and Jezebel
d. openly practiced idolatry
e. when he died, he was not buried with the kings of Judah

Ahaziah Ahaziah 853-852 B.C.
I Kings 22:51-53; II Kings 1:1-18

a. son of Ahab and Jezebel
b. reigned two years
c. served the Baals, a wicked king
d. attempted to capture Elijah, the prophet

JUDAH - (Cont.)

Ahaziah 841 B.C.
II Kings 8:25-29; II Chronicles 22:1-9

a. son of Jehoram of Judah
b. reigned one year
c. followed his father's policies
d. carried on war with Syria
e. slain by Jehu at Jezreel

Athaliah 841-835 B.C.
II Kings 11:1-21; II Chronicles 22:10-23:21

a. only woman to rule; not really a queen, but usurper of the throne
b. reigned 6 years
c. daughter of Ahab and Jezebel
d. killed all the royal family except Joash

Joash (Jehoash) 835-796 B.C.
II Kings 12:1-21; II Chronicles 24

a. son of Ahaziah
b. reigned 40 years
c. became king at 7 years of age
d. Jehoida the priest was the power behind the throne
e. after Jehoida died, Joash lost his religious fervor
f. Judah attacked by Hazael of Syria
g. assassinated by two of his servants

Eighth Century B.C.

Amaziah 796-767 B.C.
II Kings 14:1-22; II Chronicles 25

a. son of Joash
b. reigned 29 years
c. permitted the high places to remain
d. killed those who assassinated his father
e. his reign was reasonably stable
f. assassinated, but buried in Jerusalem

ISRAEL - (Cont.)

Jehoram 852-841 B.C.
II Kings 3:1-8:15

a. son of Ahab and Jezebel
b. reigned twelve years
c. evil, but he did remove the Baals
d. last king of the fourth (Omri) dynasty
e. during his reign Elisha performed many notable miracles

Jehu 841-814 B.C.
II Kings 9:1-10:36

a. established the fifth dynasty in Israel
b. reigned 28 years
c. anointed by Elisha and commissioned to destroy the house of Ahab
d. he removed the Baals, but mostly for political reasons

Jehoahaz 814-798 B.C.
II Kings 13:1-9

a. son of Jehu
b. reigned 17 years
c. followed the "sins of Jeroboam"
d. God sent Syria to afflict Israel

Eighth Century B.C.

Joash (Jehoash) 798-782 B.C.
II Kings 13:10-25

a. son of Jehoahaz
b. reigned 16 years
c. evil as Jeroboam
d. retrieved many of the cities of Israel held by Syria
e. co-regent with Jeroboam II during most of his reign (i.e. 793-782)
f. raided and sacked Jerusalem

JUDAH - (Cont.)

Uzziah (Azariah) 790-739 B.C.
II Kings 15:1-7; II Chronicles 26

a. son of Amaziah
b. reigned 52 years
c. became king at age 16
d. served Yahweh, but left high places
e. in his pride presumed to be a priest smitten with leprosy
f. co-regent with his son Jotham 751-739 and grandson Ahaz 743-739

Jotham 751-736 B.C.
II Kings 15:32-38; II Chronicles 27

a. son of Uzziah
b. reigned 16 years
c. he did little to raise the moral and religious level of the nation

ISRAEL - (Cont.)

Jeroboam II 793-753 B.C.
II Kings 14:23-29

a. son of Joash of Israel
b. reigned 41 years
c. followed the sins of Jeroboam I
d. much of the Northern coast of Israel restored during his reign
e. a reign of general prosperity
f. prophets during the time of Jeroboam were: Jonah, Amos, Hosea

Zechariah 753 B.C.
II Kings 15:8-12

a. son of Jeroboam II
b. reigned only 6 months
c. assassinated by Shallum; his death terminated the fifth (Jehu) dynasty

Shallum 752 B.C.
II Kings 15:13-15

a. reigned only 1 month
b. gained power by assassination; set up sixth dynasty - lasted only one month
c. assassinated by Menahem

Menahem 752-743 B.C.
II Kings 15:16-20

a. reigned 10 years
b. founded seventh dynasty in Israel; evil like Jeroboam
c. during his reign Israel conquered by Assyria; became a vassal of Assyria; Israel paid tribute to Tiglath-pileser (Pul)

Pekahiah 742-740 B.C.
II Kings 15:23-26

a. son of Menahem
b. reigned 2 years
c. assassinated by Pekah ending seventh dynasty

JUDAH - (Cont.)

Ahaz 743-728 B.C.
II Kings 16:1-20; II Chronicles 28

a. son of Jotham
b. reigned 16 years
c. wicked; followed the kings of Israel and offered his son as a sacrifice
d. built pagan (Damascan) altar
e. made an alliance with Assyria against directive of God's prophet Isaiah
f. died at age 36, a bad king

Hezekiah 728-696 B.C.
(co-regent 728-725) *II Kings 18:1-20:24; II Chronicles 29-32*

a. son of Ahaz
b. reigned 29 years
c. one of the best kings in Judah
  1. did away with idolatry
  2. repaired the temple
  3. reinstituted the law of Moses
  4. reaffirmed the Passover
  5. refortified Jerusalem
d. Isaiah and Micah were prophets
e. the city of Jerusalem was surrounded by Sennacherib in 701 but was spared by the intervention of God

ISRAEL - (Cont.)

Pekah 752-732 B.C.
II Kings 15:27-31

a. reigned for 20 years
b. only member of the eighth dynasty
c. co-regent with Menahem and Pekahiah
d. during his reign Assyrian conquest continued - captives taken to Assyria by Tiglath-pileser
e. assassinated by Hoshea

Hoshea 732-722 B.C.
II Kings 17:1-41

a. reigned nine years
b. only member of the ninth and last dynasty of Israel (North Kingdom)
c. Shalmanezer made Hoshea his servant; the king plotted against him and the Assyrians captured and destroyed Samaria in 722 B.C. under Sargon
d. the Kingdom of Israel came to an end
e. the ten northern tribes were deported and relocated by the Assyrians
f. the mixed population that resulted became the Samaritans

Seventh Century B.C.

JUDAH ONLY 722-586

Manasseh 696-641 B.C.
II Kings 21:1-18; II Chronicles 33:1-20

a. son of Hezekiah
b. reigned 55 years
c. very wicked, restored idolatry especially the Baals
d. in his later years he repented - see II Chronicles 33:14-20

722 B.C. End of the Northern Kingdom

JUDAH - (Cont.)

Amon 641-640 B.C.
II Kings 21:19-26; II Chronicles 33:21-25

a. son of Manasseh, reigned two years
b. did evil as his father
c. assassinated by his servants
d. people executed the assassins, made Amon's son, Josiah, king

Josiah 639-609 B.C.
II Kings 22:1-23:30; II Chronicles 34,35

a. became king at eight years of age
b. reigned 31 years
c. many reforms began in 621 B.C.
   1. repaired the Temple
   2. reaffirmed the Mosiac Law
   3. cleansed the land of idolatrous and pagan altars (even in the north)
d. one of the best kings in Judah
e. influenced by the prophets Zephaniah, Jeremiah and the priest Hilkiah; other prophets--Habakkuk Nahum
f. slain in the Battle of Megiddo against Pharoah Necho and the Egyptians

Jehoahaz 608 B.C.
II Kings 23:31-34; II Chronicles 36:1-4

a. son of Josiah
b. reigned three months
c. taken captive to Egypt by Necho

Jehoiakim (Eliakim) 608-597 B.C.
II Kings 23:34-24:6; II Chronicles 36:5-8

a. son of Josiah
b. reigned 11 years
c. placed on the throne by Pharaoh Necho
d. after three years he became the servant of Nebuchadnezzar of Babylon
e. refused to accept the guidance of the prophet Jeremiah
f. first captivity of Judah 605

JUDAH - (Cont.)

Sixth Century B.C.

Jehoiachin 597 B.C.
II Kings 24:8-17; II Chronicles 36:9-10
a. son of Jehoiakim
b. reigned 3 months
c. Nebuchadnezzar sieged Jerusalem in 597 took Jehoiachin and others, including Ezekiel, captive

Zedekiah 597-586 B.C.
II Kings 24:18-25:7; II Chronicles 36: 11-21
a. son of Josiah
b. reigned 11 years
c. last king of Judah
d. vacillating, refused to listen to the advice of the prophet Jeremiah
e. attempted to resist Babylon, this brought on the final siege and destruction of Jerusalem, including the Temple
f. the city of Jerusalem fell in 586 B.
f. the city of Jerusalem fell in 586 B.C. and the king and the leaders of the nation were taken captive to Babylon

Babylonian Exile 586-516 B.C.

Weights, Measures, and Coins in Ancient Times*

Weights

Name	Country	Class	National	U.S. or Brit.	Metric
talent	Hebr.	av.	30 maneh	110.57 lb.	50.15 kg.
talent	Gr.	tr.	60 mina	60.00 lb	27.21 kg.
maneh[1]	Hebr.	av.	100 shekels	3.68 lb.	1.67 kg.
mina	Gr.	tr.	1/60 talent	1.00 lb.	.37 kg.
shekel	Hebr.	av.	1/60 mina	258.00 gr.	16.72 g.
bekah	Hebr.	av.	8 ½ gerah	109.65 gr.	7.09 g.
gerah	Hebr.	av.	1/20 shekel	112.90 gr.	.84 g.

Money[2]

- **stater:** A standard gold coin of ancient Greece. The later silver stater was the Athenian tetradrachm containing four silver drachmae.
- **didrachm:** A greek silver coin equal to two drachmae or one-half shekel.
- **denarius:** A Roman silver or copper coin ($0.17 in U.S. money) worth ten asses.
- **as:** A Roman copper coin ($0.1 to $0.1½ in U.S. money).
- **quadrans:** A Roman coin equal to one quarter as.
- **talent:** A Hebrew coin of gold or silver. The talent contained 60 minas of 50 (or 60) shekels each. Its estimated value varied greatly in ancient times. The gold talent is valued at $32,645; the silver talent at $2,176.
- **maneh:** A Hebrew maneh has been estimated at $50. to $60. in silver.
- **shekel:** A Hebrew gold shekel has been estimated at $10.88. There were also silver shekels as well as bronze half-shekels and quarter-shekels. A silver shekel has been valued as $.50 to $.60. The first actual Jewish coins date back to the time of Simon Maccabaeus. Coins of other Maccabaean rulers have also been found. The coins of Herod and his successors have Greek inscriptions; the Romans only permitted copper coins to be minted. Later, after the introduction of minted money, we find mention of the Persian daric.

Measures

Length

cubit	1.45 ft.	
span	1/2 cubit	9 in.
handbreadth[3] (palmys)	2/9 cubit	4 in
finger	1/4 of 2/9 cubit	1 in.

Area

- **yoke:** The area of land that could be plowed in one day with a yoke of oxen. Usually rendered "acre" (cf. I Sam. 14:14).

---

*The equivalent in U.S. values are to be understood as merely approximate.

[1] In later times the maneh became 50 shekels, so that the maneh and talent were re-reduced in weight.

[2] In the earliest times money was weighed.

[3] Originally, the extreme space over which the hand could be expanded from the end of the thumb to that of the little finger.

Note--In an avoirdupois ounce there are 437.5 grains.

The Common Shekel

Comparative Value

Name	Value	Today
talent	60 manehs	75.5 lb.s
maneh	50 shekels	20 oz.
shekel	2 bekah's	.4 oz.
bekah	10 gerahs	88 gr.
gerah		9 gr.

Capacity, Dry

homer or kor	10 ephah	45 pk.
lalek	1/2 homer	22½ pk.
ephah	1/10 kor	4½ pk.
seah	1/3 ephah	11 qt.
kab	1/6 seah	2 qt.
log	1/4 kab	1 pt.

Capacity, Liquid

kor		90 gal.
bath	1/10 kor	9 gal
hin	1/6 bath	6 qt.
kab	1/3 hin	22 qt.
log	1/4 kab	1 pt.

Measures in the New Testament

bath	9 gal.
kor	90 gal.
16 sextarii (measure of corn)	8 liquid qt.
2 sextarii (small measure?)	1 qt.
metretes	8 2/3 gal.
stadium 625 Roman ft.	600 U.S. ft.
milarium (Roman mile = 8 stadia)	1600 U.S. y.
Sabbath-day's journey	5 furlongs.
measure (Luke 13:21)	13.9 liquid qt.
pound (John 12:3)	1/4 liquid qt.

Abbreviations

av.	avoirdupois	oz.		ounce, ounces	
f.	foot, feet	pk.		peck, pecks	
g.	gram, grams	pt.		pint, pints	
gal.	gallon, gallons	qt.		quart, quarts	
gr.	grain, grains	tr.		troy	
in.	inch, inches	y.		yard, yards	
kg.	kilogram				

Some Biblical Measures

Liquid

Hebrew term	equals	US liquid measures
log		2/3 pint
hin	12 logs	1 gal.
bath	6 hins	6 gal.
kor	10 baths	60 gal.

Dry

Hebrew term	equals	US dry measures
kab		2+ pints
homer	1 4/5 kabs	4 pints
seah	3 1/3 homers	1/5 bushel
ephah	3 seahs	3/5 bushel
homer	10 ephahs 100 homers	6 1/4 bushels

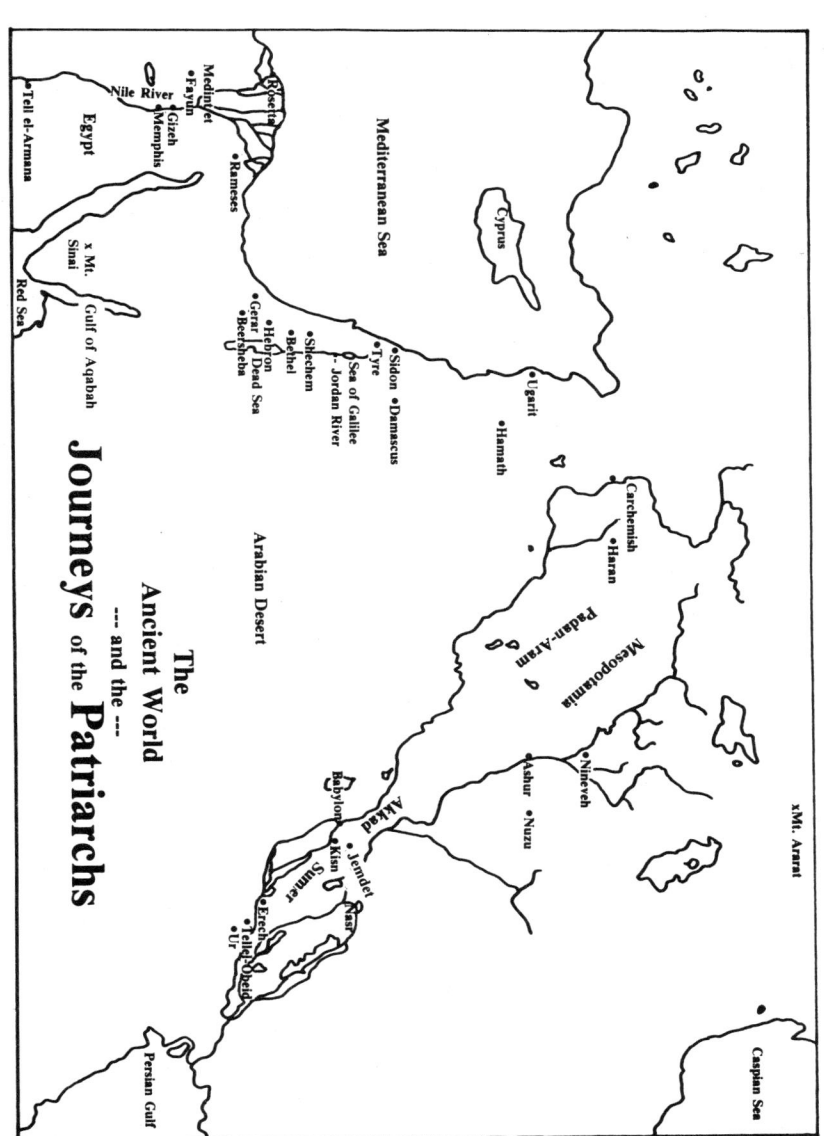

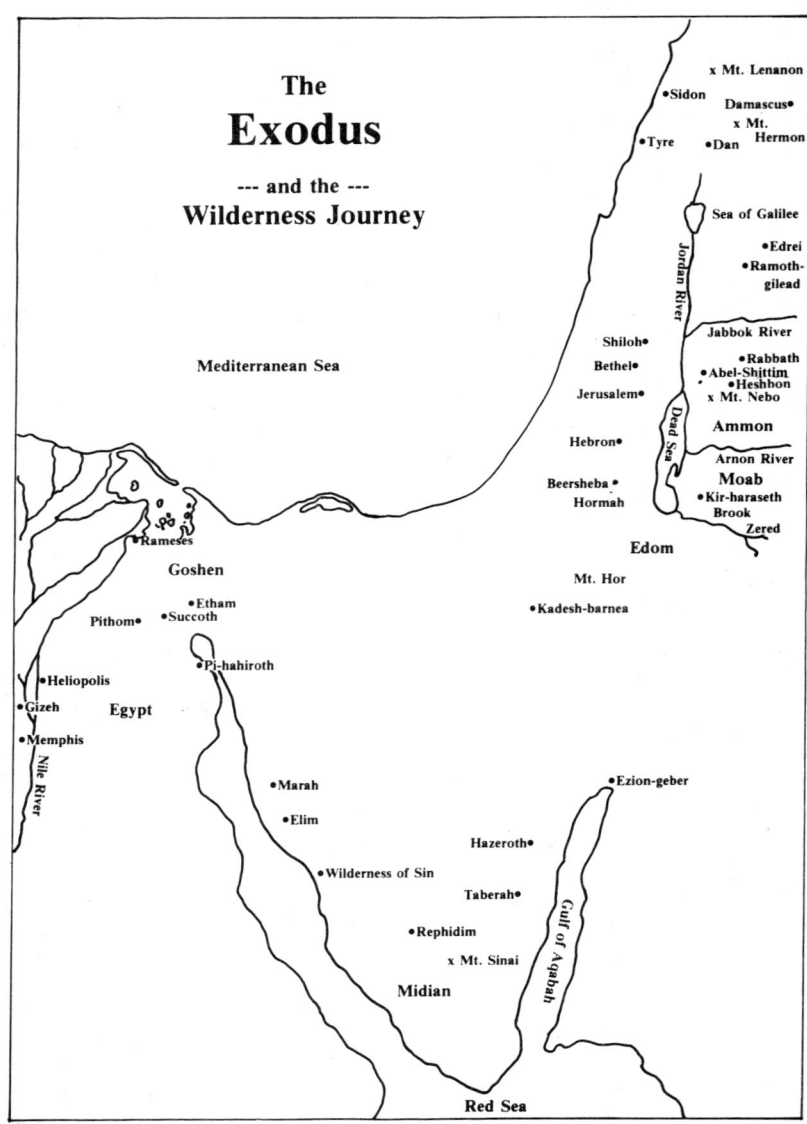

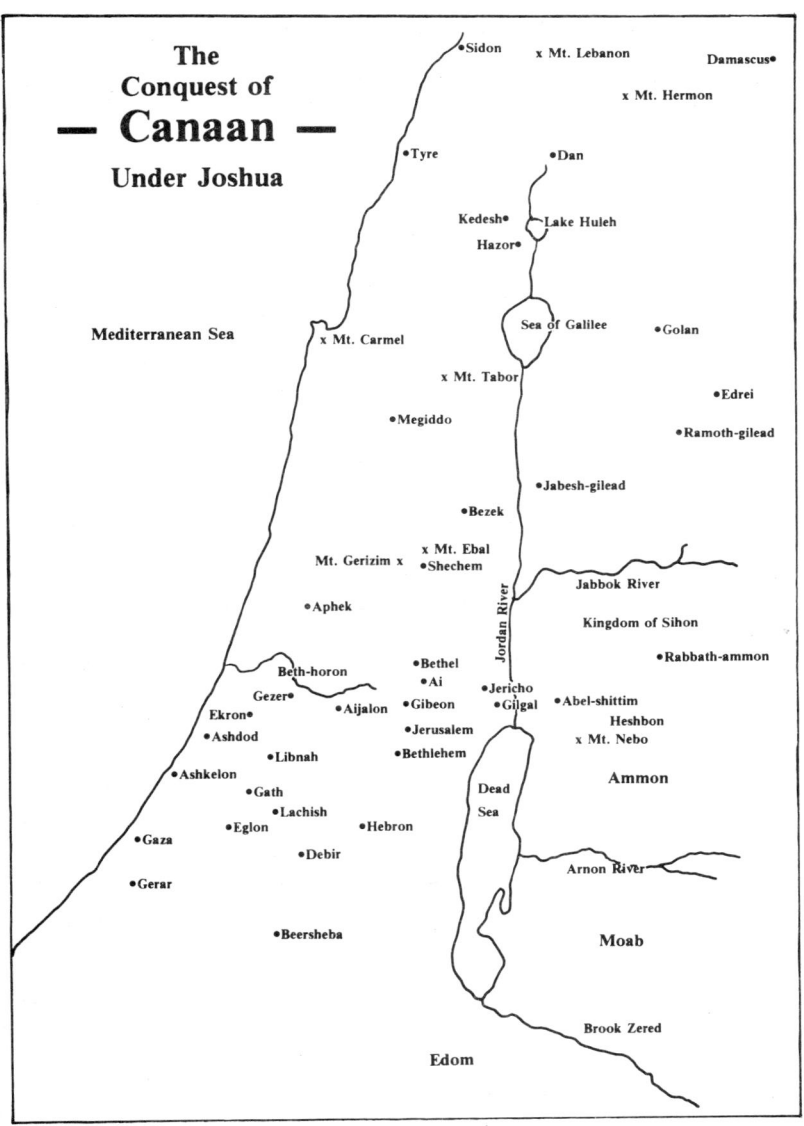

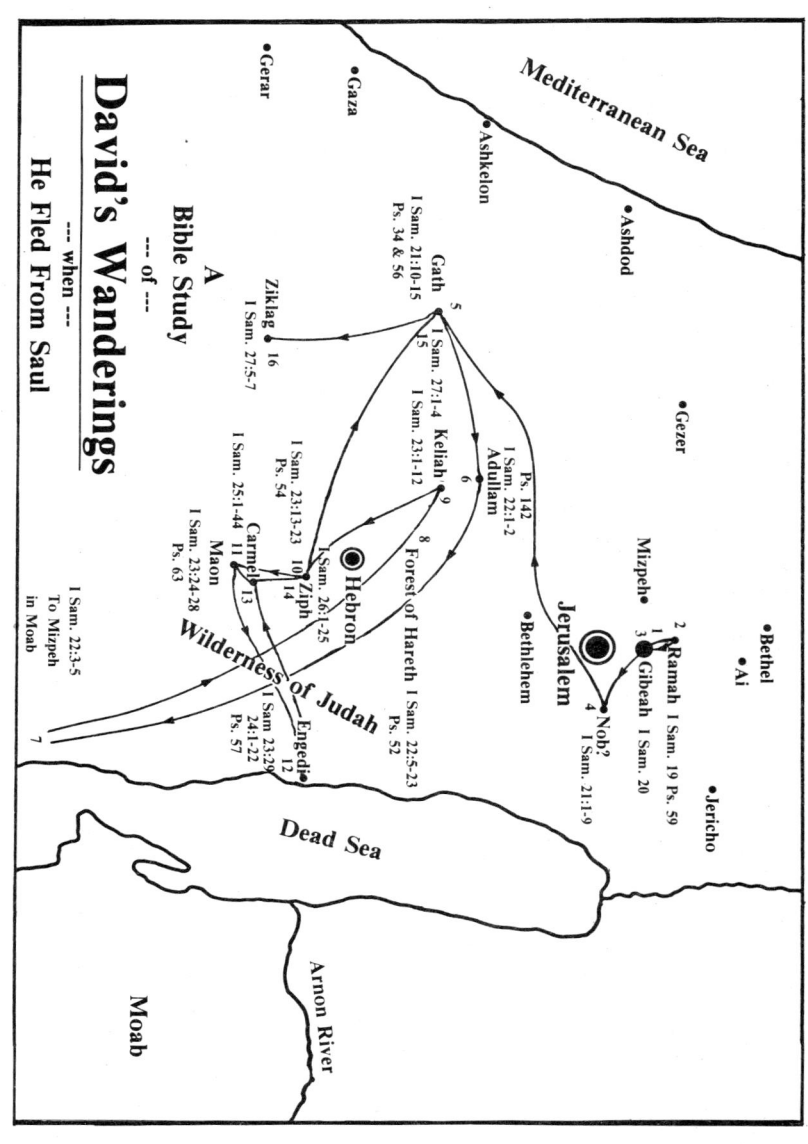

Subject Index

Aaron 44-45, 53-54, 61-63, 193
Abdon 82
Abednego 180
Abel 11-12, 55
Abiathar 85, 91, 99, 102-103
Abigail 91
Abijah 117
Abimelech 22-23, 81
Abinadab 87, 96
Abner 95, 103
Abraham 13, 21-26, 30, 41, 98, 124, 126, 201, 212
Abram 24
Absalom 98-100, 104
Achan 69-70
Achish 91
Acrostic poems 222, 226
Adad Nirari III 131
Adam 5, 8-13, 15
Adullam, Cave of 91
Adonijah 102-104
Adonizedek 70-71
Agag 90
Agagite 196
Agur 210, 212
Ahab 113-115, 117, 127-129, 141
Ahasuerus 195-196
Ahaz 118, 139, 147, 151, 155-156
Ahaziah 114, 117
Ahijah 112, 124
Ahithophel 99
Ai 69-70
Alexander the Great 180-181
Amalekites 49, 80, 89-90
Amarna Letters 47
Amaziah 118, 147
Amen-em-opet 212
Amenhotep II 47
Amnon 98
Anthropomorphic 5
Antithetic Parallelism 199-201
Antiochus (see Epiphanes)
Apocalyptic Literature 179
Apocrypha 209

Araunah 100
Aramaic 177, 180, 192
Ark of the Covenant 53, 63, 87-88, 96, 106
Ararat 16
Artaxerxes 191, 193-194
Asa 116-117
Asaph 221, 224-225
Asenath 38
Ashdod 87
Asher 30, 61, 72, 79
Asherah 127
Ashteroth 113, 141
Ashurbanipal 161
Assurdan III 131
Assyria 71, 113, 115-117, 119, 123, 131, 139, 148-149, 152-153, 155-156, 159-162
Athaliah 117
Awel-Marduk 180
Azazel 58
Azariah (see Uzziah)
Baal 72, 76-78, 80-81, 113-117, 119, 127-128, 133, 137-139, 141-142, 156, 167
Baal-zebub 114
Baasha 112
Baba Bathra 85
Babel, Tower of 19
Babylon 17, 71, 120, 123, 152, 164, 166, 160-170, 173-175, 176-181, 184, 191-192, 227
Babylonians 17, 152, 154, 161-166, 170, 177-181, 191, 216
Babylonian Exile 149, 154, 156, 167, 178, 181
Balaam 66
Balak 66
Barak 78-79
Baruch 166, 201
Barzillai 103
Bathsheba 97-98, 102
Beeri 139
Beersheba 28, 138

Bel and the Dragon 163
Belshazzar 152, 178, 180
Beltehazzar 177
Benaiah 102
Benhadad 114-115, 117
Benjamin 30, 32, 38-39, 61, 83, 88
Berechiah 186
Bethel 23, 30, 32, 55, 70, 112, 135, 138-139
Bezer 73
Bildad 203-205
Bilhah 30
Black Obelisk 115
Blood Offering 56
Boaz 83
Bronze serpent 63, 156
Burnt offering 56, 65
Buzi 174
Cain 11-12, 15, 55
Caleb 62, 66, 72
Calf Worship 112
Camp arrangement 61-62
Canaan 21, 32-33, 60-64, 66, 68-69, 71-72, 76
Canaanite 19, 21-22
Capernaum 161
Carchemish, Battle of 164, 166
Census of Israel 61
Chebar 174
Chemosh 108
Chronicles 102, 119, 192
Cities of Refuge 72-73
Clean and Unclean Animals 55, 57
Covenant 21-22, 24-26, 52, 54, 64-65, 73, 107
Covenant Renewal 64-65, 73
Creation 1-6
Crossing of Jordan 68
Cushan-rishathaim 78
Cyrus 178-181, 184, 191-192
Dagon 87
Damascus 118, 123, 136, 140, 148
Dan 30, 86, 112
Daniel 120, 177
Danites 83
Darius 178, 185-186
David, 85, 90-92, 94-100, 102-103 105-106, 108, 111-112, 165, 216, 221 ff
Davidic hymns 221 ff
Day of Atonement 58, 60, 65
Day Star 152
Day of Yahweh 130-131, 138
Days of Creation 1-5
Dead Sea Scrolls 149
Death-Bed Blessing 29
Deborah 78-79, 124
Decalogue 52
Delilah 82
Deuteronomy, Book of 65-66, 119
Dinah 32
Divided Kingdom 108, 111-120
Documentary Hypothesis v
Doeg, the Edomite 91
Dothan 35
Ebed-Melech 166
Ebenezer, Battle of 87-88
Ecclesiastes 215-217
Ecclesiasticus 209
Eden 9
Edom 63, 136-137, 152, 170, 173
Edomites 91, 96, 136
Eglon 78
Egypt 35-41, 43, 45-49, 54-55, 120 123, 137, 142, 144, 148, 152-153, 165-166, 170
Ehud 78
El 4
Elah 112
Eldad 124
Eleazar 63
Eli 85-87
Eliab 90
Eliezer 21
Elihu 201, 206
Elijah 13, 113-114, 124, 127-129, 141
"Elijah" (Malachi) 189
Eliakim (see Jehoiakim)
Elim 49
Eliphaz 203-205
Elisha 114, 124, 128-129, 141, 163
Elkanan 85
Elkosh 161
Elkush 161
Elohim 4
Elon 82

Embalming 41
Endor 92
End Time 151, 181
Engedi 91
Enoch 13, 15, 124, 128
Enrogel 102
Enuma Elish 6
Ephod 57
Ephraim 38, 41, 77, 81, 144
Epiphanes, Antiochus 181
Esau 26, 28-29, 32, 123, 136
Esther 195-196
Etham 48
Ethbaal 113
Ethiopia 152, 160
Euphrates 18, 22
Eve 5, 8-12
Exile 129, 184, 192
Exodus, Book of 43-49
Exodus, the 43-49, 167
Ezekiel 120, 124, 174-177
Eziongeber 107
Ezra 191-193
Feast of Purim 195-196
Feast of Tabernacles 106, 194
Feast of Trumpets 65
Flood (Deluge) 13, 15-18
Gad 30, 68, 73, 124
Galilee 107, 148
Gath 90
Gaza 136
Gedaliah 165, 170
Genesis, Book of 1-41
Gershonites 61
Gibeah 83
Gibeonites 70
Gideon 79-81
Gihon 103
Gilead 31, 81, 136
Gilgal 69, 71, 87, 135, 138
Gilgamesh Epic 17-18
Gittite 96-99
Golan 73
Golden Calf 54-55
Goliah 90-91
Gomer 142-143
Gomorrah 23-24, 150
Goshen 33, 40, 43
Greece 179-180

Greek 130, 181, 195-196, 215-216
Gubaru the Mede 181
Guilt Offerings 56
Habakkuk 119-120, 163-165
Habiru 47
Hadassah 196
Hagar 21, 23, 31
Haggai 184-185
Haggith 102
Ham 18-19
Haman 196
Hanani 117, 193
Hannah 85
Haran 29
Hataavah 62
Hazael 115, 118
Hazeroth 62
Hazor 71
Hebrew 147, 177-178, 181, 195, 199, 210, 212, 215, 221
Hebrew Bible 179, 192-193, 195
Hebrew Poetry 199-201, 221 ff
Hebron 24, 72-73, 95, 99
Hecka 45
Hellenistic 179
Hellenize 181
Herem 69
Herodotus 119, 149, 153
Hezekiah 106, 118-119, 147-148, 151-153, 156-157, 159, 210, 212
Hilkiah 119, 165
Hiram 105, 107, 148
Hittite 21, 26
Holy of Holies 53, 105-106
Holy Land 177, 191
Holy Place 53, 105-106
Hophni 87
Hormah 62
Hosea 118, 124, 139-144
Hoshea 116, 148
Hurrian (see Nuzi) 23, 28, 31
Hushai 99
Hyksos 40
Ibzan 82
Ichabod 87
Ikhnaton 131
"Image of god" 3-4
Immanuel 151
Imprecatory Psalms 222-223

Iraq 161
Isaac 21, 24-26, 28-30, 32, 41
Isaiah 118-119, 124, 139, 147-154
Ish-bosheth 95
Ishmael 21, 24-25, 212
Ishamelites 35-36
Israel 29, 30, 32-38, 44-49, 52-58, 60-66, 69-74, 76-83, 86-89, 95-96, 98-100, 102-103, 107-108, 111, 113-118, 123-129, 131-133, 135-144, 148-154, 157, 159, 161, 167, 169, 173, 175-177, 179, 181 186-188, 192, 218
Ittai 99
Jabesh-gilead 88
Jabin 71, 78
Jacob 28-33, 35, 38-41, 47, 98, 126
Jael 79
Jair 81
Japheth 18-19
Jashar, Book of 95
Jebus 95
Jebusites 76
Jehoash (see Joash)
Jehoahaz (Shallum) 115, 119, 165-166
Jehoiachin 120, 166, 169, 174
Johoiada 117, 130
Jehoiakim 120, 163, 166-167, 169, 177-178
Jehoram 114, 117-118, 129, 173
Jehoshaphat 114, 117
Jehosheba 117
Jehovah 44
Jehu 114-115, 117, 129, 140, 143
Jephthah 81-82
Jeremiah 119-120, 124, 165-170
Jericho 68-70, 129
Jeroboam I 108, 112-113, 116
Jeroboam II 115, 131, 135-136, 139-140, 148
Jerubbaal (see Gideon) 80
Jerusalem 95, 98, 103, 105, 108, 111-113, 129, 135, 147-149, 153-154, 159, 163-166, 168-170, 173-177, 180-182, 184, 187-188, 191-194, 216, 224
Jesse 90, 94

Jesus 139, 178, 189, 195, 204
Jethro 44, 49
Jezebel 113-114, 117, 127-128, 141
Jezreel 114, 117, 142
Joab 95, 98, 100, 103
Joash (Jehoash) 80, 115, 117, 129-130
Job 129-130, 199-207
Joel 129-131
John the Baptist 189
Jonadab 170
Jonah 125, 131-133
Jonathan 89-91, 95-96
Joram (see Jehoram)
Joseph 30, 33, 35-41, 43, 72
Josephus 149
Joshua 54, 64-66, 68-74, 76, 163, (the priest) 186-187
Joshua as Leader 68-74, 139
Josiah 106, 119-120, 159-160, 163, 165-167
Josiah's reform 159-160, 174
Jotham 81, 118, 139, 147, 155
Jubilee Year 60
Judah 30, 33, 39-41, 81, 116-120, 129-131, 135, 137, 147-153, 155-156, 159-161, 163-164, 166-170, 174-177, 184-185, 187, 192
Judges 76-83
Kadesh-barnea 62-63
Kedesh 73
Keturah 26
Ketuvim 193, 195
Kingdom of God 160, 177, 179, 181, 187
Kings, Books of 102, 111-120
Kish 88
Kohathites 61
Koheleth (see Qoheleth)
Korah 63
Korah, sons of 222, 224-225
Korahite 221 ff
Laban 30-32
Lachish 161
Lamech 11
Lamentations 181-182, 201
Law and Covenant 193-194
Law of Moses 119, 126, 160, 164-165, 189, 193-194, 201

Laws of Purity 57-58
Leah 30-31
Lemuel 210-213
Leprosy 57-58, 62
Levi 30, 55, 72-73
Levite 163, 188, 194, 221
Levitical cities 72-73
Leviticus, Book of 55 ff
Lion's Den 181
Lo-ammi 143
Lo-ruhamah 143
Lot 22-24, 26
Lucifer 152
Maccabean era 178
Maccabeus, Judas 181
Macpelah 26, 33, 41
Mahanaim 95
Maher-shalal-hash-baz 147
Makkedah 71
Malachi 128-129, 188-189
Manasseh 38, 41, 68, 80-81, (son of Hezekiah) 119, 156, 159
Manna 49, 62, 69
Marah 48
Mari 22
Mashal 210
Massa 212
Meal offering 56
Medad 124
Medes 162
Medo-Babylonian 161-162
Medo-Persia 178-180, 184, 186
Meggido, Battle of 117, 120, 166
Melchizedek 24, 26, 226
Memorial Stones 69
Memucan 196
Menahem 115, 140, 148
Mephibosheth 96, 100
Merarites 61
Merneptah Stela 47
Mesha 114, 129
Meshach 180
Messiah 24, 26, 150-152, 154, 156-157, 160, 169, 177, 179, 181, 186-189, 207
Messianic Age 153
Messianic Kingdom 150-152, 154, 156, 169, 185-189
Messianic Psalms 222-224

Methusaleh 13
Micah 118, 124, 139, 149, 155-157, 199
Micah, the Ephraimite 83
Micaiah 114, 124
Michal 91, 96
Michmash 89
Middle East 152, 177
Midian 44, 79
Midianite 35, 80
Midrash 218
Miriam 43, 48, 62-63
Mixed Marriages 188, 193
Mizpah 32, 87
Moab 64, 123, 136, 152, 160, 170
Molech 108
Monarchy 86-87
Mordecai 195-196
Moresheth-gath 155
Moses 43-49, 52-58, 193, 201, 222, 225
Mount Carmel 113, 127-128
Mt. Ebal 70
Mt. Gilboa 92, 94
Mt. Hor 63
Mt. Moriah 21, 25, 105
Mt. Sinai 48-49, 52-58
Mt. Tabor 79
Murrian 46
Naaman 129
Nabal 91
Nabi 124
Nabonidus 178-180
Naboth 113, 128
Nadab 112
Nahum 119, 161-163, 199
Nahor 23
Naphtali 30, 72, 79-80
Nathan 97-98, 124
Nature of Solomon's Wisdom 104
Nazirite 65, 82, 137
Near East 199
Nebuchadnezzar 106, 120, 164, 166, 169, 178-180
Nebuzaradan 170
Necho (see Pharaoh Necho)
Negeb 96

Nehemiah 149, 184, 193-194, 199
Neo-Babylonian 162-163
Neriglissar 180
New Israel 177
New Jerusalem 177
Nile River 43, 46
Nimshi 114
Nineveh 125, 131-133, 153, 161-163
Noah 13, 15-19, 55
NoAmon (Thebes) 161-162
Nob 91
Northern Kingdom 140, 142, 144, 148, 153, 156, 159, 167-168
Numbering of the Tribes 61
Numbers, Book of 61 ff
Nuzi 23, 28-29, 31
Obadiah 173-174
Obed-edom 96
Og 63
Omri 113-114
Omrid Dynasty 113-114
Order of the March in the Wilderness 61
Othniel 77-78
Padan-aram (see Haran)
Palestine 123, 149, 155, 184-185, 192, 201
Parallelism 199-200, 222
Pashur 168
Passover 65, 69, 119, 120, 160, 192
Peace Offering 56
Pekah 116, 140, 148
Pekahiah 116, 140
Peniel 29, 32
Pentateuch v-vi, 119
Pentecost 131
Perizzites 87
Persia 123, 178, 180-181, 186, 191, 195-196
Pethuel 129
Pharaoh 22, 43-44
Pharaoh Necho 120, 165
Philistia 123, 152, 160
Philistines 76, 86, 89-90, 96, 148, 173

Phinehas 86
Phoenicia 136, 152
Pihahiroth 48
Pithom 43
Plagues, Ten 45-46
Polygamy 98
Potiphar 36
Potiphera 38
Preacher, The 215-217
Priestly Lands 72-73
Priests 57, 125-127
Primogeniture 33
Proverbs 209-213
Psalmos 221
Psalms 221-227
Psalter (see Psalms)
Pul (see Tiglath-pileser III) 140
Purim 195-196
Qoheleth 215 ff
Queen of Sheba 107-108
Quests of Ecclesiastes 216-217
Ra 45
Rabshakeh 153
Rachel 30-32, 35
Rahab 68-69
Rainbow 18
Ramah 87, 91
Rameses 43, 48
Ramoth 73
Ramoth-gilead 114
Ras Shamra 22
Rebekah 23, 26, 28-29
Rechab 170
Rechabites 170
Red Sea 46-48
Refuge, cities of 65, 72-73
Rehoboam 108, 111-112, 116-117
Rephidim 49
Reuben 30, 35, 68, 79
Reuel (see Jethro)
Rezin 140, 148
Rome 180
Romans 188
Ruth 83
Sabbath 4-5, 52, 60
Sabbatical Year 60
Sacrifice 55-58
Salem (see Jerusalem)

Samaria 129, 135, 137, 139-140, 144, 148, 152, 155-156, 159, 161
Samaritans 116, 184, 191
Samson 82-83
Samuel 85-89, 91-92, 94, 124
Samuel, Books of 85-94
Sanballat 194
Sarah 21-26, 31
Sargon II 116, 148, 155
Satan 152, 203, 207
Satrap 178
Saul 88-92, 111
Sea of Galilee 161
Sea of Reeds 48
Second Temple 184-185, 191-192
Secularism 215
Selah 223
Seleucid 181
Semiramis 131
Sennacherib 119, 148, 153, 224
Septuagint 179
Serpent 8-11
Serug 23
Seth 12-13, 15
Shadrach 180
Shallum 115, 140
Shalmaneser 115, 116, 140, 148
Shamgar 78
Shaphat 128
Shearjashub 147
Sheba 100
Shechem 32, 55, 73, 81
Shem 18-19
Sheshbazzar 191
Shimei 100, 103-104
Shiloh 72, 85
Shishak 116
Shophet 76
Shunammite 163
Sihon 63
Siloam Tunnel 156
Simeon 30, 39, 116, 161
Sin Offering 56-58
Sinai (see Mt. Sinai)
Sisera 78-79
Soco 90
Sodom 23-24, 26, 150, 168
Sodomy 24, 83
Solomon 96, 98, 102-108, 111, 126, 209-210, 216-219, 221 ff
Sons of Jacob 33-35, 38-39, 41, 57, 64
Sons of Noah 18
Sons of Korah 224-225
Song of Deborah 79
Song of Moses 48
Song of Solomon 217-219
Song of Songs (see Song of Solomon)
Songs of Ascent 226
Songs of Praise 221
Southern Kingdom 153, 155-156, 159
Story of Two Brothers 36
Succoth 48
Supha 188
Susa 195
Synonymous parallelism 199-201
Synthetic parallelism 199-201
Syria 123, 129, 140, 148, 152, 155
Taberah 62
Tabernacle 53, 61, 72, 168
Talmud 85, 149, 193
Tamar 98
Tammuz 176
Tekoa 135
Tel-abib 174
Teman 201
Temple 100, 105-107, 116, 119-120, 168, 177, 184-186, 188, 191-192, 194
Temple Sermon (Jeremiah's) 168
Ten Commandments 52, 65
Ten Tribes 116, 144
Terah 23
Teraphim 31
Thebes (see NoAmon)
Thutmose III 47
Tiamat 6
Tiglath-Pileser III 116, 118, 140, 148, 155
Tigris 18
Timnath-serah 72-73
Tirzah 113
Tobiah 194
Tola 81
Torah v, 65, 126, 192
Transjordan 148

Tribes, allotment 72
Tribal Divisions 72
Trimphal Entry 186
Twelve Tribes 30, 57, 61
Tyre 103, 136, 148
Ugaritic 22
Upper Egypt 162
Ur 21
Uriah 97
Urim and Thummin 57, 70, 72, 89
Uz 201, 203
Uzzah 96
Uzziah 139, 147-148, 151, 155
Valley of Dry Bones 177
Valley of Jezreel 80
Valley of Rephaim 95-96
Vashti 196
Vows 65
Waters of Merom 71
Wife-sister motif 23
Wilderness Wandering 62-64
Wisdom Literature 209
Wisdom of Amen-em-opet 212
Widsom of Solomon 209
"Wise men" 125-127
Writings (Ketuvim) 193, 195
Xerxes I (see Ahasuerus) 195
Xisuthrus 17
Yahweh 64, 115, 117-119, 123-133, 136-139, 141-144, 147-157, 160-162, 164-170, 174-177, 179, 185-189, 193-194, 203, 222
Yam Suf 48
Yom Kippur 58
Zadok 99, 102
Zebulun 80, 131, 188
Zechariah 118 (son of Jehoiada)
Zechariah 115, 140 (the king); 179, 185-188, 191-192 (the prophet)
Zedekiah 120, 166, 169
Zelophehad 65
Zephaniah 120, 159-161
Zerubbabel 185-187, 191-192
Ziba 96-97, 100
Ziggurat 19
Zilpah 30
Zimri 112-113
Zion 156

Zophar 203, 205
Zoroastrianism 179